DEFENSE OR DELUSION?

DEFENSE OR DELUSION?

America's Military in the 1980s

THOMAS H. ETZOLD

1817

HARPER & ROW, PUBLISHERS, New York
Cambridge, Philadelphia, San Francisco, London
Mexico City, São Paulo, Sydney

FIRST EDITION

Designer: Sidney Feinberg

Library of Congress Cataloging in Publication Data

Etzold, Thomas H.
   Defense or delusion?
   Includes bibliographical references and index.
    1. United States—Military policy. 2. United States—
Armed Forces. I. Title.
UA23.E89   355′.033073   81-47655
ISBN 0-06-038011-X   AACR2

82 83 84 85 86 10 9 8 7 6 5 4 3 2 1

In memory of my teaching partner,
Kay Russell,
Captain, United States Navy,
1934–1979,
a long-time prisoner of war in Vietnam
and an earnest student of
America's foreign and military affairs

CONTENTS

ACKNOWLEDGMENTS

In writing this book, I have accumulated many debts to friends, colleagues, and family. My agent, Patricia Falk Feeley, suggested in 1979 that I write about America's military. Neither of us then foresaw either the events of late 1979 and 1980 or the shape this book finally assumed. But we shared a conviction that America's people needed to know more about their military. Philip A. Crowl, chairman of the Department of Strategy at the Naval War College, encouraged me to undertake this book—outside of assigned duties, to be sure. His successor as chairman, Robert S. Wood, offered similar encouragement and, to my great benefit, commented on manuscript drafts.

The Naval War College afforded me a priceless opportunity to plumb the minds of America's best military professionals, as well as to probe this nation's military institutions. In this my students and colleagues have been my teachers. I owe much to Porter Halyburton, Michael Corgan, Richard Peters, Dale Clark, Robert Svoboda, Christopher Withers, Jerome K. Holloway, Marino Bartolomei, and Alan Isaacson. Many other people elsewhere in the Department of the Navy, the Department of Defense, and other government agencies have contributed in one way or another to this book, for which I show appreciation by naming no names here.

I am obliged above all to my family. For many months, my daughter, Ingrid, made do with notice too brief to encompass all she had to show and tell. My son, Klaus, played too much basketball by himself—although he and I did catch most of the World Series. My wife, Suzanne, did without the house painting, wallpapering, landscaping, and simple attentions she deserves. I am grateful for their patience, interest, and confidence.

The views expressed here are my own. The Naval War College has a long and honorable tradition of honest investigation into the fundamentals of national defense. This tradition of intellectual and scholarly integrity is vital to the purposes of the school, and indeed to those of military education. For education, after all, encourages and equips people to think for themselves. This book should not be construed as representing the views of the Naval War College, the Department of Defense, or any other agency or official of the United States Government. I regret any errors of fact, and welcome readers' comments and corrections. In the belief that our military's interests—and our nation's—will be served best by frank and fair-minded inquiry, I remain open to discussion of judgments and interpretations ventured here.

Newport, Rhode Island
May 1981

For a great evil, a small remedy
does not produce a small result;
it simply does not produce any
result at all.

JOHN STUART MILL

I THE PROBLEM:
MILITARY MALAISE

Then Arthur learned, as all leaders are astonished to learn, that
peace, not war, is the destroyer of men.

STEINBECK/MALLORY, *Morte D'Arthur*

THE AMERICAN PEOPLE tend to leave discussion of military affairs to the experts—the military officers, defense intellectuals, and national security managers who populate government and academe. In part, this reflects traditional national ambivalence concerning the possession and use of power. In part, it manifests a belief that the experts really are expert, and that the issues of modern defense are too technical for laymen to understand. This latter impression, to be sure, receives regular support as experts present their views in inscrutable assemblages of acronyms, statistics, and abstruse reasoning.

In the 1980s, however, wide public attention to the nation's military needs and military issues is essential, even urgent. For the American military is sick. If left to the military professionals and the experts, it will remain so, incapable of meeting the nation's military needs in the coming decade. The military's people are dispirited; its equipment is obsolescent and unreliable; its leaders and bureaucrats conduct their day-to-day business and think about their long-term problems in ways likely to perpetuate present infirmities. To some extent these ailments may reflect the ordinary consequences of time passing, of the end of one generation and the passage to another. They may be normal manifestations of the malaise that in peacetime transforms warriors into bureaucrats. However explained, the maladies hold large significance for national well-being in coming years.

1

Late 1970s political events, particularly those in Iran and Afghanistan, have encouraged national consensus on the need to improve America's military capability. But these events have created much less agreement on what to do, when, and how. The first step toward answering these vital questions is, simply, careful examination of the problems. America's enlarging military liabilities, its distressed military manpower, its complex military technology, and its military modernization are issues of the coming decade. These are admittedly complicated. But they are not beyond the grasp of any citizen who approaches them with interest, intelligence, and common sense.

II THE ENVIRONMENT:
LIMITS ON
AMERICAN POWER

*I question whether anything but a military disaster will ever
make us feel our responsibilities and our possible dangers.*

THEODORE ROOSEVELT, 1893

APRIL 1980. The failed attempt to rescue American hostages in
Iran confirmed what a decade of debate over Vietnam and SALT
could not establish: America's military is inadequate to support
national interests. It is one thing for a great power to fail while
doing greatly; such is the stuff of epic, tragedy, remembrance.
But it is another for a great power to falter while doing slightly;
such is the stuff of humiliation, reappraisal, politics. The aborted
raid was a story of small failings, slight failures, and perhaps that
was its most deeply troubling aspect. In the election year, the
quest for an explanation of the muddled mission's meaning
merged almost immediately with larger concerns for the state of
America's defenses.

The rescue mission, by falling short, corroborated broader concerns about America's ability to hold its own in troubled times.
Failure in Vietnam a decade earlier had led readily to a policy
prescription sufficient to allay concern: there were to be "no more
Vietnams." The Soviet-American nuclear arms relationship,
though of increasing interest to the American public in the latter
1970s, remained a somewhat abstract issue. But the Iran rescue
mission raised distressing questions about American ability to plan
and execute even a small operation. The planning of the attempt
(too intricate), the organization (interservice rivalry), the preparation and training (too lengthy and uncoordinated), the execution

3

(helicopter inadequacies, cumbersome command and control, an accident born of confusion)—all came in for severe criticism. In Iran, defenders of the revolution gave thanks that "Allah's radar" had foiled the rescue. In Europe, German chancellor Helmut Schmidt, French political scientist Raymond Aron, and lesser luminaries observed that, in their eyes, the United States was no longer Number One. In America, anxious citizens wondered whether the Iran rescue had really been the best of which the American military was capable. Whether yes or no, the answer could scarcely have been comforting.

In the 1980s, for the third time in thirty-five years, America confronts the most fundamental of its post–World War II defense problems: the balance between nuclear and conventional forces. Three times since 1945, the United States has come to political-military crisis as a result of overconfidence in nuclear weapons and correlative underinvestment in conventional capabilities.

The first such problem arose five years after the Second World War. After 1945, American strategists devised a military posture in the Far East that depended on air-delivered atomic bombs. Military threats from mainland enemies were to be countered with nuclear weapons before the foe could venture out into the Western Pacific. With this strategy, there would be no need for bases in Japan, or anywhere on the Asian mainland. At the outbreak of war in Korea, in 1950, this nuclear strategy failed because of the paucity of atomic weapons available, the suddenness of the attack, and the difficulty of using the few clumsy weapons of the time at the battlefront. Atomic defense plans collapsed in a hurried return to an Asian strategy of interlinked bases in Korea, Japan, Taiwan, the Philippines, and even the Aleutian Islands, with large conventional ground, air, and naval forces deployed in the region. This improvised reaction was far from ideal in its consequences. It resulted in a twenty-year alienation of mainland China and in long-lived defense commitments to Asian nations. Both the breach with China and the defense commitments proved highly costly over time.[1]

After the Korean War, the United States turned again to a national strategy that was primarily nuclear in character. Under President Dwight Eisenhower, the United States adopted a strategy of "massive retaliation," which threatened to respond to military provocation with overwhelming nuclear strikes on the Soviet Union, mainland China, or other enemies. But 1950s attempts to "get more bang for the buck" through massive nuclear threats demonstrably failed to prevent serious injuries to Western interests via subversion and wars of national liberation. In 1957, Henry Kissinger summarized the problem in terms that seem disturbingly apt even in the 1980s:

> At a time when we have never been stronger, we have had to learn that power which is not clearly related to the objectives for which it is to be employed may merely serve to paralyze the will. . . . If the Soviet bloc can present its challenges in less than all-out form . . . it . . . will then pose the appalling dilemma of whether we are willing to commit suicide to prevent encroachments, which do not, each in itself, seem to threaten our existence directly but which may be steps on the road to our ultimate destruction. No more urgent task confronts American policy than to bring our power into balance with the issues for which we are most likely to have to contend.[2]

By 1960, there was wide realization that the United States needed more varied military capabilities with which to respond to political and military challenges around the world.

After the election of John F. Kennedy in 1960, the United States attempted for the second time to correct the balance of nuclear and conventional forces in American defense. There followed an era of "flexible response" strategy, in which the Kennedy and Johnson administrations expanded the nation's conventional forces by developing counterinsurgency forces and other special ground, air, and naval units. David Rees, a contemporary political-military analyst, praised the McNamara Doctrine of flexible response for being "at last a viable, detailed defense policy for the nuclear age."[3] As is well known, this refinement of the nuclear/conventional force relationship led to prolonged war which cost the United States vital domestic consensus and worldwide prestige.

In the 1980s, the causes of military inadequacy are in some respects more complex than they were in 1950 and 1960. In their most basic dimension, present problems concern the same imbalance between nuclear forces on one hand and conventional forces on the other. The question of the 1980s is whether, in its third attempt to order the nuclear/conventional force relationship, the

United States can improve on its earlier efforts, avoiding the disasters that followed on previous adjustments of this fundamental connection.

America's present military inadequacy is the product of three broad factors: (1) the growth of Soviet power from the middle 1960s to the present; (2) the political and military consequences of trends in conventional weaponry; (3) an internal military malaise resulting mainly from the way Americans have thought about their military needs in the 1970s, especially in the aftermath of the Vietnam War. Only in careful consideration of these causes of military inadequacy can the search for remedies begin.

More than any other factor, the growth of Soviet power over the past fifteen years has rendered the American military inadequate. Until the middle 1960s, the Soviet Union was not a particularly formidable threat. It would certainly have been foolhardy for the United States to try militarily to "roll back Communism" in Eastern Europe. But in the 1940s, 1950s, and early 1960s, Russia lacked the ability to challenge the United States outside Eurasia. An attack on Western Europe, so much discussed in the 1940s and 1950s, was for all practical purposes beyond Russian power. The Cuban Missile Crisis of 1962 was an exceptional effort to alter the strategic balance precisely because that balance was so unfavorable to the Soviet Union. The attempt failed, and substantial shifts in the general East-West balance of forces did not come for another decade.

Because the Soviet Union has been relatively weak for most of the period since World War II, it is especially important to set perspective on the evolution of Soviet military power and its implications for American military needs.

After World War II, Soviet military forces and naval units could not operate effectively at any distance from Central Europe or Soviet Asia. Political and military leaders of the United States did not even believe that the Red Army posed an operational threat to the democratic states of Western Europe. From the American perspective, the formation of the North Atlantic Treaty Organization—the NATO alliance—was meant to relieve Europe's fears of psychological and political collapse rather than to forestall Russian military movements to the West. It was an appropriate irony that the Marine Corps band, playing for the elaborate diplomatic ceremonies at which the NATO treaties were formally signed in 1949, performed selections from the currently popular Gershwin show *Porgy and Bess:* "I've Got Plenty of Nothin' " and "It Ain't Necessarily So."[4]

Yet immediately after World War II, the leaders and people of the United States conceptualized the Soviet threat in terms strong enough to inaugurate the Cold War. People who did not actually live through the years between the world wars, into World War II, and on into the postwar period may never appreciate fully the profundity of this change. Not World War I, not World War II, but the Cold War finally reversed classic American isolationism. This change established an importance for the peacetime military far beyond any that it had ever before possessed in American history. The Cold War also justified unprecedented peacetime collaboration between government and industry, principally for the benefit of the military. These changes of attitude and situation transformed the United States, over time, from a nation with no allies and no military commitments to a nation with eighteen allies and forty-one defense commitments; a nation in which national security policy displaces its more rustic cousin, foreign policy; a country in which Lockheed and Chrysler could not—or at least would not—be allowed to go bankrupt.

In some respects, the Cold War military relationship of the superpowers began paradoxically. Between 1945 and 1948, the Soviet Union reduced its army from over 11,000,000 men to about 2,874,000.[5] It had no long-range bombers. Its navy was war-tested but small, in sad repair, and extremely limited in range and capability. Russia possessed no atomic weapons. Its economy was in chaos, if not actual collapse. Soviet agriculture could not feed the Russian people; Soviet currency was too weak to withstand use in international trade; Soviet industry was too crude and unreliable to produce for export, much less to meet the needs of postwar recovery. There were no goods to meet the long-deferred whims of well-off consumers in Russia after World War II, no cars and refrigerators for people to purchase with piled-up wartime wages. For that matter, there were no piled-up wartime wages. The Soviet Union of the 1940s needed huge postwar loans. Soviet leaders considered the end of American Lend-Lease aid in 1945 to be a devastating and deliberate blow to Soviet security and economy.

Perhaps, as Senator J. William Fulbright argued in the 1960s, the United States came to resemble a "Crippled Giant." But for many years after World War II, the Soviet Union fit that description much more nearly.[6]

This is not to suggest that the United States had no serious quarrels with Soviet policies, or that there was nothing for the West to fear in Soviet programs after the war. It was no mistake to consider Soviet ideology inimical to the values and political institutions of Western democracies. It was no error to believe that the Soviet leadership harbored deep distrust and even deeper hostility toward Western governments and leaders. Vietnam-era doubts concerning the wisdom and motives of American leaders in the first years after World War II have caused the United States too much self-criticism and remorse for Cold War and past political practices. For this, the so-called New Left in American politics bears a heavy responsibility, for this critique of American actions has introduced hesitancy and self-doubt into American policy at a truly critical interval.

The point of recalling postwar Soviet weakness is simply this: If Western leaders fresh from the horrors and menaces of German Nazism and Japanese militarism could see in the Soviet Union of the 1940s threat enough to overturn American political, economic, and military traditions, how much more fearsome the Soviet Union of the latter 1970s and early 1980s must seem.

Since the early 1960s, Soviet economic and military power has multiplied several times over. The Soviet economy is no longer in ruins, though it remains much less sizable than that of the United States (the U.S.S.R. is usually said to have a gross national product 60 percent to 65 percent of that of the United States). Soviet agriculture still cannot feed the Russian people at a standard comparable to that in most Western countries. Although the Soviets are in a position to buy abroad food they cannot grow, their people continue to eat poorly. Most important of all, the Soviet military is backed by an economy that gives priority to military needs. The sectors of the Soviet economy devoted to military production lead the economy in efficiency and reliability.

This does not mean, however, that all is well in the Soviet military economy. Some Western analysts believe that when the Red Army orders, say, 5,000 armored personnel carriers, it is very likely to receive not 5,000 but 5,500, give or take a few dozen. Enthusiastic overproduction is one way in which factory managers attempt to avert the penalties of failure. Whether the necessary standards of quality are maintained in overproducing under deadlines; whether the resources used in overproduction might have been better invested in other ways; whether the army has a use for the equipment and people to operate it—such questions remain for the most part unasked, and unanswered. It would, in short, be a mistake to exaggerate the consistency and predictability of results in the Soviet military economy.

Despite its own problems of defense management, between the middle 1960s and 1980 the Soviet Union upgraded its military forces in every major category. Soviet military manpower increased by 1 million men, from about 3 million men to 4 million (not counting internal security and military construction forces; these would add still another million to the total in uniform).[7]

Soviet strategic nuclear forces grew even more impressively. In 1964, the Soviet Union possessed 190 intercontinental ballistic missiles (ICBMs), 29 submarine-launched ballistic missiles (SLBMs), 170 long-range bombers, and some 400 nuclear warheads for strategic delivery. By 1980 these figures had changed drastically. Soviet forces in 1980 included 1,398 ICBMs, 950 SLBMs, and 156 bombers (these have never been very important in Russian nuclear strategy). Most important for American strategic considerations, the number of Soviet strategic warheads had reached 6,000 in 1979, with every indication that the number would continue to increase. In that fifteen-year interval, the Soviets deployed five new ICBMs and three new SLBMs, and made steady advances in accuracy as well as in multiple independently targetable reentry vehicles (MIRVs).[8] American intelligence estimates anticipated that in the 1980s, Soviet warheads would double in number to some 12,000 to 13,000 while becoming still more accurate. According to an Air Force study, because of these developments the ability of the United States to retaliate against Soviet nuclear attack was cut in half between 1977 and 1979.[9] This conclusion depended on extremely technical, and indeed arcane, reasoning, which will receive extensive discussion in chapter five. The report was not a harbinger of immediate disaster; rather it provided a crude measure of the extent to which Soviet force developments were altering the Soviet-American power relationship.

In conventional forces, Soviet military development showed similar momentum. Between 1964 and 1980, Soviet tanks increased in number from about 30,000 to about 45,000. As with missiles, there were not only large increases but large improvements. In the late 1960s, to address the growing threat from China, Soviet army divisions increased from 145 to 170. Most of the new divisions went to the Far East to reinforce the long and troubled Sino-Soviet border. To this, surely, went the majority of the manpower increase mentioned above. Further, some of the new divisions did not immediately receive full equipment; a number of them remained well below the top level of combat readiness. Still, an increase of 25 divisions was more than the combat power of the entire American Army. And not all the new forces went to the Soviet Far East. Some were deployed to reinforce the Warsaw Pact where it meets NATO Europe. To round out this impressive enlargement of ground forces, Soviet artillery nearly doubled in numbers, from 11,000 pieces to about 20,000.[10]

Soviet military aviation showed similarly vigorous growth. The number of modern combat aircraft deployed grew from 3,500 in 1964 to 4,500 in 1980, again with improvements of quality. Many older aircraft were replaced with newer, more capable ones, so that the real enhancement of air capability was greater than numbers alone might suggest.[11]

Finally, and of very high importance, between the middle 1960s and the middle 1970s, the Soviet Navy came into its own. Although it is far from the equal of the combined navies of the NATO allies, it possesses—and has demonstrated—the ability to operate in all the world's oceans. The navy has become a symbol of Soviet power, a challenge to traditional Western dominance of the seas as well as to the quasi-imperial style that flowed from dominance at sea. As a prestigious study of the NATO–Warsaw Pact naval balance noted in 1979: "It was primarily because of Allied success in establishing supremacy at sea that the postwar balance of power almost defied the logic of distance and geography."[12] The balance of power no longer flies in the face of such logic.

Yet in naval matters, assessment of Soviet force developments is more complex than in other forces. Raw numbers are not as revealing, because Soviet forces have grown only modestly in terms of numbers of ships. In 1969, the naval order of battle totaled 1,670 ships for the Soviets; in 1979, it added up to 1,764. But in that interval, retirement of aging ships in the United States reduced the American Navy from its 1969 total of 926 active ships to a 1979 total of 462. As Admiral Elmo R. Zumwalt, former Chief of Naval Operations, wrote in his 1975 memoir, the United States Navy had not fallen below 500 active ships since 1939; since that year the United States had taken on defense commitments to many nations and had acquired a powerful peacetime enemy while reducing the Navy's size. Further, the total tonnage of Soviet naval vessels increased at a larger rate than the increase in numbers of ships, indicating that Soviet ships were becoming larger and more effective. It was notable that almost the entire increase in Soviet naval forces occurred in the category of mobile logistics support ships. These vessels enable Soviet warships to operate far from bases. They thus give the Soviet Navy its most important new characteristic: a worldwide operating capability.[13]

Today, when American warships call at Dakar, Senegal, or Lagos, Nigeria, or virtually any other African port, they are certain to find several newer and—at least to the uninformed eye—more impressive Soviet warships there as well. The significance of Soviet naval development has by no means been lost on the governments and nations in whose harbors Soviet warships linger and Soviet merchantmen bid energetically for cargoes.

All this is not to suggest that the United States has stood still, ignoring its defense while the Soviets have grabbed for power. In the middle 1960s, when Soviet forces began their sharp expansion, American strategic forces had already taken on their modern proportions. In 1966, the United States had more than 900 ICBMs, nearly 600 SLBMs, and some 5,000 strategic warheads, including those carried by the B-52 bombers of the Strategic Air Command. Since 1967, the overall number of launchers in the ICBM forces and SLBM forces has not increased—1,054 and 656° respectively; the number of warheads has almost doubled, to about 9,200. This increase in deliverable warheads has come about through ad-

---

° In 1981, U.S. SLBM launchers declined in number as older missile submarines were retired.

vances in MIRV technology; the second-generation Minuteman ICBMs and the later SLBMs all carry several warheads, many capable of being delivered on entirely separate targets. While Soviet improvements in missile accuracy have been important in the last several years, it is generally conceded that the United States retains the lead in this vital technology.[14]

The point, therefore, is not that the United States has become powerless; rather, the Soviet Union has become much more powerful than it was when Soviet-American and East-West relations took their post–World War II shape. This development was, in any reasonable outlook, certain to occur as the Soviet Union recovered from World War II and consolidated its political, economic, and military institutions. Now that it has occurred, the growth of Soviet power is equally certain to have important effects.

Changing power relationships inevitably mean changing political relationships. The signs of the times have been both prominent and disturbing in the latter 1970s. In 1946, for instance, when Russian troops refused to leave Iran in the face of American demands to do so, President Harry S. Truman told the Soviet ambassador in Washington that if Russian troops were not out of Iran within forty-eight hours, the United States would use its "super bomb." (The United States then possessed a nuclear monopoly.) "We're going to drop it on you," Truman said, and Russian troops were on their way out of Iran twenty-four hours later. More interesting, however, was the way in which President Truman's threat became a wry and nostalgic comment on America's inability to force the Soviets to withdraw from Afghanistan, as Senator Henry "Scoop" Jackson in 1980 told *Time* magazine what President Truman had told him and, earlier, the Russians.[15]

Throughout the Cold War, Soviet intransigence in negotiation had been a formidable problem. In the latter 1970s, however, this trait of Soviet diplomacy took on new strategic significance. From 1948 through 1961, in a series of crises over Western access to Berlin, the United States faced down the Russians time after time. In the greatest test of Cold War resolution, Russians and Americans came "eyeball to eyeball" in October 1962, in the Cuban Missile Crisis. As American leaders bragged thereafter, again the Soviets "blinked first." But sometime after the Cuban Missile Crisis, the constellation of political and psychological factors favorable to the United States shifted.

In one sense, it is true that the United States has always been relatively weak on Russia's borders, and it is an irony of American foreign policy that so many of the nation's vital interests have been defined in close proximity to Soviet territory and, correspondingly, to Soviet power. The special poignance of late 1970s events in Iran reflected an appreciation that the United States might no longer be able to sustain its interests in areas of earlier success. When Russian combat troops were "discovered" in Cuba in the fall of 1979, President Jimmy Carter pronounced their deployment completely unacceptable to the United States. But within a few weeks, he had quietly dropped the issue in the face of Soviet intransigence. Later in the year, with Americans hostage in Iran, the President met the Soviet invasion of Afghanistan with boycotts on food and athletic contests rather than with more traditional instruments of great power influence. There were no appreciable effects on the Russian stance.

The growth of Soviet military power has large but complex implications for American military adequacy. In the most general sense, it is evident that Soviet power now counterbalances that of the United States, so that the superpowers must avoid direct conflict with its threats of escalation and nuclear exchange. In practice, this has meant the transformation of struggle in ways that make it both inefficient and ineffective. Many observers have noted that counterbalance in Soviet-American power relations forces both superpowers to contend through proxies, over small issues, and often in remote locations. Such conflicts keep the risks of direct engagement at arm's length and minimize risks of escalation.

It has seldom been recognized, however, that superpower struggles of this nature make it very cumbersome to bring military power to bear. In turn, this makes it hard to be reliable or efficient in using power under such circumstances. In this sense, Vietnam was far from ideal as a location from either the Russian or the American perspective. It was remote not only from the United States but from Soviet resupply as well. Soviet war matériel sent overland was subject to interruption by Chinese forces, through whose territory such shipments had to pass. The years of the Vietnam War were also years of worsening Sino-Soviet relations and, in 1971, of the Nixon-Kissinger "opening" to China. The Soviets could supply North Vietnam by sea no more easily than by land. It was a long route for Soviet ships, many of which had to steam from ports in Europe and the Mediterranean (the Soviet Far East is not the location of significant productive facilities, transportation routes, or indeed much of anything). Further, the sea lanes of supply were always vulnerable to interdiction by superior American air and naval forces. Out of caution, American forces refrained from interrupting Soviet seaborne trade with North Vietnam until President Nixon ordered the mining of Haiphong harbor in 1969.

The need to manage risk by contesting small issues in remote places means that the great powers in effect must fight with at least one and sometimes both hands tied behind their backs. This can only be strenuous, clumsy, and unproductive.

In diverting their struggles into peripheral issues and areas, the powers also risk miscalculating the importance of a given issue to the opponent—sometimes while overestimating their own ability to carry through to success. Vietnam showed over and over again how trying it was for American political and military leaders to see what it would take to create favorable conditions for negotiation with North Vietnam, not to speak of conditions for victory. For the Russians, the 1979 invasion of Afghanistan has surely provided a classic example of both propositions. In the first weeks following the move, it seemed that Soviet leaders had thoroughly miscalculated American reaction, world opinion, even the political reflexes of client states in Eastern Europe and the Third World. Although outside observers remain divided on the issue, it also appeared likely that Soviet officials had underestimated the physical difficulty of doing what they had planned. The caution of both Soviet and American leaders in the early days of war between Iran and Iraq in September 1980 doubtless reflected an appreciation of such risks.

In one of its most painful consequences for Americans, the superpower standoff resulting from the growth of Soviet power greatly reduces the room for error in political-military affairs. This new limitation has been agonizing as well as confusing for Americans. For about twenty years after World War II, the

United States and its allies enjoyed such a preponderance of power—military and economic—that the United States rarely paid much of a price for politico-military mistakes. It was like having a checking account with a very large balance: no service charges, and even with errors in computation, no bounced checks. The United States could—and did—override the feelings and interests of lesser nations in every continent, usually without immediate or serious consequences. But in so doing, it drew more heavily than it realized on its fund of goodwill and political resources. American ability to topple governments and sustain friendly rulers obscured questions of whether the United States was using its resources and influence wisely. As John L. Gaddis, a prominent student of Soviet-American relations, has written: "Persistent success . . . is intoxicating; it blurs objectivity and fosters an illusion of infallibility."[16] In this sense, the Iranian revolution of 1979 was truly a sobering experience.

Now, in contrast to early Cold War years, the Soviet Union can deploy forces into regions in which the United States has important interests. Soviet military presence in and around Asia and Africa and the Middle East reduces or eliminates American ability to bring local issues to quick and favorable conclusions simply by maintaining American forces in the region. Nearby Soviet forces may offer freedom of hand to small regional states involved in controversy or crisis. Recent developments in Iran were an apt, if distressing, example. American intelligence and defense experts interpreted the positioning of Soviet troops in western Afghanistan early in 1980 as a warning that the Soviets would not permit significant American intervention in Iran. This factor was one of the most important considerations dictating absolute operational security, smallness, and precision in the hostage rescue attempt. In turn, the attempt to make the mission small, supersecret, and precise contributed greatly to its failure.

The growth of Soviet power has deprived the West, and especially the United States, of the ability to make mistakes without penalty. The global reach, military power, and political outlook of Russian leaders in the 1980s has made it certain that the United States will be brought to book for every mistake in determining and defending its interests around the world.

In addition, the growth of Soviet power has notably increased the military cost of possessing vital interests in areas that lie close to Soviet territory. America's commitments to major allies in Europe and Asia were acquired a generation ago, when the Soviet Union was much weaker and the United States much stronger at least in relative terms. As Soviet power has increased, the potential cost of projecting military power into areas peripheral to Soviet territory has increased even more quickly. A political scientist or Pentagon analyst could probably invent some clever mathematical representation of this problem. Some strategic analysts suggest that effective military power falls off in logarithmic proportion to the distance it is from national territory. In any case, it is clear that the power of the Soviet Union today has vastly increased the American military liabilities incurred through commitment to NATO defense, the defense of Japan, the Philippines, and other allies. According to the French proverb, "The more things change, the more they remain the same." But in American defense, the more commitments remain the same, the more the real burden of meeting them increases.

The American military has become inadequate, further, because of the effects on warfare of important developments in conventional weaponry. One has been the invention since World War II of so-called smart weapons—precision guided munitions. Into this category fall the bombs, rockets, projectiles, and missiles using sensors and small computers to "see," select, and attack targets. These weapons are vastly increasing the rates at which men and weapons may be consumed in combat. They are also changing the equations of power between traditional great powers such as the United States and many lesser powers around the world.

The other notable development has been an astounding increase in the complexity of military engagements, in part as a function of the evolution of sophisticated weapons. Wars of the 1970s and now the early 1980s have provided sobering evidence of the rising costs of conventional war—and of the penalties the new weapon technologies may impose even on large, modern military forces. In 1967, in an early indication of the coming problem, the Israeli destroyer *Elath* was sunk by a single surface-to-surface missile. The destroyer cost $150 million; the missile, Soviet-made, cost the equivalent of about $20,000.

In the Arab-Israeli war of 1973, further evidence accumulated to suggest the increasing deadliness and expense of war with the new weapons. Within a few hours, in a single engagement, 130 Israeli tanks were destroyed by Russian-made antitank weapons— 25-pound explosive warheads on rocket launchers not much more sophisticated than World War II German bazooka rounds. In that same war, obsolescent surface-to-air missiles in Egyptian hands brought down 90 Israeli aircraft in two days. In that war, the Israelis lost 2,500 killed, 7,500 wounded, and 300 taken prisoner. In all, Israel lost 109 advanced combat aircraft. Further, 835 tanks and armored personnel carriers were hit in action, of which about half were later repaired and put back into service at least for the duration of the war emergency. Thereafter, some undoubtedly were scrapped. On the Arab side, 16,000 people were killed, 45,000 wounded, 9,000 taken prisoner. In equipment, the war cost the Egyptians and Syrians and their Soviet sponsors 450 aircraft, 2,200 tanks (300 were repaired and used by the Israelis in the last days of the war), and about 1,000 armored personnel carriers.

The 1973 war lasted only seventeen days. But that brief conflict cost the United States more than $5 billion in military equipment and supplies provided to Israel during the course of the war and afterward to compensate for losses. These were the costs of backing the winner in a short war in which the United States was not even engaged. Egyptian losses far exceeded those of Israel, which means that the immediate military cost alone considerably exceeded $10 billion.

In the Middle East in 1980, in the war between Iran and Iraq, similar results soon were evident. The opening days of that war lacked the intensity and coordination of the Arab-Israeli war of 1973, but losses of aircraft ran high. In the first two to three days of fighting, some 100 aircraft were lost on the two sides. Iraq had begun the war with 337 modern airplanes, Iran with 449.[17] Of those totals, some planes were surely unready. Military organizations around the world face similar problems of maintenance, spare parts, and repair, so that some proportion of the nominal order of battle must always be unavailable. In Iran, after the turmoil of the revolution and the disruption of relations with the United States, aircraft availability fell below 50 percent. Indeed, one Western military expert, Drew Middleton of *The New York Times*, asserted that only 10 percent of the Iranian Air Force's F-

14s were battle ready when the war with Iraq opened.[18]

The point, simply, was this: war with modern weapons had the potential to consume staggering amounts of equipment, people, and wealth without necessarily leading to quick victory or to resolution of underlying political and strategic concerns.

The proliferation of the modern weapons that make war so intense and expensive—the aircraft, missiles, and precision guided munitions—may well be the most important military development since World War II. It exceeds, in some respects, the significance of evolution in the nuclear forces of the superpowers, and it possesses higher consequences than the problem of nuclear proliferation.

From the middle 1960s to the late 1970s, indexes of world military investment and military power increased in every major category. World military expenditures rose substantially even after adjustment for inflation, climbing by a full half despite the end of the Vietnam War. The figures used to describe this growth are confusing, because they are usually expressed in dollar terms adjusted to the inflation indexes of the year in which the statistics were assembled. The latest calendar year for which full statistics were available at time of writing was 1977; expressed in 1976 constant dollars, the world had spent $221.8 billion on armed forces in 1968, and $433.9 in 1977.[19]

Similarly, world military manpower in all the globe's armed services increased, from 20.7 million in 1965 to 26.3 million in 1977. Shipments of arms in international transfers—bureaucratic terminology for the business of those who used to be called merchants of death—approximately doubled, from about $8 billion in 1968 to about $16 billion in 1977 (figures again expressed in 1976 constant dollars).[20]

Most interesting and certainly most worrisome about all these aspects of world military activity, the NATO countries in every case either increased less or actually decreased their level of spending. Warsaw Pact and developing nations showed sharp increases. Between 1968 and 1977, annual American military expenditures fell $34.7 billion in constant dollars, in part because of the end of the Vietnam War. Spending of the NATO allies rose by $11.2 billion. Military spending by the Soviet Union and the Warsaw Pact increased $36.7 billion. Developing countries increased their overall military expenditures by almost 3 percent in constant dollars from 1976 to 1977; the military costs of developed countries actually declined slightly, by 1 percent, in that same year. Even taking the Vietnam spending bulge into account, in both absolute and relative terms the world's militaries are becoming more formidable in relation to the military capabilities of the United States and its allies.[21]

For the American military, recent conflicts and world military trends hold several important implications.

First, it is clear that small powers can impose high military costs on much larger powers. Today, the most sophisticated and expensive surface naval units in the world can be brought under attack by airplanes and submarines armed with missiles. An aircraft carrier with its air wing costs nearly $5 billion; aircraft capable of attacking it cost $10 million to $15 million; submarines cost more, on the order of $200 million to $300 million; but missiles are cheap, ranging in cost from $20,000 to $100,000,000. New American tanks cost $2.7 million; they can be destroyed by anti-tank weapons costing from a few hundred dollars to perhaps $5,000. The newest American fighter and attack aircraft cost from $18 million to about $40 million; they, too, are vulnerable to destruction by cheap missiles. As the world's leading exporter of such weapons, the Soviet Union has made cheap modern missiles a mainstay of the international arms trade. Between 1973 and 1977, the Soviet Union delivered 14,870 surface-to-air missiles to countries around the world.[22] In 1979, the Soviets in addition exported an all-time record number of advanced aircraft: 600 of them, worth between $2 billion and $3 billion.[23] In many parts of the world, even in war against relatively small states, the United States would have to expect substantial losses of equipment and, possibly, high casualties.

Further, the potential costs of modern war mean that the United States probably cannot meet its formal strategic requirements of being able to fight "one and a half wars" simultaneously. From World War II to about 1969, the United States maintained a military supposedly strong enough to fight two and a half wars at once: war in NATO Europe, war in Asia, and a lesser military action. At the time of the Korean War, for example, the few atomic weapons on hand and the majority of first-line troops in the American military were withheld from the war in the belief that Korea might turn out to be only a Soviet feint, with larger and more important war to come in Europe once the United States had committed forces to Korea. Variations of this strategic nightmare, the two-front war, have continued to shape American defense planning. The Vietnam War's high costs, however, showed that a two-and-a-half war capability was an impractically high expectation for the peacetime American military. Rather than call for an expansion of the military to support the two-and-a-half war strategic posture, President Nixon revised American strategic requirements. In the Nixon Doctrine, he acknowledged that the United States had become overextended, and that it would be necessary to reduce American commitments to a point commensurate with American military capabilities.

Since 1969, the American military has been required to maintain the ability to fight a large war in Europe, presumably against Soviet and Warsaw Pact forces, while fighting a lesser war elsewhere in the world. But experts have doubted that in the past ten years, the United States really has possessed forces adequate for one and a half wars.[24]

Now the high costs of war with modern conventional weapons and the high levels of military investment in many of the world's smaller countries are forcing an increasing realization that the United States probably cannot meet this test of adequacy. Indeed, the deadliness of modern weaponry and rising world militarization make it unlikely that the United States could fight even its "half" war without serious strain. The easy interventions of the 1950s and 1960s may be a thing of the past. In Lebanon in 1958, 8,000 Marines waded ashore, to be met by the ice cream vendors of Beirut. But if they had met a more intimidating reception, the military establishment of the time would have been capable of dealing with the problem without running out of ammunition or amphibious shipping. It would not have needed to call for extraordinary measures impinging on the peacetime economy or the home front. In the Dominican Republic in 1965, a few thousand Marines went into a more hazardous situation. They encountered little trouble, as things turned out, but if they had met serious opposition the nation would have felt no strain. In Vietnam, there may have been a glimpse of the coming problem: one common explanation for failure to do better in that war was the Johnson administration's effort to have both guns and butter, to fight a demanding war without putting the nation on a wartime footing. The increasing expense of warfare may be putting an end to America's era of "little wars." Modern war, even against very small powers, may have become so costly that the nation cannot be left on a peacetime footing when engaged.

The new Rapid Deployment Force (RDF), created by President Carter early in 1980 in response to the Soviet invasion of Afghanistan, gives evidence of the way in which American thinking and expectations are being shaped by the new realities of warfare. Pegged originally at 100,000 men, the new RDF has already risen in nominal size to about 200,000 men. This is almost half the number of troops in Vietnam at the height of that war. In part, this may reflect the possibility that in places like the Middle East the RDF could have to fight against enemies reinforced by Soviet troops. But in a more fundamental sense, the creation of an RDF on this scale illustrates the height to which modern technology has driven even small conventional wars. The days are past in which a great power could steam a battleship up to within a few miles of the coasts and harbors of a state that had gone into default on its international debts and fire off a few rounds to underline its overdue-payment notice.

Individually, the growth of Soviet power and the rising costs of conventional conflict are bad enough. But in practice, they often combine to pose nearly intractable problems for the United States. Developments in Iran and the Persian Gulf amply demonstrated this difficulty in 1979 and 1980. To defeat Iran in outright war would have been well within the ability of the United States; to defeat Iraq in straightforward engagement similarly would have been possible; but in war with either state, Soviet intervention would have strained American regional capabilities beyond breaking. As the Iranian-Iraqi war broke out in September 1980, reports indicated that the Soviet Union had some 23 reinforced divisions ready to move into Iran if necessary. To deal with Russian attack into Iran toward the Persian Gulf, the United States would have needed air-dropped land mines; the Air Force had none on hand. To meet the Russian troops available for use in the Persian Gulf area, the United States would have had to deploy troops from the United States; the Air Force had troop carriers and cargo planes to move one third of an army division at any one time.[25] These numbers—and others—make only too clear that America's military capability has become inadequate to contend against enlarging Soviet power and increasingly expensive conventional warfare.

In its present condition, the American military simply cannot be brought to bear in many of the world's regions and on many of the nation's problems. In some situations, the costs may outweigh the importance of the issue. In others, the chances of success are much reduced. In both contexts, a policymaker's prudence will likely incline him toward inaction. The peacetime status of the American military no longer permits it to deal with problems of routine dimension, because new weapons and Soviet power have so enlarged the dimensions of routine situations.

Another large reason for our present military inadequacy is the way Americans have tended to think about military power and military institutions for the past fifteen years. There has been nothing secret about the Soviet military buildup, except for technical details inessential for appreciation of the magnitude of the enterprise. New weapons and their effects have similarly been widely remarked. In a very real sense, the United States has the military it deserves, shortcomings and all. For the nation's own thinking about military power and military institutions has impeded its ability to recognize and respond to causes of military inadequacy.

In military matters, the United States is caught between its ideals, its experience, and its emotions. Its ideals, passed down from founding philosophers, tell the American people that it is immoral to rely on violence in pursuit of democratic purposes. Its recent experience, such as that in Vietnam and Iran, tells the public that reliance on force is counterproductive, unlikely to work. But its emotions tell the nation that violence may be the only answer in a world of intractable problems and implacable enemies.

The Vietnam War encouraged the revival of an intellectual tradition long central to American political philosophy, the idea that force is not particularly useful or usable in the rational pursuit of national interests. This is an old theme of American diplomacy. The earliest American diplomatic documents expressed skepticism about the use of force. They exalted instead economic intercourse as the path to peace, and economic pressure as a more productive alternative to armed conflict.

In the 1960s and throughout the 1970s, largely under the impetus of the Vietnam War, there flourished in American academic and government circles a "new school" of international relations. This new school's chief doctrine emphasized the declining utility of force as a political instrument. A prominent professor of political science, Klaus Knorr, published a seminal book, *On the Uses of Military Power in the Nuclear Age.*[26] Appearing in 1966, this work contended that the "usability and usefulness of military force in interstate relations, compared with previous historical periods, had been diminished." Professor Knorr argued that "some traditionally important goals for going to war had lost appeal, that the anticipated costs of doing so had risen, and that the expected utility of using military forces internationally had therefore probably declined." Territorial conquest, for instance, a traditional goal of military action, had formerly meant an increased share of the people, resources, markets, investment opportunities, and geographic position that translated into enhanced national power. But the modern international economy permitted states to enjoy all these benefits without necessarily owning territories important to their economic and political well-being. Military technology was becoming more important as a determinant of strength than mere manpower or resources. Concurrently, military technology was making territory a less effective insulator against attack.

Further, nuclear weapons made the use of force even less promising. Their existence, and the possibilities for escalation of small wars into thermonuclear exchange, emphasized the potential costliness of war. To many observers, nuclear weapons seemed so destructive that they were simply unusable, good only for deterrence, for inhibiting the resort to war.

Finally, postwar political trends appeared to reduce the promise of resorting to force. Nationalism remained the predominant political force in world politics. The nationalist enthusiasm of many of the world's smaller states made them potentially formidable enemies, "unattractive targets for intervention or conquest by the great powers." There was also, Knorr noted, a fundamental change in world attitudes toward war. At the end of the nine-teenth century, war had widely been regarded as natural, legiti-mate, and inevitable. It seemed then no more than a social mani-festation of natural laws beyond human power to change. But in the latter twentieth century, by contrast, war increasingly seemed wrong, illegitimate, avoidable—a view that indeed had been em-bedded in the charter of the United Nations.

In the ten years following the appearance of this important book, many other scholars and government officials elaborated on Professor Knorr's arguments. In one proposition, adherents of the new school of international relations argued that the superpowers were completely "self-deterred," unable to take significant mili-tary actions anywhere in the world without fear of counterinter-vention by the other superpower. In a second and more important point, adherents of the new school emphasized that the issues of international affairs were changing in ways that rendered the re-sort to force meaningless, irrelevant. Formerly states had quar-reled over territory, prestige, and power. Now states were con-cerned with social and economic development, with domestic priorities and their international implications. In contrast to the old issues of security and power, the new issues were not suscepti-ble to resolution in war. Third, there was great emphasis on the ways in which growing economic interdependence made war irra-tional. It was more and more difficult to think of wars that would not harm the interests of the participants more than help them.

This new school of international relations converged with America's political and social reaction against the Vietnam War. After Vietnam, the American people turned to an all-volunteer military force and sought ways to limit military expenditures. The American policy outlook was given over to the "three D's" of the 1970s: Détente, Development, Dependence (or interdependence). In Soviet-American relations, this policy orientation resolved into a focus on arms control, on management of the increasingly ex-pensive and dangerous nuclear arms race. The Army got out of the counterinsurgency business, eliminating the kinds of special forces, the "flexibilities," that had created the opportunities to en-ter the unprogressive wars of the 1960s and 1970s. By July of 1976, the Army had issued new field manuals stressing its mission to fight and win in NATO Europe.[27] Counterinsurgency schools and units folded up their tents and disappeared into an army once more devoted to traditional tactics, forces, and missions. The Navy was encouraged to continue retiring ships, including some that had been reactivated to help supply the Vietnam War. And as General Sir John Hackett mockingly wrote in *The Third World War:* "It became fashionable . . . to suppose that a main object of diplomacy would always be to make friends of the rulers of Iran and the Arab oil countries." In a moment of prescience, General Hackett added: "But billionaire shahs and sheikhs are not likely to be the most popular folk heroes for the last decade of the twentieth century."[28]

In 1976, presidential candidate Jimmy Carter won support by promising to trim $5 billion to $7 billion from the defense budget, to withdraw troops from Korea, and to make arms control work. To much popular acclaim, Carter as President canceled the B-1 bomber program in 1977, opposed construction of a new aircraft carrier from 1977 through 1979, imposed pay caps on the military, and directed that any new land-based missile be designed so that 200 launchers—the President's minimum-deterrence arms control campaign figure—could do the job. In the Carter years, the post-Vietnam size of the Army was fixed at 16⅔ divisions, nearly all earmarked for NATO in the event of war.

In speeches and pronouncements, as well as in military policies, the administration's principal figures manifested their belief in the new school's ideas about the diminished role of force in international relations. In one statement characteristic of the administration's outlook, the President's national security adviser, Zbigniew Brzezinski, told *The New York Times* in 1978:

> The proper role of the United States . . . is to try to create global policies which are responsive to the fact that the global population is now politically awakened and in most cases living in very unfair conditions. This means ultimately an active effort genuinely to shape a stable world of diversity with many centers of power and many ideological systems. . . . I am optimistic about our role because I think our vision of the future and our definitions of our role correspond more accurately to genuine global dynamics than [does the vision] of the Soviets.[29]

In his January 1980 State of the Union message, President Carter defined American interests in terms of avoiding nuclear war, showing restraint in the use of force, and making America strong at home. In presenting a defense budget calling for significant increases in forces and, therefore, in spending, the Secretary of Defense, Harold Brown, said explicitly in the opening pages of the Fiscal 1981 Defense Department Annual Report that such increases "did not reflect a single sudden change in the world situation, or a sudden conversion on the part of the Administration."[30]

Yet revolution in Iran and Soviet troops in Afghanistan for a time seemed to introduce a certain ambivalence into public policy and public attitudes on the military. In a gesture widely interpreted as the end of America's post-Vietnam rejection of military instruments of power, Congress and the President set aside public land for a Vietnam memorial. President Carter's words at the ceremony were quoted as evidence of a new and more positive attitude toward the nation's military: "A long and painful process has brought us to this moment. Our nation was divided by this war. For too long, we tried to put that division behind us by forgetting the Viet Nam War. In the process, we ignored those who bravely answered their nation's call. We are ready at last to acknowledge more deeply the debt which we can never fully pay to those who served."[31] In another break with the administration's previous military policy, the Secretary of Defense testified to Congress on January 29, 1980: "We face a decision that we have been deferring far too long; we can defer it no longer. We must decide whether we intend to remain the strongest nation in the world."[32]

Despite the implications of presidential speeches and cabinet officer testimony, the administration continued, early in 1980, to emphasize that it had ruled out the use of force in the hostage crisis. The April 1980 raid aimed at releasing the hostages in Tehran was a virtually complete surprise to Iran, probably to the Soviets, and certainly to the American people precisely because it was inconsistent with the avowed philosophy of the Carter administration. That unmilitary, unmilitant philosophy had received reaffirmation even amid the collapse of SALT II, the invasion of Afghanistan, and the revolution in Iran. It was a philosophy in which the nation had come to believe, with only a small number of diehard dissenters.

In a sense, failure of the attempt to rescue hostages in Iran

confirmed earlier beliefs in the tenets of the new school in international relations. A psychologist might wonder whether, or to
what extent, a subconscious need for failure influenced the impo-
sition of crippling constraints of secrecy and size on the mission. It
is certain that such thoughts crossed the minds of many military
professionals disappointed and embarrassed by the desert fiasco.
One Marine colonel remarked to me in October 1980: "When I
think about what could have been done, and wasn't, and what was
done, and how it was done, I sometimes think that the mission
was intended to fail. I just can't see it any other way."

Failure of the raid seemed to prove the validity of the view
that military action could rarely be the answer to American problems. Even in failure, the attempted rescue had a cathartic effect.
The President left the Rose Garden to begin campaigning in earnest for reelection. In the mission's aftermath, but before the
Olympic boycott inspired by the Soviet invasion of Afghanistan
had run its course, the administration renewed its call for passage
of the SALT II treaty. The hostage issue receded quickly to secondary levels of public and media attention, only to be revived
when, in August 1980, news columnist Jack Anderson broke a
story alleging possible preparations for another, larger attempt to
be made just before the election.

After the failed hostage rescue attempt, the President's closest
advisers, including press secretary Jody Powell, told reporters that
the White House had been engaged in a grand strategic deception. The President's repeated emphasis on the inappropriateness
of force in the Iran crisis had been a deliberate cover for the
rescue operation being prepared. But in truth, the reiterated
theme that force would not advance America's interests in Iran
was much more than strategic deception. It was an attempt to
keep the faith of the new school, whose depreciation of the utility
of military force seemed of fading relevance and conviction amid
worsening Soviet-American relations and intolerable provocations
from Third World nations.

Ironically, one of the founders of the faith, Professor Klaus
Knorr, had already renounced it in a series of articles in 1977.[33]
Recapitulating his sanguine conclusions of 1965 regarding the di-
minishing usefulness of force as a political instrument, Professor
Knorr confessed his heresy. Rising world military expenditures,

increasing numbers of civil wars, regional conflicts, and other forms of violent struggle around the world had forced him to recant his optimistic projections about a political order in which national interests could be satisfied without war. That great illusion of Western culture, the rational actor, the economic man, had not yet evolved to a state of perfection permitting him to dispense with violence in politics. The Age of Aquarius, it seemed, had not yet arrived.

But Professor Knorr's change of heart had less immediate political effect than had his earlier hopes. In September 1980, when Iraq and Iran went to war, American policy again reflected the judgment that inaction was preferable to action, that American interests would be best served by standing hopefully on the sidelines. The cutoff of oil shipments from Iran and Iraq—the second and fourth largest suppliers of Middle East oil—threatened the vitality of economies in Japan, France, and other European partners of the United States. When the President proposed use of American and allied naval units to keep the vital Strait of Hormuz open, only the British among America's major allies responded favorably. The Germans and Japanese declined to take part in any such joint action, citing technical provisions in their constitutions as reasons for nonparticipation. But it was clear that they feared alienation of Arab oil suppliers in the long run, and the risks of leaning on a weakened United States in the short run. The French, with fourteen naval vessels in the Indian Ocean, as usual remained uncommitted and unpredictable.

The explanation for the failure of the rescue attempt in Iran, when all was officially said and done, was not timidity or incompetence in the nation's political leaders, not military mismanagement, not lack of national will. Rather, the mission's failure was ascribed in the most general way to the presumed fact that the problem was simply too hard. The mission's failure, so it was said, reflected present-day limits on power and on the utility of force. No other military in the world could have attempted the mission, the evaluation committee and administration spokesmen concluded. The President, Jimmy Carter, insisted on describing the rescue attempt not as a failure but as an "incomplete success." That linguistic legerdemain earned him an award at the end of 1980, for conspicuous abuse of the English language. Then Secretary of the

Navy Edward Hidalgo called the rescue attempt not a disaster but a "triumph of American technology." This locution, if it had become better known, would surely have been at least a runner-up to President Carter's.

President Carter and the high-level military leaders he assembled to evaluate the mission praised the professionalism of those who had planned and executed the operation. In the face of criticism of the mission's failure, the Chief of Naval Operations asserted that American military professionals of 1980 were as good as any in the nation's history.[34]

But the report of the military committee formed to assess the mission—the Special Operations Review Committee—showed numerous and real shortcomings in the military's operational capability and in the mission's planning, training, and execution. The tight operational security that prevented using more helicopters was forced in large part by Soviet capability to monitor American military activities and to obstruct the operation once it became known. Service jealousies made it necessary for each of the four services to take part in the mission—to share the credit in the event of success, to spread the blame in the event of failure. The participation of all services increased the difficulties of training, command, and organization. These in turn produced confusion on the ground at Desert One, leading to the deadly collision of a helicopter and a C-130. Some of the pilots originally assigned to the mission proved incapable of mastering the night flying and other techniques deemed essential to the mission; they had to be replaced after several weeks of training. Although the mission was in preparation for months, elementary safeguards for classified material and equipment were overlooked; autodestruct devices were not implanted into the helicopters flown on the mission, and in the chaos into which Desert One evolved, highly sensitive papers and equipment, not to mention several virtually intact helicopters, were left for the enemy to find.[35]

However hard the problem—and there is no doubt that it was very difficult—the Iran raid did not show a military in the peak of condition doing its best against insuperable obstacles and odds. Rather, it portrayed a military in crisis, unsuccessful in small matters, unfit, perhaps, to attempt larger ones. In the months following the Iran rescue effort, most of the nation's major newspapers and magazines conducted lengthy surveys of the state of America's defenses. In every case, the conclusions were similar and somber.

The portrait of the American military drawn in the election year was a picture of inadequacy. In personnel, morale was low, turnover high. In equipment, shortages were high, maintenance and reliability low. One of Sir John Hackett's comments, dating back to 1962, seemed distressingly apt: "What a society gets in its armed services is exactly what it asks for, no more and no less. What it asks for tends to be a reflection of what it is. When a country looks at its fighting forces it is looking in a mirror; if the mirror is a true one the face that it sees there will be its own."[36] In the 1970s, the American nation thought about military power and military institutions in ways that, at last, prevented a timely and correct response to a changing strategic environment.

Remedies for the troubled American military stand high on the list of national priorities for the 1980s. Like most remedies, these must be chosen and administered with care. More money in itself will not restore the nation's military competence. Continuing public attention to military issues and military institutions is vital.

The military organizations of democratic states have a special problem, rarely recognized in the United States. Democracies and standing military organizations are instinctive enemies. For democracies, at least in theory, war is an unnatural state; for militaries, peace is abnormal and, in its own way, dangerous. The military of a democracy at peace is virtually certain to lose its sense of purpose, to lapse into shortsighted political and bureaucratic machinations. In the American military from Vietnam to Afghanistan, these difficulties have taken concrete shape as obstacles to military adequacy and military reform.

III THE PEOPLE:
LOVING THE MILITARY
AND LEAVING IT

Of all the things that exist between heaven and earth, there is nothing as valuable as man.

SUN PIN, C. 400 B.C.

IN THE GENERATION from 1957 to the present, the moments at which people have loomed larger than hardware in American defense have been both rare and brief. The United States has spent the years since Sputnik worrying about its technological edge, or lack thereof. Year after year, in appropriations hearings, publicity snow jobs, and even in officer education requirements, the military's worst fears, best hopes, and biggest-ticket budget concerns have all centered on high-technology hardware.

With its draft calls, the Vietnam War raised "people" issues in a way that the military, and for that matter the country, probably would have preferred to avoid. But termination of the draft at the end of 1972—Congress's revenge on the presidency for the deceptions that led to the Gulf of Tonkin Resolution, and perhaps Congress's apology to the nation for its part in supporting the war—was supposed to end manpower issues as well. Armed with enlarged advertising budgets and enlightened personnel policies, the services were charged to find their own men for the national defense, beginning in January 1973. The all-volunteer force was, in short, a device to prevent military manpower needs from ever becoming an important issue.

In 1979, for the first time since the all-volunteer force had come into being in 1973, all four services—Army, Navy, Air Force, and Marine Corps—failed to meet recruiting goals. In

31

1980, manpower concerns picked up tempo. In January, the Chief of Naval Operations, Admiral Thomas B. Hayward, reported to Congress that "adverse trends in retention of our key supervisory talent—our most experienced middlegrade leaders—are fast becoming *the* critical constraint on the size, capability, and readiness of the Navy. . . . The talent drain occasioned by inadequate compensation is clearly the single most serious concern I have about the present state of the Navy."[1] In the same month, the Carter administration called for renewal of draft registration, though not the draft itself, to signify American displeasure over the Soviet invasion of Afghanistan in December 1979.

Early in April 1980, as Navy forces kept station in the Indian Ocean to manifest American interest in goings-on in Iran and Afghanistan, a supply ship, the *Canisteo,* could not get under way from the United States because its crew lacked essential boiler technicians and machinists. During the first four months of the year, the rate at which warships of the Atlantic Fleet had been rated unsafe for deployment because of manpower shortages tripled.[2]

Other figures seemed even more ominous, for it was becoming evident that such problems were neither isolated nor transient. In increasing numbers, men and women with irreplaceable training and experience were leaving the service, and doing so years early. In the nine years from 1971 to 1979, reenlistment rates of the Navy's career people fell from about 90 percent to just over 62 percent. The Marines suffered a similarly precipitous falloff in reenlistments, although the Army actually showed a slight improvement in its rate and the Air Force showed only a comparatively modest 10 percent decline.[3]

Later in April, the attempt to rescue hostages in Iran gave even sharper point to manpower concerns. Failure, of course, brought much criticism upon the military, and even where criticism was restrained, still there were questions about the competence of the men in the field and the judgment of the men in the background. After the rescue effort, the Chief of Naval Operations clearly took the lead on manpower matters among the service chiefs. This was only natural; of all the services, the Navy's problems were the most acute.

Lashing out at the military's critics just two days after the Iran rescue operation, Admiral Hayward complained that a national "penchant for headhunting and thirst for scapegoats have added to our internal divisiveness at a moment when we should be showing our strength by linking arms and supporting our government." He quarreled with a press statement that "the professionals of the American military have compiled a record replete with failure and catastrophe," asserting that those professionals "are as good today as they have ever been." He preached a sermon drawn from Theodore Roosevelt's muscled prose and even more muscular outlook: "It is not the critic who counts," Admiral Hayward quoted TR, "not the man who points out how the strong man stumbled or where the doer of deeds could have done better. The credit belongs to the man who is actually in the arena; whose face is marred by dust and sweat and blood . . . and who, at the worst, if he fails, at least fails while doing greatly, so that his place shall never be with those cold and timid souls who know neither victory nor defeat." [4]

Then Admiral Hayward suggested his own interpretation of the intersection between manpower concerns and the aborted rescue mission: "Are we," he asked, "so short of skilled personnel in the all-volunteer force that we couldn't run a successful rescue mission without taking excessive risks?" [5] It was a suggestion worth pondering. A few weeks later, presumably in a personal answer to his own question, the admiral broke ranks with his fellow chiefs of service—and more surprisingly, with presidential policy—to call for renewal of the peacetime draft.

"The all-volunteer force, set up in 1973, is threatening to turn into the biggest military fiasco since Little Big Horn." So wrote Walter Guzzardi, Jr., in *Fortune,* as summer drew to a close in 1980. [6] In July, in a country deeply divided over the necessity and desirability of considering a revived draft, thousands of young Americans born in 1960 and 1961 registered with the Selective Service System, the draft board. Thousands more, born in those same years, declined to obey the registration order.

Friends and foes of the draft argued well into the fall about the success of the sign-up, and the scale of resistance to it. In their election-year platforms, the Republican and Democratic parties said as little about the subject as they decently could. Even though it earned him loud jeers from the convention crowd, President

Carter maintained even in accepting the presidential nomination
that registration of men was necessary, but not that of women. In
any case, as the Carter administration stressed, no draft was in
sight. The American Civil Liberties Union went to court to contest
the legality of a Selective Service System that discriminated
against women; for a day or so, just before registration was to
begin, the ACLU seemed on the verge of victory. Former Vietnam activists girded for a familiar fight. Congress, also inclined
toward prudence in election season, voted funds to register young
men but none to ensure that those required to register would either do so or be called to account.

Somehow, in America, military manpower issues always seem
to come around to the draft. In the last two years, the draft as
panacea has become a virtual fixture of national security discussions. Do you want to get the Russians' attention? Revive the
draft. How about reassuring America's allies? Reinstitute the
draft. Meet recruiting quotas? Enlarge the Army? Draft some
bodies. Reduce manpower costs? Return to the draft. Improve the
overall quality of the enlisted ranks? Draft some more high school
graduates and perhaps, for good measure, a few college boys too.
It would not be difficult, on the basis of recent news features and
defense-related writings, to get the impression that quite a few
people have begun with an answer—the draft—rather than with
the questions—America's military manpower problems: the fact
that recruiting numbers have been down; the educational level of
recruits is sinking; social and demographic trends seem likely to
make things worse; retention figures are slipping. More important
than all the rest, the recent showings of the American military
have not been good. Vietnam gave the military a reputation for
poor discipline; 1970s cost overruns added a reputation for medio-
cre management; the hostage rescue attempt in Iran appended
one of incompetence.

Would it be prudent, timely, helpful, to resuscitate the draft
now? The answer depends on the extent to which a draft would
alleviate the specific aspects of manpower difficulties: recruitment, retention, mobilization, political-military image, and cost.

Recruiting difficulties revolve around the numbers and the
quality of recruits. Under the all-volunteer force, planners initial-

ly expected to maintain a military of about 2.5 million people. Each year since 1973, the overall force has declined in size, but there has been no clear policy decision that such reductions reflected America's reasoned and reasonable interests.[7] In 1979, the Department of Defense was authorized to have 2,050,000 people in uniform; it ended the fiscal year with 2,025,000, a shortfall of only 25,000, or about 1.25 percent. Plans for 1980 called for no growth, again a target figure of 2,050,000. The Defense Department met this target, reporting in the first quarter of fiscal 1981 an active-duty force of just that size. For fiscal 1981, Defense planned modest growth, to 2,059,000.[8]

To maintain present size, the military needs to recruit about 340,000 people per year. This has been difficult enough in the past, as witness the recruiting scandals of 1979, when some 393 recruiters were charged with taking 12,700 fraudulent enlistments, that is, helping prospective enlistees to pass admission tests, falsifying high school diplomas, or in other ways concealing disqualifications for service. Recruiting in the coming decade will be more difficult than in the past, because the number of American males turning eighteen in any given year peaked in 1978, will decline through 1992, and will rise only slowly thereafter.

But it is important to remember that in the United States the principal limitations on manpower for the military have always been political. They stem not from demographic but from political, social, and economic conditions. The American public is not antimilitary; but it continues to be definitely *un*military. Thousands of young men and women capable enough to meet the military's entrance standards now neither attend school nor hold full-time employment. In May 1980, the national unemployment rate was 7.8 percent; for youths of military service age, the rate was between 12.7 percent and 17.4 percent, depending on exact age. The inescapable conclusion was, simply, that many young men prefer unemployment to military service.[9]

The recruiting problem also concerns the usability of the people entering the military. Amid criticism on this point in 1980, the Defense Department insisted that "the quality of our recruits, in terms of their ability to learn military skills and perform successfully as members of military units, has been roughly comparable, since 1973, to what we experienced in the pre-Vietnam period."[10]

But the customary indexes of quality gave reason for worry. In the first half of 1979, for instance, 68 percent of all enlistees had high school diplomas; in the first half of 1980, only 58 percent were high school graduates. In 1964, 13.9 percent of those brought into the service had at least some college; in 1979, for enlistees, this percentage had dropped to 3.2 percent, although it improved slightly in 1980.[11]

Less scientific evaluations of recruit quality occasioned even more concern. One Marine lieutenant colonel with long experience in recruiting bemoaned the diminishing abilities of service enlistees. "Thank God for the Mag-card typewriter," he said to me, referring to the marginal skills even of his enlisted clerks. "Without it we could never get a clean copy of anything." A Navy captain echoed this view, but with more alarm: "We have probably reached the point where this country could not rearm itself if it wanted to," he remarked to me. "Kids today can't take orders; they are used to arguing their way out of doing things they don't like. Today's youth attitudes of questioning and rebellion cannot be dealt with in the traditional military framework." In a more detached but equally disturbing report, the Boston *Globe* ran a story on the fall 1980 maneuvers of the NATO alliance, in which the poor performance of American troops caused Dutch military men literally to laugh at them.

In this declining trend, the military's methods of assessing the quality of recruits came in for scrutiny. For decades the military has given all prospective entrants the Armed Forces Qualification Test, a general test of verbal ability, mechanical aptitude, and simple mathematics and reasoning. On the basis of this test, the military categorizes potential recruits into five groups: Category I contains those with above-average abilities as shown by the test; Category IIs are average in ability; Category IIIs might be called low average; Category IVs are below average in intelligence and ability, and Category Vs are those judged too low in promise to be inducted.

Of the recruits entering the service in 1972, the last year of the draft, 35 percent were in mental categories I and II, 48 percent in category III, and 17 percent in category IV. By 1978, things were much worse: 57 percent of the Army's male recruits that year were in mental categories IV and IIIb, that is, well below average intelligence in the United States. In 1979, almost as bad, 29 percent of the volunteers qualified in categories I and II, 66 percent in category III, and 5 percent in category IV.[12]

Then in 1980, the issue of recruit quality took on an added dimension of controversy and concern. Early in the year, former Under Secretary of the Navy R. James Woolsey testified to Congress that recently found flaws in the military's entry tests meant that recruits of the last few years were still weaker in ability than test scores had indicated. By midsummer of 1980, the Department of Defense had admitted that such testing flaws had been substantial indeed. It now seemed that 30 percent of 1979's recruits had been mental category IVs, not the 5 percent earlier claimed and widely publicized as a sign of successful recruitment policy. Still later in the year, the figure was revised again; the Army alone had taken in 46 percent category IVs in 1979. The Defense Department explained that the test in use for the last several years had been "miscalibrated," and that this problem had been promptly corrected upon discovery earlier in the year.

The military's reaction to these 1980 recruitment statistics took yet another turn, this a classic bureaucratic maneuver. The Secretary of the Army, Clifford Alexander, announced that the Army would no longer use the test, period. "Whatever category they [the new recruits] happen to be in that silly-ass test," he said, "bears no relationship to their performance as soldiers."[13] Fearing that upward revision of minimum entrance standards would make it impossible to meet recruiting goals, Defense officials refused to permit the services to alter their minimum passing scores to compensate for the "calibration" errors discovered in the Armed Forces Qualification Test. Robert B. Pirie, the Assistant Secretary of Defense for Manpower and Reserve Affairs, refused the Air Force permission to raise standards, arguing that this would be a mistake unless and until it could be proved that those who had entered the military under the flawed test really could not make it as soldiers. An unnamed Air Force official, quoted in the *Air Force Times* of November 3, 1980, explained his service's view on this policy. It's like having a car, he said, that needs 90-octane gasoline. You find out that it has in fact been getting 85-octane gas for some time. The question: Do you then give it the 90-octane gas it requires or do you continue giving it 85-octane fuel, waiting to see if the engine breaks down?

The Congress also took note of the trends in manpower quality as measured by traditional tests. Without passing on the merits of the testing system, Congress simply imposed new restrictions within which the services would have to devise recruiting policies. In fiscal 1981, Congress required that no more than 25 percent of all enlistees be Category IVs. For fiscal 1982, Congress is applying this 25 percent limitation to each individual service, so that shortcomings of one or another service cannot be averaged out against the superior performance of others. For fiscal 1983, Congress is tightening standards still more: no more than 20 percent Category IV recruits for each service.[14] How this new direction would work out against the Secretary of the Army's unwillingness to continue using the AFQT at all remained unclear.

The quality problem is not simply a matter of abstract concern. It has serious implications for military effectiveness. Declining quality—as measured in terms of intellectual ability, mechanical aptitude, even reading competence and mathematical facility—increases the training burden on the services. One Navy commander told *Time* magazine early in 1980: "There is no need anymore for the so-called able-bodied seaman. What we need are technicians."[15] A couple of years ago, of the soldiers specializing in the maintenance of nuclear weapons, 90 percent of those tested failed the skill-qualification test for this specialization. In 1976, 53 percent of the infantrymen tested at Fort Benning, Georgia, could read only at fifth-grade level.[16] And there is the story, told to me as true, about a frustrated East Coast recruiter who started giving a simple test to prospective recruits. The question: "Recite the alphabet." Out of thirty men, two succeeded.

In a decade of diminishing age-eligible young men, the best the services could hope for, according to Defense Department guidance for 1981, was to keep their proportionate share of the nation's high school graduating classes. This meant that in the 1980s, the military would have to adjust to having fewer and fewer high school graduates in its ranks, and possibly to fewer and fewer people.

Further, as Secretary of Defense Harold Brown noted in his

January 1980 message to Congress, "those in the lowest mental categories have historically accounted for a disproportionate share of disciplinary problems."[17] The most important result of this historical showing has been a startlingly high "first-term attrition," that is, failure of enlistees to complete their initial three-year term. In the latter 1970s, about one out of every three people who joined the military did not complete even one term of service. This figure was worse earlier in the 1970s; it was clearly improving at the end of the decade, but it was not good. It meant, in simple terms, that about one third of the entire recruiting effort was going to waste. In 1979, for instance, non-marijuana drug offenses among Army enlistees climbed 21 percent over 1976, and desertions rose 18 percent.

Results aside, recruiting itself has been extremely difficult. A 1979 Army study showed that at 47 percent of the nation's high schools, military recruiters were refused information on student names and addresses. At 2 percent of the high schools, they were barred altogether. Although in the state of Washington, in June 1980, a new statute gave military recruiters the same rights of access to and information about students as might be extended to any other recruiters—say, from colleges or businesses—how far such laws would spread remained to be seen.

Officer recruiting is, if anything, still more difficult. 1979, the Air Force had its best year in a long time as far as recruiting engineers for its officer corps; it got 202 out of the 642 it was seeking. The Navy funds about 6,000 ROTC scholarships at 55 ROTC units around the country. Forty-five percent of those obtaining scholarships drop out of the program before their junior year, at that point still owing the government nothing in return for two years' worth of tuition, books, and subsistence payments.

Thomas Jefferson once said that the Navy was aristocratic, imperialistic, and expensive. Today, it is only expensive. In 1978, it cost $80,000 to train an officer at the Naval Academy in Annapolis. The average cost of officers obtained through the NROTC programs on the nation's college campuses was $30,000. Even college graduates, officers already educated, cost $6,000 each to send through the brief orientation course known as Officer Indoctrination School.

Moreover, the officer corps is being drawn increasingly not

from the top of American society, or even from the middle, but from the lower portion of the spectrum. As one Navy captain heading a large ROTC unit explained it to me, the ROTC scholarships and a large proportion of the service academy appointments were being sought by—and going to—young people of very limited background, kids who need the money. In a talk to a Rotary club in a large midwestern city, this naval officer asked the sixty Rotarians in attendance how many had children between the ages of eighteen and twenty-three; of the thirty who did, only one had a child in the military or in officer training.

"When kids apply for ROTC scholarships," the captain told me, "they have to supply letters of recommendation to the selection committee. Naturally, they try to get letters from the 'heaviest hitters' they know. We're seeing letters of recommendation written by Amy of Amy's Diner, who tells us, 'This is a good kid; he don't smoke no dope.' The officers corps is becoming lower middle class, or simply lower class, in makeup. The rich and upper-middle-class segments of American society are increasingly unconnected to the military. They don't know about military pay, military conditions, military quality, or about the nation's potential military uses."

Recruiting is difficult, but without doubt the number one manpower problem is retention. The issue here is not that of getting people to reenlist after one term in the service. Since 1969, the numbers of people reenlisting have risen year by year. In 1979, 94,465 men and women reenlisted, about 30 percent of those making the choice that year to stay in or get out at the end of their first enlistment. Still more reenlisted in 1980. But people with seven to ten years of service, officers as well as enlisted, are leaving the military at an unprecedented and increasing rate. The Air Force cannot keep its pilots and engineers; the Navy cannot keep its nuclear power officers and aviators; throughout the officer and enlisted ranks, people with marketable skills, training, and experience are getting out of the military—mostly to improve their financial circumstances.

Retention problems pervade the services, although they take slightly different forms in each. In the fall of 1980, the Army was short 7,000 noncommissioned officers, most of them in the combat arms—infantry, armor, artillery, and combat engineers. At the end of fiscal 1979, the Navy calculated that it was short 23,369 petty officers, and 2,300 midcareer pilots. As fiscal 1980 drew to a close, these numbers had changed only slightly. In 1979, the Navy lost 102 out of 138 nuclear-qualified petty officers up for reenlistment; late in 1980, the rate of reenlistment for Navy nuclear engineers facing their third term dropped to a staggering 7 percent, with 60 percent the necessary rate for the Navy to maintain its minimum requirements for nuclear manning. Between 1975 and 1979, Air Force third-term reenlistments dropped 20 percent. The Air Force needs to retain 59 percent of the pilots and 50 percent of the navigators who have between six and eleven years of service. Late in 1980, it was managing to keep only 26 percent and 44 percent respectively. In 1980, the Air Force considered itself 2,100 pilots and 900 navigators below requirements, and expected these figures to increase appreciably by 1982.[19] It takes three to six years of repeated training and constant flying to produce a frontline combat aviator. It takes five to seven years to train a first-class electronics repairman, about the same to develop the skills of many other technicians essential for keeping the military's machines and weapons in operable condition.

The midcareer officers who are leaving in such numbers are the "operators" and middle managers of the military. They fly $25 million airplanes, drive ships that cost $200 million or more, hold direct custody of nuclear weapons, fill important staff jobs, and administer programs and organizations with annual budgets running into the millions of dollars. The petty officers—and their counterparts, the sergeants—are the direct supervisors for hundreds of thousands of soldiers, sailors, airmen, and marines. The "foremen" of the military, they provide the age, experience, leadership, on-the-job supervision and training that stabilize and improve the military work force. Every military in the world depends on its noncommissioned officers to make things work, to provide the essential link between tradition and organization on one hand and people on the other. Generals may lead armies, but noncoms run them.

An article in the *Wall Street Journal* on October 30, 1980, described the effects of the manpower problem on the aircraft carrier *Kennedy*, deployed to the Indian Ocean for operations in the context of events in Afghanistan and the Persian Gulf. Like every other ship in the Navy, the *Kennedy* is undermanned by about one third. Just to deploy, the *Kennedy* had to "borrow" about fifty sailors from other ships and units. *Kennedy* is supposed to have three chief petty officers in the aviation stores department, which cares for an inventory of 60,000 aircraft parts for the carrier's air wing. There wasn't a single one there at the time of the article. Less experienced petty officers were taking longer to do the work. "A squadron of aircraft," said a supply officer on board, "instead of getting a part in one hour, will have to wait four hours." *Kennedy* had to stop using one of its four catapults for launching aircraft because its deck crew was too inexperienced to move aircraft around the deck in ways that would keep the area clear for operations. Such deficiencies slow down aircraft repairs, retard routine maintenance, and reduce the number of missions that *Kennedy*'s planes can fly. "In war," the *Journal* cautiously observed, "such compromises might be dangerous."

"This manpower problem reminds me of what it was like just after World War II," one naval officer veteran of that war told me after reading the *Wall Street Journal*'s story on the *Kennedy*. "All the chiefs and the first-class petty officers had a lot of points, and so they went home first. To keep the battleships and other big ones going, they pulled people from all over—other ships, shore jobs, everywhere. Radarmen and other skilled types were concentrated on the most important ships. But the result was wide deterioration of the whole Navy's organization and capability."

All this experience walking out the door is very costly indeed. To begin with the lesser dimensions of cost, only 55 percent of the Naval Academy graduates brought into service at a cost exceeding $80,000 each stay very long. In 1980, fully 45 percent of the Naval Academy's graduates were staying on commissioned service for an average of only two years beyond their initial four-year obligation. The figures were similar for officers obtained through NROTC: 44 percent were remaining in only about two years beyond their required initial period of service. The longer an officer is in, however, the more the military stands to lose by his early departure from the service. The Air Force estimates that when a pilot with twelve years service leaves to take a job with the airlines, he has received pay, allowances, and training worth $4 million, money and training invested in him in the hope that he would give the military—and the nation—twenty to thirty good years of service. In 1979, of people with between six and eleven years of service, the Air Force lost 71 percent of the pilots, 50 percent of the navigators, and 66 percent of the engineers. It was losing enlisted people at the rate of one every six minutes; in fiscal 1979, the Air Force calculated, it lost the equivalent of half a million man-years of experience. Again, by the Air Force's own calculations, the loss of an F-15 pilot costs $1,137,000, that of a C-130 pilot $350,000; to replace a first-rate F-15 pilot might take as much as eight years and $8 million.[19] In the Navy, one captain told me late in 1980, in some squadrons, ships, and units, *everyone* was planning to get out at the earliest opportunity—all the enlisted, and most of the officers—almost literally a zero percent retention rate in those units.

Thus the quality problem in the military revolves as much, if not more, around the instability of its noncommissioned technicians and its officer corps as around the mental test scores of recruits. It is simply impossible to build and sustain a competent, improving military when those who have been in the service long enough to reach advanced schooling and long enough to have had varied experience leave at such rates. To deal with this in the short term, the military has resorted to some truly extraordinary measures. In 1980, the military began serious efforts to recruit recently separated officer pilots, asking them to return to active duty. The Air Force literally had more planes than pilots, and was receiving large numbers of new F-15 and F-16 fighters. In earlier years, the Air Force had had some 5,000 pilots available; in early 1981, this number was down to about 2,000. In fiscal 1981, the Air Force hoped to attract 550 former officer pilots back to active duty, although response to its campaign was not particularly good in early months. In the Navy, a pilot shortage of similar dimensions inspired a resort to expedients usually seen only in war: sending enlisted personnel to flight school to make up for the pilot shortage. These actions, it must be said, suggest the military's desperation, considering that officers who have once resigned, in effect turning their backs on their brother officers and on the military way of life, have not always been regarded with enthusiasm by the senior military leadership. The Air Force is experimenting with a program for retaining enlisted technicians beyond their normal retirement dates, another revolutionary expedient in the tradition-bound military. It takes an act of Congress to keep Admiral Rickover on active duty past his retirement date; and it took World War II to keep officers and men in the service past their regular retirement dates in any significant numbers.

The inability to retain enough trained people in the service makes the recruiting burden heavier. In the last two years, it has become something of an occasion when one of the services meets its monthly recruiting quota. Usually this achievement—the military code word for almost anything done by almost anybody—receives service-wide publicity. Occasionally, retention and recruitment strains lead to imaginative, if not always feasible, programs. Not long ago, someone in the Navy Department thought of raffling 1,000 Corvette Stingrays per year to reenlisting sailors. Each sailor was to get three chances to win, one in the first month of the new enlistment and one each on the following Fourth of July and Navy Day, days on which a bonanza of 100 cars would be raffled off at once. It was a wonderful idea—the sexiest car in America, and as it is often said, most sailors will bet on most anything. The hitch: federal regulations would have required the Navy to invite competitive bids for 1,000 cars and to buy from the lowest bidder. The regulations would doubtless have resulted in raffles featuring stripped-down Ramblers, the mainstay of many a government motor pool, but as an inducement to reenlist not quite in the same class as a navy-blue-and-gold-striped Stingray.

The pressures sometimes lead less to imagination than to efforts to do the impossible by means of the ill-conceived. An Army spokesman in 1979, for instance, announced a considerable lowering of the Army's minimum mental requirements for entry as a "substantial widening of opportunities for women." In exquisitely opaque prose, the report of the Chief of Naval Operations to Congress early in 1980 referred to measures easing entry standards as a new recruiting policy "which would expand the recruiting market." The Marines, ever individualistic, commissioned the J. Walter Thompson advertising agency, one of Madison Avenue's most prestigious, to devise new recruiting ads. Among other efforts, the

Thompson agency hired a cookbook writer to create food spreads for recruiting posters and ads, presumably to suggest that food in the Marines is so good that people should willingly enlist to get theirs. It remained to see whether anyone would believe that food in the Marines would be as good as that depicted in $1,000-per-day-plus-expenses publicity photos. And it was even more in question whether the Marine Corps would find that ads appealing to hedonism if not gluttony would bring them recruits with the same desirable toughness attracted by the appeal for "a few good men."

The gimmicks in recruiting campaigns are signs of what many old soldiers believe to be a distortion, a disturbance, permeating the services. A good many officers flatly believe—and will loudly maintain—that the Army has no business spending good money and good people on recruiting. Some in the Congress seem to agree. Senator John Stennis, chairman of the Senate Armed Services Committee, observed after the Iran rescue effort that "Recruiting has become a grave contest, an ordeal—much of it is not in keeping with the dignity of the military services."[20] Further, the stress placed on increasing reenlistments has contributed, so it sometimes seems, to an erosion of military discipline, a "babying" of servicemen to get them to "re-up." Some officers believe that in the all-volunteer force they are coming to be evaluated and promoted less for ability to lead a command in carrying out its missions than for avoiding racial incidents among subordinates and for improving reenlistment rates. "What we are lacking," Senator Stennis said in the same speech, "are things that money can't buy—discipline, character, dedication, and many other personal qualities."[21]

The Navy and the Marine Corps are now assigning top officers to recruiting duty in line with current priorities and needs. But many of these officers have told me of their fear that the "system" will let them down when they next come up for promotion. Recruiting duty traditionally has been peripheral to officer career development, not the job for a "hot-runner," and promotion boards are notorious for esteeming tradition above current guidance in selecting officers for advancement.

The Marine Corps, populated by volunteers for most of its years, has probably found adjustment to the all-volunteer era less strenuous than have the other services. Perhaps for this reason, the

Marine Corps seems to have seen the handwriting on the wall sooner than the others. After failing to make its recruiting goal in 1979, along with the rest of the services, the Marine Corps voluntarily reduced its size by about 5,000 men, from 190,000 to 185,500. This can be construed two ways: (1) as sound managerial philosophy. The move might have reflected convictions that good is better than big, that declining manpower and coming fiscal constraints called for this kind of adjustment. Or it could have seemed a commitment to keep that lean, mean Marine image hard and bright through a healthy consolidation of the sort that Senator Sam Nunn seemed about to force on the Army by proposing a 25,000-man cut in strength in 1980. And (2) as bureaucratic politics of the highest order. By the drawdown in forces—a reduction mostly on paper, since it was in fact already about 4,900 men short—the Marine Corps brought itself to 100 percent of authorized strength. This permitted it to lower the following year's recruiting goal, which in turn made it the only service in 1980 to reach its target. In either interpretation, it is clear that the Marines are fighting Washington's battles every bit as skillfully as any they have ever fought on foreign shores.

There is large potential confusion in the recruiting and retention problem. On one hand, the Department of Defense ended fiscal 1979 only about 25,000 men short, and fiscal 1980 with scarcely any shortage at all; on the other, the Navy alone claimed to be more than 23,000 petty officers and 2,300 commissioned officers below strength, while the other services had commensurate if not worse personnel deficiencies. What explains this apparent discrepancy?

In part, the military simply has not adjusted internally to the shrinking overall size of America's armed forces. In some respects—though this is surely an oversimplification—it is still organized as if it were a 2.5-million-man force. But there is another problem. Simply put, the military has a far from ideal personnel distribution across its rank, rating, and specialization groups. In the officer corps, there are plenty of admirals and generals, as many as the law and budget permit; there are only a few less Navy captains and colonels than authorized; there are enough ensigns and lieutenants; but there are far too few lieutenants, captains, majors, lieutenant commanders, commanders, and lieutenant colonels. The enlisted ranks show similar distortions.

As one would expect, the military organization encounters serious difficulties in absorbing such problems of distribution among ranks and skills. In the Navy in 1979, certain units were designated to receive only 71 percent of the replacements they would ordinarily have received as people left in normal rotation to new assignments. Similarly, in confronting its 1980 pilot shortages the Air Force manned its operational units while "gapping"—leaving unfilled—staff and support jobs. In its own words: "Thus the flying mission will be maintained by supervision and career-broadening opportunities will be degraded."[22] In other words, the kinds of education, responsibility, and experience that make for competent senior officers in the future were being sacrificed to keep men in cockpits for the moment. However desirable it sometimes seems to cut the fat out of government, an organization can scarcely be expected to perform at its best when it receives personnel cuts on such a scale, especially when these are the result of uncontrollable forces, rather than part of some more permanent and more deliberate scheme to streamline operations and improve results.

As the 1970s came to a close, manpower concerns arose in still another form: the problem of mobilization for war. This version of the manpower problem received special attention because of the Carter administration's emphasis on America's commitment to NATO.

Adopted at the end of the decade, new criteria for mobilization—derived and approved well before the foreign-policy setbacks in Iran and Afghanistan—sharply raised the burdens that an order for mobilization would place on the Selective Service System, and through it on the nation. Where previously the Selective Service System had been required to produce the first inductees on the 110th day after mobilization, it would be expected to do so on the thirtieth; where previously Selective Service was to provide at least 100,000 men by the 150th day after mobilization, now it was to do so by the sixtieth; and where previously the military had expected Selective Service to make available 390,000 men in six months, the military now called for 650,000 men in the same interval.

But new requirements were one thing, new capabilities another. For in some respects, even old capabilities had become chimerical. A spokesman for forty-nine adjutants general of state national guards said in May 1980 that the United States "couldn't mobilize a force strong enough to beat Snow White and the Seven Dwarfs."[23] America's reserve forces, supposedly available for early use before the tide of wartime draftees could reach readiness, had sunk into disrepair. With the end of the draft, there was considerably less incentive to join reserve military units. Further, many Vietnam veterans, disenchanted with their military experiences, did not stay in the reserve beyond their minimum obligations. Then too, fiscal pressures of the middle 1970s encouraged the military, for a time, to skimp on pay for reservists as well as on equipment and operating expenses for reserve units. All these things cost the reserves people, competence, and readiness. As a result, by 1977, the Army's National Guard and Reserve were 100,000 men under authorized peacetime strength, which in turn was only 75 percent of expected wartime strength. By 1980, figures on shortfalls in reserve manpower were ranging from an official Army figure of 276,000 to figures of 370,000 from experts quoted in the press. There is no need to argue about the specific numbers. The score is not encouraging by either count. The only bright aspect of this dour concern was that by the end of the decade the sharp losses the reserve sustained when the draft ended had pretty well come to a halt.[24]

In the late 1970s, moreover, Selective Service itself had been placed into "deep standby," so deep that at the end of the decade it could not have produced the first draftee for training in less than four months from the date of mobilization. It would have taken three months more for minimum military training of the initial draftees. Hence no draftee could have reached, say, Europe in a NATO emergency in much less than seven months.

In present manpower discussions, cost issues have a special place. To be sure, cost pervades all national security concerns, but there is more. Soviet military personnel costs are much lower than comparable American costs. The United States now spends slightly more than half its defense dollar for personnel, including the pay of defense civilians and retired military, while in the judgment of some military analysts something less than a fourth of Soviet military costs are imputable to manpower. This permits a larger proportion of Soviet military spending to go for weapons, training, and readiness. In budgets of equal size, such a differential would mean that the Soviets were outspending the United States on weapons by about a third. In actuality, the Soviet Union may have been spending substantially more on defense than the United States has been doing, which means that Soviet spending on weapons might conceivably approach a level double that of American procurement, at least in recent years. Yet all this needs to be qualified, for Western analysts have experienced great difficulty in reaching a consensus on these matters.[25] Statistics on Soviet military spending are developed by comparison and inference, notoriously unreliable methods. This leaves considerable room for variation in conclusions, and requires great caution in arriving at them.

In 1979 and 1980, the manpower problem also became a factor important for the political-military image of the United States abroad. The United States and Great Britain are the only NATO countries that have significant military forces without having as well some form of compulsory military training or service for a substantial portion of their young men. Because the world is questioning the power, leadership, vision, policies, and interests of the United States, this fact has especially complex consequences. As the principal political and military counterweight to Soviet power around the world, and as a power with worldwide interests and involvements in its own right, the United States cannot fail to be concerned about the inferences other nations and their leaders draw from a disinclination to revive the draft.

Is the draft necessary? Is it wise? Recruiting, retention, mobilization, image, and cost considerations make at best a mixed case for any return to the draft. To be sure, the draft would ease or eliminate some important portions of the problem. It would ensure that, year by year, the military would receive the number of recruits or inductees needed, planned for, and budgeted; it would ease the strains of recruiting, and prevent one year's shortfalls from increasing the difficulties of following years; it would permit a return to higher entry standards of basic intelligence and mechanical aptitude. Further, a draft could be so constructed as to encourage participation in the reserves, thus contributing to mobilization needs. Finally, a draft would unmistakably signal both to the American people and to the outside world a change in the tenor of American foreign and security policy.

Against these possible—and by no means trivial—advantages from resumption of the draft, certain disadvantages weigh. The draft would not eliminate recruiting problems entirely, and perhaps not very much; any draft likely to come out of present political concerns would probably be of modest dimension, a supplement, not replacement, for vigorous recruiting efforts. Unless the United States undertook a considerable expansion of its forces or ceased to recruit seriously, a draft would probably need to produce only about 20,000 people a year. Even if every single draftee were a mental giant and a high school graduate, a draft of that size would not transform the quality of a 2-million-man military, especially since the draftees would work at the bottom of the system and leave it as soon as possible.

As suggested above, I believe that the number and quality aspects of manpower problems are as much or more a function of retention than of recruitment, and this fact sharply limits the potential usefulness of a draft. Shortages in the middle and upper reaches of the officer and enlisted groups cannot be adequately offset simply by larger numbers of people taken in at the bottom of the personnel pyramid. Failures of retention set the dimensions of recruiting needs and cost the military its best-trained, most experienced, and potentially most stable people. No draft can change that.

As for mobilization, unless a revived draft is coupled with sharp expansion of the military, or with a much shortened term of service tied to a long reserve obligation, or with a system of deferment that encourages young men to join reserve units, it seems to me that a draft can do little to reduce the problems of quick reaction in war or crisis. A draft might, however, very well be appropriate when such an emergency was at hand, and I think it would be desirable to clear away any legal obstacles to such action in the course simply of draft registration.

For now, I believe, only registration is clearly essential. There is no possibility that Selective Service can meet estimated needs if it has to start without even the names and addresses of potential draftees. The present goal of the Selective Service System is to be able to begin draft calls within seventy-two hours of a mobilization order. As things stand, it will have a very difficult time coming anywhere near that target even with the help of the Army reservists and recruiters designated to assist for the first forty-five days or so of an emergency.

Because of the problems remaining in mobilizing manpower for war, the success of the summer 1980 draft registration and the January 1981 follow-up registration for young men born in 1962 remains highly interesting—and highly political. Joan Lamb, a spokesperson for Selective Service, said shortly before the presidential election that 3.64 million men had registered, out of the 3.88 million estimated to be eligible, for a 94 percent rate of success. (The Selective Service Administration estimated that there were 4.3 million American males born in 1960 and 1961; 370,000 were in the military; 70,000 were in institutions such as prisons and hospitals.) Against these optimistic judgments, opponents of registration argued that far more men were eligible, and that the registration count had included thousands of false and duplicated registrations. The Boston *Globe* estimated that only 75 percent of those eligible had actually registered. The Committee Against Registration and the Draft, which had tried to organize national opposition to the registration call, maintained that at least 3.95 million men had been eligible. Although the debate remained inconclusive, figures assembled in the course of post-Vietnam clemency proceedings confirmed that Census Bureau data contained large enough errors to be unsound as a basis for Selective Service estimates.[26]

In another approach to the mobilization aspect of manpower problems, Dr. Kenneth J. Coffey, formerly an official of the Selective Service Administration, suggested initiating a draft directly for the reserves if not for the active forces.[27] But in view of political and legal uncertainties surrounding even simple registration, this proposal seemed premature. Although it evoked a certain interest in the small community of manpower experts, it led to no important consequences.

There remains the consideration of cost, an extremely complex matter in the context of manpower concerns. Proponents of the draft like to assert that the turn to an all-volunteer force after Vietnam tripled or quadrupled military personnel costs; that a return to the draft in the 1980s would reduce or limit those costs;

and that such limits would help in military competition with the Soviet Union as well as in domestic fiscal circumstances.

But the increased military personnel costs of the 1970s are not all attributable to the all-volunteer force. These costs had several components. First, there were pay raises to keep officers and enlisted careerists in the service during the Vietnam War. In the late 1960s, officer pay rose at a rate of about 7 percent per year, well ahead of wages in the civilian economy and also ahead of inflation. Then, in the early 1970s, congressional reformers assaulted the complex system of fringe benefits enjoyed by the military, again granting offsetting pay raises. Next, the Vietnam War added heavily to the rolls of military retired and disabled, which helped to boost costs for retired pay. Finally, post-Vietnam inflation increased the burden of military compensation, even though pay increases lagged well behind the inflation rate.

If the figures are adjusted for inflation, between 1964 and 1981 the aggregate costs of active duty and reserve military personnel actually declined, from just under $40 billion in 1964 to just over $33 billion in fiscal 1981 (figures here in fiscal 1981 dollars). The Department of Defense had 600,000 more people in uniform in 1964 than it planned to have in fiscal 1981. After adjusting for inflation and for the difference in force levels, rule-of-thumb calculation suggests that active-duty and reserve military personnel cost something less than a third more in 1981 than in 1964. That is bad enough, but it is a far cry from a quadrupling of costs.

As an attempt to reduce the costs of military manpower, a resort to the draft would be completely mistaken at best, disastrous at worst. Unless the draft is revived not as a complement to energetic recruiting but as a complete replacement for volunteerism, draftees will, as mentioned, form only a small part of the military. Correspondingly, only modest proportions of military pay could be held down in any scheme to pay draftees at nominal rates. Using the draft to limit manpower costs will inevitably force enlargement of the draft as volunteerism collapses into economic madness.

America's military manpower problems—recruitment, retention, mobilization, image, and cost—are serious and immediate, but I do not believe they make a case for the draft. For the foreseeable future, reintroduction of the draft will in my opinion be neither necessary nor wise. If reintroduced, the draft will have no positive effect on the most urgent and consequential manpower problem—shortages of career enlisted personnel and officers, especially those with critical skills; it will impose social and political costs of an order unjustified by military results; it will save money, if at all, on a scale much lower than that commonly suggested by its proponents. Any potential benefits of a renewed draft, moreover, would be offset in some measure by costs likely from resuscitation of a nationwide draft resistance organization.

Rather than a draft, improved retention of those in the service must remain the focus of efforts to resolve the manpower problem. The beginning of that necessary effort to improve retention lies in accepting as fact that the United States has irreversibly entered an era in which manpower is expensive and getting more so. This development is akin, in its way, to America's recent transition to an era of expensive energy. In the long run, I believe, this will require the military to make do with fewer people still, to find new ways of mixing people and machines, men and weapons, in practicing the military arts. In the near term, this new manpower era requires three things: (1) skepticism about the extent to which a return to the draft might ease manpower difficulties under present conditions; (2) forthright, public, and official assessments of necessary force size, including a thorough rationale; and (3) long, hard thought about relieving the military of direct responsibility for recruiting.

The provision of adequate manpower for defense is a national responsibility, not simply an obligation of the military services and departments. Recruitment should have been transferred to a civilian agency in 1973, at the turn to the all-volunteer force, in order to keep broad national responsibilities in this area clear. The military should also be relieved of the costs of recruiting. This may seem no more than a suggestion for fiscal sleight of hand; in the end, the taxpayer always pays for it all, and such a proposal would probably not save any money. On the line where one year's defense budget said $614 million for recruiting, next year's budget might say $0 for recruiting; the budget of the new recruiting agency might say $625 million. But even if no more than this took place, it would be worthwhile. There is a large psychological

problem here, for the military feels that ballooning costs of recruiting under the all-volunteer-force concept have required the
use of money and men in untraditional ways. Senator Stennis
surely echoed the sentiments of senior military leaders when he
said, as noted above, that recruiting had become an ordeal, a
"grave contest" inconsistent with the dignity of the armed forces.

Further, there is reason to think that the military's highly cen-
tralized recruiting commands may not be the ideal mechanisms
for the recruiting effort. Recruitment is to a great extent dependent for success on intimate knowledge of local and regional social, economic, educational, and other conditions. Local committees along the lines of Selective Service boards might meet much
greater success in tailoring recruitment appeals to the people of
their own cities, schools, and outlying regions. It is at least possible
that in recruiting, as in so many other areas, the military suffers
from over-centralization. In the absence of a revised recruiting
method for the volunteer force, the Council on Foreign Relations'
conclusion that volunteerism cannot work seems premature if not
perverse.[28]

Finally, manpower policy, because it is also social and economic policy, should probably be coordinated outside the Department of Defense. Already it is clear that many decisions made in
other policy areas bear directly on the likely success or failure of
each year's recruiting efforts. If the military were succeeding in
recruitment and not, as now, failing, prudence might restrain
thoughts of reordering a system that worked merely to obtain one
that is more ideal. As it is, the military should be both encouraged
and allowed to concentrate on retention issues while turning recruitment over to a civilian organization reporting either to the
White House or to the National Security Council.

And whether the military releases or retains its grip on recruitment, it must be very careful to deal with manpower problems in
ways that do nothing whatsoever to confirm the public's suspicion
that America's generals and admirals are simply bent on giving
the country a haircut.

As we have said, the heart of the military manpower problem
is retention. By itself, improved retention will not eliminate or
ease all personnel ills; it will do little immediately for issues of

mobilization; it will cost more not less money; it may have only modest effects on America's potential image if indeed it has any effect on it at all. But improved retention will work wonders in the critical areas of numbers and quality—the adequacy and competence of the American military. Improved retention is not the only solution to present difficulties, and certainly it is not a complete solution; but without improved retention there can be no solution at all.

Retention problems reflect the strains of military life—financial, social, professional. Of these, pay is beyond doubt the most urgent and sensitive. "There are lots of reasons for resignations listed on those letters to Washington," Navy Lieutenant Mark T. Brown wrote in mid-1980. "But if each of them doesn't say 'The Navy doesn't pay enough,' then the author is not telling the truth. Inadequate pay is not just one of the reasons for opting to leave the service: it is *the* reason. Everything else is secondary."[29] Recent studies have shown that a 1 percent real decline in military pay will produce a 1 percent to 3 percent drop in retention rates. For every 1 percent that military pay drops in real terms, according to another study, the military can expect to lose 5,000 more people than it otherwise would.[30] "Personal satisfaction doesn't help pay for the rapidly rising cost of living," one noncom, R. L. Wiebe, recently wrote in a letter to *Navy Times*, "nor does it help explain to your children why college may be out of the question, or why you have to continue to drive an eight-year-old car, or why many service families are forced to use food stamps, or why many service mothers do most of their shopping at garage sales and flea markets for clothing and other needed items."[31] The service chiefs have summed it up: People don't expect to get rich in the service, but they don't expect to become welfare cases either.

It has been difficult to get across to the American people just what is wrong with military pay. On the surface, the military compensation system looks very attractive. Officers and enlisted men receive basic pay, an allowance for housing, an allowance for food, and complete medical care. Their retirement system pays them half their base pay upon retirement at twenty years of service, and up to three-quarters pay after thirty years, this with no contribution out of the individual's earnings over the years. Military people enjoy shopping privileges in government-run discount grocery and general merchandise stores, gas stations, and auto repair shops. They have access at nominal or no cost to recreational facilities, hobby shops, and more. Married military officers and enlisted personnel receive higher housing allowances to help support their dependents, together with free medical care for those dependents. When transferred, military personnel are entitled to have their household moved at government expense, and their travel costs, as well as those of their families, are also paid by the government. Of all these allowances and benefits, only basic pay is subject to income tax (retirement pay, of course, may also be taxed).

Yet, as I will explain, military pay is inadequate, and the military compensation system is worse. Military compensation has become incredibly complex, a nightmarish tangle of tradition, bureaucracy, and inequity. Few outsiders ever grasp its intricacies, and for that matter many in the military go through an entire career without ever finding their way fully through the money maze that Congress and the military together have constructed over the years. Friends of the military in Congress regularly call for higher pay, but even the military's best friends have been too timid to call for thoroughgoing reform—simplification of the compensation mess. The military needs a combination of more money and less hassle.

To some extent, statistics tell the story of the relative decline in military pay.[32] Between 1972 and 1980, the consumer price index has risen by 76 percent, and military compensation by 51 percent. Average military pay has fallen over this term by about 14 percent, with sharper reductions for servicemen and officers at some points on the pay scale. From 1953 to 1980, officer pay dropped overall about 12 percent, that of the enlisted ranks 24 percent. In 1973, base pay for an E-1, that is, a new recruit, equaled 110.8 percent of the federal minimum wage; in 1980, it amounted to only 83.5 percent of the minimum wage.

As of late 1979, average enlisted pay was $9,900, about 17 percent below the Bureau of Labor Statistics minimum figure for a "lower" standard of living and more than 50 percent below a moderate standard for a family of four. Thirty-two percent of the enlisted force, about 600,000 people, were receiving pay less than that established in the federal minimum wage, no matter how many hours a week they had to work, or how hard they had to work, or where in the world they had to do the work. The Marines guarding the American embassy in Iran when it was seized were earning an average of $8,200 per year, nearly 30 percent less than the "lower" standard of living figure and less than the minimum wage as well. As an Air Force general noted early in 1980: "A good sharp youngster can do better working at McDonald's."[33]

These hard facts have set large changes in motion in the military. One such change involves the resort to outside employment. According to one recent survey, 86 percent of enlisted personnel were either moonlighting or had a working spouse in 1980. That same year, 22 percent of the Air Force's enlisted people were working at least eighteen hours a week at an additional job. Some enlisted people were working at two extra jobs, and many were reporting for their military duties so weary that they could scarcely put in a good day's work. Still another set of figures showed that in 1980, about 20 percent of the entire enlisted force was working at a second job for between eleven and thirty hours per week. Considering that a substantial portion of the enlisted force is based abroad or otherwise assigned to jobs in locations where outside employment is unavailable, this is a very substantial percentage indeed.

Many military people earn more in moonlighting part time than they do working for the government full time. An E-5 stationed, say, at Moffett Field in California can make about 20 percent more fixing electronic equipment for sixteen hours a week than his annual base pay—$12,000 a year for sixteen hours a week, and $10,000 a year for sixty or seventy hours a week. And of course, many in the military have the ability to earn much more in full-time civilian employ than they can earn by remaining in the service. A military computer programmer may earn $12,000 per year; on the outside, he or she could find comparable work at $25,000 annually. Boiler technicians in the military earn perhaps $12,000; in civilian companies, comparably skilled technicians start at $23,000. The newspapers that the military's men and women read most faithfully, *Army Times*, *Navy Times*, and *Air Force Times*, carry pages of ads every week in which companies of every description advertise for people who have been trained by the military, at government expense, but who can do much better for themselves by leaving the service.

The *Navy Times* of June 2, 1980, carried a typical series of ads soliciting helicopter pilots, aircraft technicians, electronics technicians, computer operators, facilities engineers, test engineers, program managers, aerospace engineers, boilermen, nuclear technicians—even medical technicians. Salaries offered ranged up to $40,000 or more, with featured promises of choice of assignments and even permanent job locations. In the November 3, 1980, issue of *Air Force Times,* similar attractions filled the ad pages at the back of the paper. Ads called for a variety of skilled military people similar to that in the *Navy Times* of June. "Put your military training to good use," one ad urged. Indeed, that was the general message of most of the ads.

One Marine colonel told me how economic realities had begun to change military verities: "A few years ago we court-martialed or discharged guys for having a second job because they were clearly not giving the Corps 100 percent. Now company commanders help their enlisted men get part-time jobs."

Pay trends have brought another change to the military, this nothing short of a national scandal: the evolution of a welfare military. Sixteen percent of the Air Force's enlisted people qualified for welfare in 1980. About one third of the average stateside Army battalion was either using food stamps or eligible for them. The services have been sending instructions around to all officers on how to assist their enlisted people in applying for food stamps and other possible welfare programs for which their low salaries made them eligible. The base commissary at Fort Campbell, Kentucky, was collecting about $30,000 in food stamps every month as of October 1980. Annually, as of mid-1980, the military commissaries were taking in about $10 million in food stamps from about 30,000 military families.[34]

Officers have told me of their chagrin and shame at this. One told me of a recent tour as a recruiting officer. The public building out of which he worked had other government and military offices in it, and one day he walked into the corridor to see, just underneath his exciting new recruiting poster, a small sign directing enlisted military personnel to an office that would help them process welfare applications.

"If the government can give me $71 a month in food stamps," one Army enlistee asked, "why can't it give it to me in salary?"[35] Wrote a Navy technician: "I was brought up by parents who had pride. My father . . . would turn over in his grave knowing that one of his sons had [accepted welfare]. If anyone had to accept welfare it was due to one of three things: lack of pride, laziness, or a physical defect. . . . This is just one of the many reasons the Navy is losing its best. The best have pride and they refuse to accept a handout."[36]

The wives of servicemen similarly feel the embarrassment of their predicament. At a large meeting called by Navy personnel officials to invite the airing of grievances, the wife of a chief petty officer spoke of the distress she felt when her children's school notified her that her husband's low income made her children qualify for the school's free lunch program. She no longer felt the pride, she commented, that had sustained her through "so many endless deployments and could not continue to justify these separations . . . with ideals of honor and service to a nation which no longer cares."[37]

The captain of the *Texas*, as his ship returned from the Indian Ocean with the *Nimitz* in spring 1980, after a long and strenuous deployment, cabled what his contemporaries in the officer corps all felt keenly: "It is very hard for a commanding officer to recommend to his men that they apply for food stamps or other welfare and at the same time ask them to be ready to fight."[38]

Late in 1980, Staff Sergeant Louis Loman, a B-52 mechanic, summed it up for *Time* magazine. With a take-home pay of $704 per month, Sergeant Loman and his family used food stamps until his wife found a job. They cannot afford to buy a house, and must therefore live in government quarters on base. "I'm missing the American dream," Sergeant Loman said, "by serving in the Air Force."[39]

It is the job of commanding officers to counsel those who face a decision about whether to reenlist or to get out. One Marine colonel told me bluntly: "You have to maintain your credibility with the troops if you want to be any good or do any good. When they ask, 'Should I get out or stay in," I tell them honestly that if they have a skill they can sell they should get out. The only reason that doesn't simply cost you all your men is that many of them really do not have a place to go. For some of them, that outside job is an illusion. A good commander can help a guy see that. Some of them really need the discipline and structure of the military life. You can show them that as well. But some of them can walk out the door today and double their pay tomorrow, and never look back. You have to tell them that too. It's the right thing. Of course, those are usually the ones we could most use."

There are some important differences in the pay problem for officers and for enlisted personnel. For the enlisted ranks, inadequate pay means food stamps, welfare, outside work, and ultimately attractive alternative job opportunities. For officers, there are also the attractions of outside jobs, and many officers—51 percent, according to the most recent study—have working spouses. But few officers themselves have additional part-time jobs. The Army captain whom CBS News found pumping gas in the summer of 1980 was unusual if not unique. And officers' families do not qualify for welfare or food stamps. But officers and their families, in addition to suffering the same losses of real income as the enlisted ranks, find that the system of pay, allowances, and benefits works less and less well. The military is not just a job; it is a way of life. Today in the United States, it is becoming a way of life that does not meet the needs of those who follow it.

The military compensation system is, on the surface, extremely attractive. In addition to the various forms of pay and allowances, medical care, shopping and other privileges, and retirement provisions, military people receive various forms of educational benefits both in the service and after leaving it; they are entitled to thirty days of annual leave, or vacation; they can obtain VA or FHA loans for house purchases, usually at terms more advantageous than those being offered through regular consumer channels; and they are covered by a government insurance plan that includes survivors' and dependents' benefits. The most recent survey conducted for the Department of Defense has been interpreted to mean that these benefits add the equivalent of about $15,000 per year to the effective salaries of the average man or woman in the military, which to be sure is no small sum.[40]

Unfortunately, almost none of this complex and expensive system works to the satisfaction of those within the military. They voice several types of complaints, pointing to substantive shortcomings in the delivery and value of promised advantages, services, and privileges.

One large category of complaints might be called "consumerist complaints." Military families increasingly find that the commissaries and exchanges in their base or area offer no better prices than local supermarkets and discount stores. Sometimes, in fact, the military's private stores are more expensive. Almost always the selection of merchandise leaves something to be desired by comparison with what is readily available in nearby civilian shopping facilities.

Problems of merchandise selection in the military exchange system are the inevitable consequence of doing business the government way, a fact that does nothing to alleviate the irritations of those whose shopping privileges are supposed to make up part of their compensation. If an exchange has been carrying a particular type of photo album, for instance, and a family has invested in several of them to hold its growing snapshot collection, one day it may find that the exchange doesn't have any more, can't get any more, and doesn't much care. To keep everyone happy, the exchange has given the contract for photographic supplies to another company. Government regulations require the government's enterprises, such as post exchanges, to spread out purchases and contracts for goods and services in accord with the time-honored principle that everyone is entitled to make money from the government. New products may not be inferior; but they will be different. Thus any hope of consistent availability of materials, supplies, and the like is simply illusory.

Problems of availability and choice are one thing, but problems of price are another. There would seem to be no reason why a government store run to provide a certain subsidy to augment military salaries could not do so in a reasonably consistent way. Yet this aspect of exchange and commissary operations also becomes convoluted and correspondingly less reliable than it ought to be. Price savings in military exchanges are extremely uneven. On some items there are very considerable savings; flashlight batteries, for instance, usually sell for about half the standard retail price. On others, savings may be minimal; food and liquor prices hover relatively close to the prices a careful shopper could obtain in local stores in most areas. Clothing may be attractively discounted, while durable goods and electronics items actually sell for more than one would have to pay in a nearby civilian store.

Despite this, when the government calculates the value of such shopping to military families, it averages or in other ways aggregates the theoretical savings this system makes available. Recent government figures indicate that, at least from this perspective, the commissary and exchange system provides about 20 percent savings on all the shopping needs of an average military family. Here a certain credibility gap opens, for most military families do not see savings of that magnitude. Some families might; those that use more flashlight batteries than lettuce, for instance, probably find the shopping savings quite worthwhile. But families whose composition, life style, eating habits, and pattern of major purchases fail to coincide with the idealized government shopping profile do not benefit from this system in anything like the degree commonly asserted by the government.

Similar consumerist problems abound in every area in which the government is providing services. The medical services to which military dependents are theoretically entitled now cause the most pervasive and serious complaints next to those about shopping. The Army, for instance, late in 1980, boasted only 24 percent of the desired number of general practitioners, 32 percent of the ear, nose and throat specialists necessary, and only 36 percent of the orthopedic surgeons required.

Shortages of doctors in the military have created real problems; adequate medical care for military families is in point of fact not now available. Early in 1980, in an attempt to induce more doctors to remain in the service, Congress passed a bill increasing the special pay increments paid to medical professionals in the military. President Carter vetoed the bill, despite the fact that military doctors earn only about half what most of them could expect to make outside the service. This veto earned the President no little censure. Military personnel generally regarded it as one more indication of the President's—and the nation's—lack of commitment to providing adequate and effective benefits to the military. Military doctors, understandably, took it somewhat more personally. A few days after the veto, one doctor, stationed at Walter Reed in Washington, was asked for his comment on the bill and the presidential veto. "We hope," he replied, "that the next time President Carter needs treatment for his hemorrhoids, he comes to Walter Reed."[41]

In some respects, the doctor problem was indeed serious. One military surgeon wrote a letter to the *Navy Times*—a newspaper read by hundreds of thousands of military personnel and their families—saying that "Some of the military doctors who stay in at current pay scales are either lazy or could not make it on the outside. . . . and the troops just plain get lousy care when they are seen by those physicians."[42] People leaving the military now routinely cite poor or unavailable medical care as one of the principal reasons for their decision to get out. There are growing numbers of horror stories—tales of inferior surgeries, misdiagnosis, delays, botched emergency treatment, military hospitals stripped to the bone of people and equipment so that they simply prove inadequate when suddenly subjected to out-of-the-ordinary demands. For those who have reached the retirement point, of course, getting out is not much of an answer to the problem. Retired military personnel these days can rarely get to a doctor at the military medical facilities they are entitled to use; they must settle for a medical assistant and hope for the best.

Shortages of physicians in the military have consequences that extend beyond the concerns of military dependents and retirees; these shortages also have implications and effects of concern for the health and safety of the active force. They are forcing some of the medical personnel remaining in the service into jobs and situations for which they are not qualified. Early in 1980, in a case that made national headlines, one Navy doctor spent four months in jail for refusing an assignment for which he felt unqualified. In the Air Force and the Navy, doctors are being assigned as flight surgeons without adequate preparation in the special aspects of pharmacology and physiology vital to the care of men undergoing the physical and mental stresses of supersonic flight. Medical care for soldiers and sailors deployed overseas, or at sea, falls further and further short of prudent and adequate levels, especially considering the hazards of routine operations and training.

These days consumer complaints are by no means exclusive to the military. They have become a fixture of American life. Perhaps a latter-day Karl Marx would explain the inevitability of such annoyances in American society—consumer complaints as the logical consequence, the highest stage, of a consumption-oriented, materialistic society.

The problem is that the ordinary forms of recourse open to civilians in dealing with consumerist dissatisfactions are not as readily available to those in the military. Unless they choose not to patronize the military shopping system, they have great difficulty in getting satisfaction. After all, they are dealing with career government employees in those stores and shops, people whose jobs are secure and who can take refuge behind government procedures and regulations cumbersome enough to thwart even the most determined. The Better Business Bureau, the state attorney general, Ralph Nader—all are irrelevant, no help to the military consumer contending with the commissary and exchange system.

Military personnel and their families are captives of a rank structure and a bureaucracy that are impervious to normal procedures for obtaining redress or making improvements. On one New England military installation in 1980, the base auto repair shop was so incompetent and difficult to deal with that administrators of organizations based there were advising newcomers to use other garages. Or, to return for a moment to the problems of medical care, it seems more and more that getting proper medical attention has become a matter not of entitlement but of manipulation. To get an appointment with a specialist in Newport, Rhode Island, an officer may have to call a personal friend in the medical corps in Florida, one who has enough rank to call back to Rhode Island and direct local medical officers to assist rather than obstruct those seeking the care due them. In all, it is very much like being on the "outside," a mere civilian, hoping that a friend of a friend will be able to open otherwise closed doors. For the military, expecting efficient, high-quality service as its due, there could be no more damning indictment.

Apart from consumer-style difficulties, there are substantial "hidden costs" for being in—and staying in—the military. As military families now see it, they pay in several ways for the privilege of remaining in government service and accepting the financial penalties levied on them by the inadequacies of the compensation and benefits system.

One hidden cost relates again to the problem of medical benefits and medical care. As military medical facilities have become incapable of meeting the health care requirements of military dependents, the government has gradually established family health "insurance" similar to many plans offered to civilians through company groups. Under the provisions of this plan—called CHAMPUS, for Civilian Health and Medical Program for the Uniformed Services—military personnel and dependents can go to civilian doctors and hospitals. The insurance plan will pay varying portions of the costs.

Military families feel, however, that their plan leaves an inordinate share of the costs on the family itself. Twenty to 25 percent of the cost usually falls to the individual, 75 to 80 percent to the insurer, in many cases no more than those costs civilian families must pay under comparable health insurance plans. But such comparisons are in a sense inappropriate, for the military family at least in theory is entitled to good medical care at no cost. In the most recent survey, in early 1980, 83 percent of the military families polled said they would leave the CHAMPUS program if the government provided an alternative.[43]

Military families also regularly lose money on moves ordered by the government. In one recent estimate endorsed by former Secretary of Defense Melvin Laird, military people being transferred were subsidizing government-ordered moves with at least $600 million per year of their own money—and possibly as much as $1 billion. An E-7 moving about 1,500 miles with his family might expect to have to spend $3,835 exclusive of the costs of buying and selling a house (something that on an enlisted man's pay he will probably not be worrying about in any case). Of this amount, under the regulations and rates in force at the end of 1979, he could have recovered about $644 from the government. In other words, he would have had to spend between 20 percent and 30 percent of a year's pay to subsidize his government-ordered change of duty.[44] October 1980 changes in compensation provisions would reduce that out-of-pocket figure slightly by paying more for personal and family travel expenses. But these changes are far from enough to eliminate the more serious dimensions of this problem.

In a profession that is characterized by frequent moves, people have come to expect significant out-of-pocket costs every couple of years. It is not unusual for a military family to move fifteen, eighteen, or twenty times in the course of twenty-five to thirty years. Many families, especially those of Marine Corps personnel, move nearly every year, year after year. Each time, they make up from their salaries, savings, or other moneys the difference between the government's moving allowance and the actual costs of the household move. There are, as most Americans have had cause to discover, always additional costs in damaged furnishings, household fix-up, and the like involved in household moves. These are incalculable, but surely of large dimensions, especially when added to the differential between direct moving costs and government reimbursement levels.

There are also substantial hidden costs associated with housing the military. Military families are supposed to receive not only free and adequate medical care but adequate housing at government expense. The quarters allowance paid to military personnel theoretically fulfills the government's obligation to house the military service member and his dependents. Set according to rank, the quarters allowance is withheld when a military family lives in government-owned housing. Outside of government housing, the family uses its quarters allowance to offset the costs of rent, house payments, and utilities. If the military family has been ordered to a city such as Washington, D.C., or San Diego, its housing allowance will fall considerably short of covering rental costs or house payments. The military family will simply have to go out of pocket for any difference—if it can manage to do so. Again, the actual levels of pay for enlisted people make this a chancy situation.

One Marine colonel explained to me just what this could mean: "Some places, living costs are so bad that the government, the military, probably operates right at the edge of the law, leasing apartments, mostly one-room efficiency types, and renting them back to servicemen at a loss. If they didn't, these guys couldn't afford to live anyplace at all. One of my guys I found living with his wife and a new baby in a little camper on the back of a pickup truck, which he parked under a bridge abutment every evening. He had been at his new assignment for more than a month, and had not been able to find any housing at all that he could afford."

In practice, military officers and enlisted men are subsidizing their own housing costs; again, Melvin Laird's recent calculations indicate that they may be spending about $1 billion per year to do so.[45] What makes it worse is that most of the time military families will have little choice about whether or not to live in government quarters. Sometimes, rarely these days, a military family will find housing that costs them less than their quarters allowances, so that they show a modest net gain; sometimes they will be assigned to highly unsatisfactory quarters, for which they will nevertheless have to surrender their quarters allowance and about which they may be able to do little or nothing. As with the exchanges, so with housing—no tenants' organizations to put pressure on the landlord here. If anything, the government puts pressure on its tenants. Government inspectors can and do come around to make sure that central thermostats are turned no higher than 65 degrees in winter, whether or not the bathrooms at the edges of the buildings drop to 37 degrees overnight in winter. In the last several years, military officers have been required to perform minor—and sometimes not so minor—maintenance on government housing that had been allowed to slide from peak condition. There are only a few places where modern, livable quarters are in adequate supply; and as we have seen, there are many places, including many overseas, to which assignment guarantees that the military family will lose a considerable sum of money in subsidizing housing that the government theoretically owes them.

The economic strains of frequent moves and of housing costs are forcing more and more military personnel to leave their families behind when they are ordered to new jobs in new locations. Military personnel assigned to tours aboard deploying ships, or to tours in dangerous foreign locations, or to short periods of special duty of one sort or another, have always had to leave families behind for a time. But economic considerations are now causing family separations that operational requirements—the jobs themselves—do not demand. "In family terms," as one senior military officer remarked to me, "this development is a disaster waiting to happen." Many families do not wait for that disaster to strike; they decide to forsake the military profession, even at significant sacrifice of accrued time toward pension rights, and they get out.

Another large complaint about the military compensation system is that it is discriminatory. Amazing as it sounds in this era of equal opportunity, the military does not provide equal pay for equal work. Discrimination in pay matters takes three forms, each of a different character as concerns particulars, but all important as causes of dissatisfaction in the active force: discrimination against single military personnel in favor of those married; discrimination against active-duty personnel in favor of those retired; and discrimination against those in noncritical skill or job classifications in favor of those in critical areas.

Pay discrimination between married and single military personnel has large consequences in terms of dissatisfaction and morale in officer and enlisted ranks. In its deliberations about pay increases and reforms, Congress regularly ignores the simple fact that married officers and enlisted persons make more money than single ones. This fact is a remnant of paternalist traditions central to the military way of life—and of personnel management. Time was that when a man joined the military, the government in effect promised to take care of him—and if he married, of his family as well. Time was when the government kept this promise more fully than it does today. It was natural, therefore, to structure the system of pay and benefits to do a little more for the man who needed a little more by virtue of having dependents. Hence, although base pay remains the same, married persons have larger quarters allowances than single persons; they are entitled to more flexibility in drawing and using quarters allowances; and of course, they draw proportionately more benefit from the entire structure of privileges and services bound up in the military compensation system.

Changing times have rendered this traditional approach to the needs of married service personnel both anachronistic and inequitable. For one thing, as indicated in the foregoing pages, military people do not consider the government successful, or even very interested, in meeting their needs and those of their families for such basics as housing and medical care. For another, substantial social changes in the last generation have strongly reinforced the idea that people who do the same work should receive the same pay.

It is important to realize, however, that this idea is more than an abstract concept of justice, more than an offshoot of recent social and political fads. Real financial injury may be done to people caught in this problem; inevitably, such financial injuries return to diminish the effectiveness of the military itself, either through damaged morale or through its consequences: resigned commissions and decisions to quit rather than reenlist.

Consider the case of a naval officer assigned to sea duty, still the essential building block of a naval career, the only path to advancement. You might think this prospect would excite, gladden, and encourage a young officer. Except for the necessary family separation, a married officer might very well look at sea duty in this way. His family will continue to live in government quarters while he is at sea, their utilities paid for—including heat, which is no small item these days. If not in quarters, the family will continue to draw quarters allowance, using it to meet house payments or rental expenses.

A single officer, on the other hand, may justifiably regard assignment to sea with somewhat less enthusiasm. "What does that [the order to sea] mean to me financially?" As Navy lieutenant Mark T. Brown wrote in middle 1980: "It means that I lose my BAQ [quarters allowance] to go back to sea to the most demanding, difficult, and time-consuming job I have yet had in the Navy. It means that I will get 'adequate government quarters' (one half of a 12 by 6 foot room, one half of a closet, one desk, one chair, and one bed), and a $2,710 per year cut in take-home pay [his lost BAQ]. It means I will get $3,409 per year less than my contemporaries who are married. It means I will make a gross $19,249 per year for a three-year job after six years of experience with the same company, which previously paid me $21,132 per year after only fours years with the company. . . . with my 15% real income loss due to BAQ and a conservative 10% because of inflation, . . . I am looking at a 25% pay cut just to stay in the Navy. My orders should read: 'Go directly to sea. Do not pass *Go*. Do not collect

BAQ. Tighten your belt. Smile, you are being given the opportunity to make a further personal financial sacrifice in the behalf of your country."[46]

The manifest unfairness of pay discrimination in favor of married and against single military personnel cannot be excused by reference to tradition. Single officers and enlisted are entitled to establish themselves financially through purchase of homes, or to live as comfortably as they can manage in the civilian housing market, just as their married colleagues do. What began as tradition now continues as a cost-saving device, with direct and damaging effects on morale and retention.

In the last several years, as a result of the 1970s inflation, a form of pay discrimination between retired military and those on active duty has equaled if not exceeded the importance of that concerning marital status. *Pay for military retirees is indexed to the consumer price index; pay for active-duty military personnel is not indexed at all;* rather, it is set year by year in a complex negotiation between the President and the Congress.

The inflation of the 1970s combined with the "pay caps" imposed by President Carter on the pay and benefits of all federal employees has caused military retiree pay to rise at a rate much faster than that of active-duty personnel. The heart of the present problem is that people who retired between 1974 and 1978 are making more in retirement in the 1980s than are active-duty people of equal rank and seniority, who are still, of course, working full time. The retirees, in addition, can seek additional income, which many of them, if not most, do. In 1979 and 1980, therefore, people were discovering government-wide that immediate retirement would bring them higher pay than they could expect from continued work, and this in short order, often within as little as one to two years. The September 1980 pay of a Navy captain or a colonel from another service who had retired in middle 1974 with thirty years service slightly exceeded the base pay of an active-duty officer of the same rank and seniority, and outreached the retirement pay of a newly retired thirty-year captain by about $600 per month.

Rome and retention: somehow all roads seem to lead to them. In a time of inflation-induced economic dissatisfaction, active-duty military officers and enlisted persons saw many incentives to retire early rather than to continue working for less money than others, completely retired, were receiving. Those on active duty, of course, continued to receive allowances for quarters and food, no trivial sums, since these allowances are, as mentioned, tax free. But base pay, which is the centerpiece of military pay comparisons, showed such a divergence that even some who would have liked to stay in the military felt stupid for doing so. Further, the possibility for employment in addition to military retirement pay seemed to hold more hope of financial comfort than did any pious promises of the Congress or of national leaders.

The costs of military retirement pay grew so large so fast in the 1970s that by the early 1980s, reform of the military retirement system was already in progress. In 1964, there were 435,000 military retirees drawing pay; in 1981 there were about 1,370,000. In 1964, pay for military retirees cost $1.2 billion (in 1964 dollars); in 1981, it was expected to cost about $14 billion (in 1981 dollars). Despite the inflation factor, this burden seemed to many military analysts to have grown to excessive size. In 1964, pay for retirees had amounted to only 9.8 per cent as much as the payroll for the active-duty force; in 1981, pay for military retirees equaled 45 percent of the payroll for the entire active-duty military. Many of the pressures pushing retired pay up have eased. The bulge of retirees from World War II and Korea years has passed; that from Vietnam has not yet come. But inflation continues high, and all those retiring now draw retirement benefits based on the relatively high military pay scales drawn up in the late 1960s and early 1970s to help with manning in Vietnam and in the transition to the all-volunteer force.

Because in the long run the retirement costs seem likely to grow unacceptably large, important features of the military retirement system are certain to change over the next several years. In one proposal under discussion, active-duty personnel may be allowed, after ten years of service, to draw a lump sum against their future pension rights; people separating from the service between ten and twenty years of seniority would be entitled to deferred pensions, beginning at age sixty; those retiring at the twenty-year mark or after would receive immediate annuities, smaller ones than at present but rising to approach current benefit levels when the retiree reached age sixty. The avowed intention of the reforms is to encourage more people to stay beyond ten years, even if fewer stay until twenty.[47]

In effect, however, the main thrust—and motive—of the reform is to reduce the rate of increase in retired pay costs. I believe this to be wise, even though it will meet strenuous opposition from those already in the military. Since almost 30 percent of the approximately 50,000 able-bodied military retirees year by year are not yet forty years of age, some such reforms are surely necessary. After the October 1980 pay increase, a chief petty officer who retired on twenty years service, making a base pay of $1,596.20 per month, would have received a pension of $798.10—half his base pay—the equivalent of the income from a trust fund of $120,000 yielding 8 percent. An Army colonel who retired with twenty years service, making a monthly base pay of $2,934.60, would have received a pension of $1,467.30—equivalent to the income from a capital sum of nearly $200,000 invested at 8 percent. A thirty-seven-year-old retiree has an actuarial life expectancy of more than thirty-six years in which to draw and enjoy this "legacy." To fund a full pension for such a span—and for someone completely capable of continued gainful employment—hardly seems either necessary or sensible.

Pension reform is overdue; it must be high on the agenda of the 1980s. Walter Guzzardi, Jr., writing in *Fortune,* has come to this flat conclusion: "The venerable policy that people in the armed services may work for 20 years, retire regardless of age, and for the rest of their lives get pensions amounting to half their final annual salary, indexed to the CPI [consumer price index], is a ludicrous tradition. It has to go."[48] This is doubtless correct. The question is how to reform the pension system without driving needed people away from the military.

In distinguishing financially between those with critical skills or jobs and those in less critical positions, the differentiations are of two types: those drawn on the basis of jobs—actual work and work conditions at any given time—and those drawn on the basis of skills. Both lead to noticeable effects on morale. These features of the pay system mean that some officers, petty officers, and others receive more pay than colleagues of identical rank and years of experience. Aviators, for instance, are paid from $125 to $306 more per month than their nonflying associates, whether or not their job of the moment actually requires them to fly. Over twenty-five years of service, the span for which aviators are eligible for flight pay, that kind of differential really adds up. At the rates put into effect in fall 1980, an aviator earns $77,000 more than his colleagues of similar rank and time in service over that twenty-five years of flight-pay eligibility.

There are also various bonuses, one-time special payments rather than long-term monthly additions to income. Nuclear-qualified personnel facing a reenlistment decision now might find that they are being offered $12,000 to sign on for another tour, while an equally experienced noncommissioned officer in another specialty is being offered only $2,000—or perhaps nothing at all. The reasoning behind variations in bonuses is straightforward: some jobs are harder to fill—and to keep filled—than others. In 1980, for example, Air Force sheet metal workers were being offered $2,000 to reenlist, while an air traffic controller would receive $8,000 for signing on again. A Navy boiler technician could command a $10,000 bonus, a Marine microwave repairman $6,000.

Sometimes the job or the duty itself leads to extra pay. This perhaps makes the most sense of all. Several types of hazardous duty bring bonus or incentive pay—including combat duty, even though the good sense of this provision is somewhat reduced by the ridiculously low levels at which these bonuses are set. In Vietnam, combat pay amounted to $65 per month, about $2 per day—not much of a compensation for inconvenience and none at all for risk. America's prisoners of war in the Vietnam War received the munificent sum of $3.50 per day as a bonus for their ordeal, a gesture of thanks from a rich and grateful nation. And most recently, sailors and their commanding officers have become eligible for sea pay and responsibility pay, again in amounts that scarcely relate to the demands being placed on individuals and their families by arduous tours and long separations. Enlisted people receive a mere pittance—$30 per month—as "family separation allowance" when they are deployed. Perhaps that covers postage and telephone calls; more likely, not.

Still, it makes sense to pay a premium to people on the flight deck of the aircraft carrier out in the Indian Ocean. There people work—truly—100 or more hours a week, taking all the risks that go with flight deck operations and accepting all the penalties that deployment imposes. It makes a good deal less sense, especially from the point of view of the taxpayer, to pay every other lieutenant commander and chief petty officer in the Navy the hefty premium that might be required to keep people working at demanding front-line operational jobs. The question is whether it makes sense to expect present compensation rates to help with this—the Navy's Career Sea Pay now ranges from $29 to $115 per month, depending on years of sea duty.

In one sense, this is the heart of the pay issue: the real problem is not military pay per se but how to differentiate rates of pay so as to reflect the demands placed on individuals and at the same time provide a structure of incentives related to personnel requirements. A revolutionary thought is being voiced more often in recent years—the idea that not all lieutenants, or sergeants, or even privates need to be paid at the same rate, that job, not rank, should determine pay. But the military fears this idea, because of the implicit connection between pay, status, and influence. In an organization that runs—at least in war—on discipline and rank structure, it is dangerous to explore this financial ground. However promising it may seem in terms of labor economics, pay based on job rather than rank is a distant prospect for the American military.

Apart from the dead hand of tradition, pay issues are incredibly complex once we move beyond the elementary. This in itself is a barrier to change or improvement. The circumstances of those in the military—years of service, time till retirement, financial condition, financial values, preference for quarters or for civilian housing, and many more—these things ensure that pay and compensation provisions cannot and do not affect everyone the same way. For everyone who is helped by some particular proposal or measure, someone is injured, or at least not helped as much. Congress has found, as experts in the Congressional Budget Office will confirm, that it simply does not have the staff and expertise to analyze in full the consequences of differentiated pay packages. Congress must therefore rely on the military for analysis of pay issues. It can deal only with very broad pay initiatives on one hand and trivial concerns on the other. Hence congressional pay proposals typically include a highly trumpeted gross percentage raise and a dozen or so third- and fourth-order concerns, such as the small changes in sea pay, flight pay, and travel allowances included in the 1980 pay package.

Still another general complaint about the military compensation system turns not on government benefits but on government good faith. There is a widespread feeling in the military that in matters of pay and compensation, the government does not deal in good faith. Such doubts about the government's—or the administration's—good faith are the principal reasons why it is not enough, and will never be enough, to say that compensation problems are difficult, that variations in circumstance and situation simply prevent justice, equal treatment, or even satisfaction for a large portion of the military from issue to issue.

What causes such suspicion?

For one thing, the White House and the Office of the Secretary of Defense do considerable preaching to the military, telling them what a good deal they have and how thankful they should be. Military personnel are regularly reminded, in study after publicized study, of how valuable their many special benefits are. I have already mentioned that the latest such study, done in the summer of 1979, concluded that the thirteen principal benefits might be worth as much as $15,000 per year to the average military family. But to arrive at this dollar figure, the Department of Defense did nothing as straightforward as asking a representative sample of military personnel to calculate the value of these benefits; nor did they do anything as relatively simple as calculate what it costs the government to provide them; not did it even ask a couple of good economists to calculate their value in the marketplace. Instead, the Defense Department hired an opinion research firm, which administered a questionnaire to about 2,400 military people, asking them to rank order their benefits. So far, so good; but here the good-sense quotient fell sharply. "Test answers were converted into an arbitrary unit of measurement called 'bennies' (for benefits), which allow comparisons between the perceived benefits values. A bennie, however, means nothing by itself. Analysts used another complex formula to convert bennies into a dollar value."[49] The rank ordering of the benefits that came out of this survey seemed to make sense; the dollar values attached in this mystical two-stage number crunch, however, seemed simply ridiculous. Taken literally, the survey indicated either that military people had not the faintest idea what their various forms of insurance, privileges, and the like were worth on the open market, or—and this is far more likely—that the game was rigged, simply another in a long series of official attempts to allay military concerns about pay by pointing to the value of the fringe benefits.

In driving home to the military this point about relative privilege and advantage, the government even goes to the extent of printing out little computer messages on monthly leave and earnings statements of people in the military. As mentioned, the quarters and food allowances of military compensation are untaxed. Several times a year, in computer capital letters across the bottom of the leave and earnings statement, there appears this line: "If BAQ and BAS were taxed your take-home pay would be $— less." Never mind that BAQ, or quarters allowance, falls a couple of hundred dollars short of meeting monthly housing costs; and never mind that the BAS, the food allowance, for officers was, in 1980-81, $82.58, somewhat less than it takes to complete weekly grocery shopping for a family of four, and scarcely enough to take a family of four out for a restaurant meal. It is small comfort to someone who is buying and selling a house every two to three years, losing money on moves, trying to send children to college and cope with inflation, to be told that he is better off than he feels.

A similar problem of credibility shows in the trial reintroduction, in 1980, of slot machines in officers and enlisted clubs overseas. These devices were withdrawn from the clubs in the backwash of scandal as Vietnam drew to a close and some of the larger illegal money-making operations in clubs, messes, and supply organizations came to light. Like the profits from the exchange and commissary system, those from clubs are used for recreation facilities and activities not funded by Congress. The reintroduction of a mere 275 machines on a trial basis was expected to net $375,000 in the first year. Later on, in full-scale operations, "slots" are expected to produce some $7 million per year for the Army and only a little less again for the Air Force. The money, however much, will by and large be spent to improve the clubs themselves and to hold down prices for military patrons. In one sense, and especially since tax moneys are not appropriated for this, it sounds good both for military-club users and for taxpayers. But in another sense, I find this disturbing: at a time when military pay levels are forcing the lower ranks to and over the brink of poverty, the financing of "morale, welfare, and recreation" activities from the gambling losings of military personnel smacks of bad judgment. If the trial of the 275 machines is a "success"—that is, if the profits are high enough—the plan is to reintroduce them into 128 clubs at 45 different bases.

Even when a big pay raise seems to be in the offing, good faith can become a substantial issue. In 1980, by midyear it seemed likely that the Congress and the President would agree on an 11.7 percent pay raise for the military. Some spokesmen for the administration were suggesting that a pay raise of this size would make up for the "pay caps" of 1977 and 1978, a somewhat ingenuous proposition since the 11.7 percent under discussion did not even equal the current year's inflation rate, much less begin to compensate for earlier inflation damage to military pay. Despite this fact, it promised to be a healthy raise, one that the President's people probably expected the military to greet with enthusiasm. Yet as the year drew on, worried and critical comments on the pending pay raise far outnumbered approving ones. The reasons were complex, rooted in the intricacies of the military compensation system.

Since 1976, Presidents have had the authority to apportion military pay raises, within limits, between the two largest components of military compensation, the base pay component and the quarters allowance. In 1976, President Ford took advantage of this authority; so did President Carter in 1977. In 1980, after President Carter finally committed himself to a substantial pay boost, it seemed likely that he would allocate 25 percent—the maximum possible—to the quarters allowance portion of compensation. This meant that rather than seeing an 11.7 percent increase in each area—quarters allowance, base pay and subsistence allowance—the military would receive proportionally larger increases in quarters allowance and smaller ones in base pay.

For military personnel not in quarters, such a reallocation of raises could be advantageous; the untaxed portion of compensation would grow, and they would enjoy the full benefit of the raise. For people in quarters, however, additions to quarters allowance at the expense of base pay increases meant that they would receive somewhat less than the full 11.7 percent raise; their quarters allowance would simply go back to the government. In effect, increases in quarters allowance are increases in the "rent" the government charges military families for quarters. Stories in service-oriented newspapers made most military personnel only too well aware of what consequences had come from earlier real-locations in 1976 and 1977; by the summer of 1980, according to some calculations, these reallocations had already saved the government—and cost the military—about $500 million.[50]

Most important, however, were the implications of pay reallocations on retirement pay. Since military retirement pay is computed in relation only to base pay, allocations of money to quarters allowance was widely regarded as an attempt to hold down long-term retirement obligations. Military personnel with long service, whether in or out of quarters, therefore opposed reallocations of coming raises in no uncertain terms. Hence even the relatively generous pay package in view for fiscal 1981 created ill will within the military in far larger proportions than it created gratitude or satisfaction. It was one more illustration, and an accurate one, of the way in which the complexity of military pay issues under the prevailing system of pay and benefits prevented universal and equitable provisions from being one and the same. What was universally applicable was not universally equitable, and what might have been equitable could rarely if ever be universally suitable.

In their sometimes well-meant manipulations of the pay and benefits provisions, it seems to me that the military leadership and its friends in Congress have been missing the point. In simplest terms, the psychological contract between military officers and military enlisted people on one hand, and the government on the other, has been broken since Vietnam. Because of the uncertainties, difficulties, and financial hardships built into the military system of pay, frequent moves, and unreliable benefits, a serving military man or woman can never push family and home considerations far out of mind.

"There is only one thing that basically separates the military from other jobs," one Marine colonel told me last fall. "Someone can literally order me to go out and be brave, to go out and die—tonight, tomorrow, next week. And I will go. But a man can't do a good job when he has to worry about whether the wife and kids are going to have trouble with quarters, or medical care, or even just money while he's gone. For a man who takes his family responsibilities seriously, staying in the military for twenty to thirty years is possible only if he has confidence that his family will have what they need. If they don't have it while he's home, it's hard to believe they'll have it when he's gone."

Perhaps because of election year considerations, the pay package of 1980, when it came in October, did not include a presidental reallocation of the 11.7 percent pay raise. Base pay, housing, and subsistence payments all rose in equal measure. In addition, Congress for the first time appropriated money for "variable housing allowances," supplemental payments for military families living where housing costs exceeded the averages used to calculate the standard quarters allowance. For Newport, Rhode Island, for instance, this variable housing allowance added $190 per month to the $468.60 housing allowance of a colonel with dependents. But for those in government quarters, as suggested earlier, it only added to their rent. The first response I heard, when asking a group of officers about their views on the new variable housing allowance, was this: "All it means is that I am now paying almost $200 more per month for those lousy quarters."

There is another side to the military compensation issue: Some people in government, as well as some outside it, suspect the military of wanting to be the highest-paid entity in the government. Leaving aside for the moment the question of pay for enlisted people, that suspicion does not far miss the mark as concerns the officer corps. The salaries now being paid to military officers of any seniority and rank are by no means trivial. The limitations on pay for federal executives established in accordance with the level of congressional pay apply only to the base pay portion of military compensation. Allowances for quarters, food, specialty pay, privileges, and benefits accrue on top of that. In this sense, and it is a real one, senior military officers earn considerably more than their rank and grade equivalents elsewhere in government service.

The present level of military compensation for officers in this sense constitutes one of the biggest barriers to a forthright approach to the shortcomings of military compensation.

The simplest, and in many ways the best, thing to do about the whole problem of military compensation would be to eliminate the entire system of military benefits and pay the military a straight salary adjusted initially to compensate for the surrendered privileges and benefits. Savings to the government would almost certainly be enormous. It takes thousands of people and hundreds of millions of dollars to operate the bureaucratically convoluted military compensation system, with its commissaries, exchanges, recreation facilities, pay, allowances, moving reimbursements, medical services, and all the rest. Further, the government is well known as an inefficient provider of goods and services. It is an iron law of American political economy that the government *never* gets what it pays for.

But any attempt to pay the military straight salaries and provide fringe benefits on the scale available to other federal employees would raise the issue of military compensation in politically explosive terms. Within the military, of course, there would be the fear that the government, the nation, would shortchange the hard-pressed and sacrificing military once again, as always. Outside the military—and this is by far the more serious prospect—any adjustment of base pay that really compensated for surrendered fringe benefits would highlight the fact that the officer corps already makes more money than any other group in federal employ, with the possible exception of Supreme Court justices and a handful of other officials. To have military compensation debated on that basis, however, would not particularly serve the national interest, and it certainly would not serve the interests of the military.

It is essential to remain clear on one point: the real question is not which federal employees either should or do make the highest salaries; rather, the question concerns the compensation levels essential to securing a stable, competent, and adequately populated officer corps and enlisted military. For now, military compensation is too low to produce these necessary results.

In this situation, there is much to gain from establishing a small number of clear principles to guide military compensation adjustments in the next several years. There will, of course, be many such adjustments. For all the reasons mentioned in preced-

ing pages—complexity of issues, variations in circumstances of
military personnel, limitations on congressional ability to analyze
pay issues, the love of political gimmickry and paternalist traditions—such proposals will possess a diversity and an ingenuity
paralleled only by their relentless triviality. There is a great need
for principles, reference points by which to judge the direction
and progress of the marginal and incremental adjustments certain
to come in military pay in the 1980s. It is true that in Washington,
when people start talking about principles it is a sure sign that one
should put a hand over his wallet, keep an eye on his coat and hat,
and say no to every proposal put to him. Principles are expensive;
there is no getting around that. Nevertheless, the ills of military
compensation and the lack of confidence the military now feels
not only in the ability but in the goodwill of national leaders require strict adherence to a few pertinent guidelines in compensation matters.

1. It should be a matter of principle that no one in the American
military, beginning with the lowliest private or rating, should
qualify for any form of welfare in any state in the Union.
2. It should be a matter of principle that new enlistees in the
military be paid at least at the rate of the federally established
minimum wage, calculated on the basis of the average work week
in the military.
3. It should be a matter of principle that active-duty military personnel be paid no less in base pay for full-time work than is paid
in retirement benefits to a person of equal rank and seniority.
4. It should be a matter of principle that military personnel be
paid equally for equal work, regardless of marital status.
5. It should be a matter of principle that, even in times of economic stress, military pay be permitted to decline in real terms at
rates no faster than those in the civilian economy.
6. It should be a matter of principle that the military compensation system be so structured as to provide incentives for continued
service rather than for premature retirement.

Even to a military inflamed over pay issues, money isn't everything; social and professional concerns also exert great influence on retention rates.
Perhaps the biggest revolution in the all-volunteer force has

been the transformation of the enlisted force from largely single to largely married. America's peacetime, volunteer military is more than half married, and the military has just begun to adjust to that development. In times past, it did not matter as much when the military required its enlisted people to move to new duty stations or to deploy overseas for months at a time. The jobs, to be sure, were just as demanding. But the concerns—personal, familial, and financial—of such relocations and dislocations were more limited and certainly more manageable. The new situation has several effects. Some of the old hands in the military now complain that the aspects of service life that used to pull people together are slipping away. People drift away after work and no longer spend their off-duty time together. This lament over vanishing cameraderie is in fact a veiled comment on the "marriage" of the enlisted service. In the old days, everybody ran, drank, gambled, and fought together up and down town, whether stateside or overseas. Now, for the most part, they go home to wife and family.

With its present manpower difficulties, deployment patterns, and operating routines, the military is not prepared to accommodate such a high proportion of married personnel in the enlisted ranks. In many overseas assignments, the government simply does not provide for enlisted people to take their families along.

An enlisted technician—a specialist in antitank weapons, for instance—can expect to spend most of his career in Germany; that's where the Army's antitank forces are largely deployed, to meet a possible Soviet invasion threat. In most cases, he will have to transport his family at his own expense, and because no quarters are available, house them in the expensive German market. The dollar has weakened sharply against the mark through the 1970s; the enlistee may be making on the order of $10,000 plus, say, $3,000 in quarters allowance; he can expect to be rotated back to the United States every two years or so; if he is lucky, he will get to stay in the United States for a year before his specialty makes him eligible for reassignment to Germany; he will find it impossible to obtain outside employment in Europe, as will his wife.

There are only three choices open to him: abandon his family for the majority of his time in the service—this in peacetime;

bankrupt himself and live at the very margin of subsistence, but with his family; or get out of the military. It takes little imagination to guess which choice looks best after eight years in the service.

The crews of Navy ships face similarly demanding deployment schedules. There is, of course, no possibility of taking families on shipboard. But many of the Navy's vessels are "home-ported" overseas—that is, the ships spend their port time not in the continental United States but in the Mediterranean or Japan. The government in such instances may authorize military personnel to move their families at government expense to these home ports, so that at least when the ships are in port—normally about half of any given year (except for the aircraft carriers, which have a more intensive schedule)—there can be some semblance of normal family life.

The present political environment has stepped up the pace of naval deployments and operations still further. As national news stressed in 1980, the carrier *Nimitz* spent 144 days at sea in response to events in Iran and Afghanistan. And, as reported, shipboard morale was high during the deployment and even into the return. It was not reported, however, how morale plummeted when after a few weeks in Norfolk word went around that *Nimitz* would head for the North Atlantic in August, only three months after returning from its record deployment to the Indian Ocean.

There should have been nothing surprising in the morale problems of such long deployments. Indeed, the popularizer of American navalism, the great Alfred Thayer Mahan, himself complained when reassigned to sea after many years of more comfortable positions ashore. After being given command of the *Chicago*, the Navy's newest and best cruiser, Mahan wrote to his daughter Ellen in 1893: "I had forgotten what a beastly thing a ship is, and what a fool a man is who frequents one."[51]

Some shore duty is just about as bad as a deployment. Officers assigned to duty in the Pentagon can expect to put in twelve-to-fourteen-hour days, not always because the job itself requires that but because office politics do. It is part of the elaborate military bureaucratic etiquette—mirrored, to be sure, in many corporations across the country and memorialized in Robert Morse's wonderful portrayal of how to succeed in business without really try-

ing—to be at the office before one's superior and to stay until, or
after, he leaves. Failure to demonstrate this kind of dedication to
the job—and to the boss—cannot be made up by any amount of
efficiency, brilliance, or consistency of endeavor. Coupled with
the forty-five-minute or more commute to and from work common to Pentagon workers, such a schedule makes fathers and hus-
bands virtual absentees, men who leave the house before their
family is awake, and who arrive home well after children and
spouses have eaten and gone on if not to bed at least to evening
activities. Many of the military's administrative jobs in bases
around the world show this same ritual of long hours, whether
they are needed or not.

The military, of course, is not completely blind to the pressures its work load and work habits place on family life. But its
ways of dealing with those pressures are limited, and in some respects, ironically, they only exacerbate the strains. Ships in port,
for instance, in their contribution to better family life for military
personnel, may send married officers and crews home at the end
of the normal working day, except for that small proportion actually assigned to late evening or overnight duty shifts; the bachelors
have to stay to finish, or at least to carry on with, the unending
work.

Senior officers and even senior civilian officials in Washington's manifold bureaucracies now customarily take office with the
promise to hold the work of their agency to a sensible eight-to-
five workday; they encourage their subordinates to come in on
time, and then to leave on time as well, so that government jobs
and especially military service do not automatically mean forfei-
ture of all family roles and responsibilities.

But the corridors of the Pentagon, like the road to hell, are
paved with such good intentions, and still the bureaucratic ethic
retains its tradition-strengthened grip: coming in early and staying
late count when it comes time to write fitness reports, the make-
or-break evaluations of officers. Being a good family man doesn't
count, and likely never will. Being at the office early enough in
the morning to be prepared to brief the boss the moment he ar-
rives counts. Staying late enough to sustain the impression that the
boss is running a hard-driving organization, and the even more
important impression that one is working at least as hard as the
boss, if less brilliantly—that counts too.

In the frequent reassignments and family moves of military service, the economic pressures mentioned above and the family pressures discussed here come together to create some of the worst strains of military life—and hence to provide some of the strongest reasons for leaving the military. Nationwide inflation has made it impossible for many military families to move without drastic reductions in living style and living standard. Military officers ordered to Washington and other high-cost areas in the last several years have sold comfortable houses to scrape together a minimum down payment on a lesser but more expensive house at their new duty station, accepting out of necessity mortgage payments that eliminate all possibility of living the comfortable middle-class life they may have been living up to that point, the life they had every reason to expect when they made their professional commitments fifteen or twenty years ago. Among military families, there are dozens of horror stories circulating; everyone knows someone who has recently undergone the shock of a plainly unaffordable move to Washington, Honolulu, or San Diego. Some families are ending up with monthly mortgages of well over a thousand dollars at a time when their military breadwinner is netting little more than two thousand dollars per month. Lieutenant colonels transferring to Washington with nineteen or twenty years of government service find that they cannot, on their salaries, even qualify for mortgage loans on houses that in many respects are less substantial than the ones they sold to move to the Washington area. The nationwide education crisis, the often-remarked but little eased collapse of standards in schools, has made military families especially sensitive as well to the penalties they often pay in terms of their children's education. As many psychological studies have shown, family moves are about as stressful as the death of parents. In these situations, more and more military families are choosing not to move with the job. As mentioned earlier, some of these leave the service; many others accept long family separations dictated not by the physical restrictions inherent in operational deployments but by the financial restrictions that now frame even normal rotations from job to job within the continental U.S. military establishment.

Large corporations such as IBM and Xerox have long faced similar requirements for mobility in management. Many of these companies have done a great deal more than has the government to come to terms with the inevitable penalties—financial, emotional, and professional. Today it is standard practice for large companies transferring executives to buy their employee's house at a fair market price, later reselling it, if necessary at a modest loss, and to help the employee find adequate replacement housing in his new location. This protects the employee not only from the financial losses that come from having to buy and sell without regard to the condition of the local real estate market, timing instead being determined by the company transfer; it protects him as well from the drawdown of his personal real estate investment caused by paying frequent real estate commissions; and it relieves him of all the personal worries, time-consuming activities, and emotional strains that go with such financial concerns. Such things have, of course, the most direct bearing on the morale and, correspondingly, on the work, of people so treated.

The military is simply not equipped to provide similar support to its executives on the move. In 1980, the Air Force attempted to inaugurate a program in some respects paralleling this corporate-style move support. The plan was to use service lawyers at bases and installations to handle real estate transactions for transferring service members and to use government computers to establish a real estate information net to help those buying and selling at a distance. Whether such activities would withstand the inevitable outrage and pressure of real estate agents and lawyers whose fees and commissions were thus threatened remained an open question. Whether the military could carry through such a program on a scale that would much diminish the pangs of moving—and the costs—for officers was even less clear. And there was no help at all in sight for enlisted service members, whose problems were, if anything, more severe than those of officers.

In view of the high price military families are paying for the mobility traditionally associated with the military personnel system, with its frequent rotations, its overseas deployments, and its interplay between operational and support jobs, the question is whether all this moving is worth it, whether it is necessary. And the answer is: Probably not. A certain amount of such movement is not only inevitable but essential. For enlisted people and officers in the warfare specialties—the people who will be in the front lines or in command in combat—there is an essential, quick-paced, and strenuous round of schooling, weapons training, operational seasoning, and supervisory experience that can be attained only in rapid progression from assignment to assignment.

There is in addition a tendency in all the services to foster the myth that every young officer has the potential—and the opportunity—to become chief of his service, that is, if he does everything right and is just a little bit lucky. It's the military's own special version of the great American egalitarian tradition, the idea that literally anyone can grow up to be President of the United States. Frequent rotation through a variety of jobs and assignments is the personnel system's institutionalization of this military myth, a dizzying and increasingly troublesome career progression that pulls people apart on the dilemmas of specialization versus generalization, operational versus administrative skills, political versus technical concerns.

The problem is that the majority of the people in the officers corps and in the enlisted ranks do not fall into the category of either front-line operators or potential chiefs of service, and the price paid in personnel management terms, not to mention financial terms, is very high, and almost certainly out of scale. Navy dentists, for example, move just about as often as naval aviators. The officer in charge of the dental clinic in Newport, Rhode Island, recently took command of the dental clinic in Seattle, Washington; another Navy dentist came from afar to take over in Newport; there were doubtless six or seven other moves in this daisy chain, and for what? How essential can it be to the military to rotate its dentists across the country and around the world at an average dollar cost well in excess of $5,000 per move and with all the strains on people such moves entail?

The military personnel system has become so infused with the proposition that military people must rotate every two to three years that people who choose for personal reasons not to do so, who indicate to their personnel manager that they would like to remain where they are, letting their children finish school, or enjoying the community and work ties they have established, or simply appreciating the climate and surroundings they have found, will discover that they are no longer considered to be serious about their military duties. They become marked as unpromotable; in this manner, they "select themselves out" of future opportunities either for advancement or for good assignments.

Military families with children in the teen years, when high school associates and programs become so important and family moves so devastating, regularly face the choice between moving or shunting themselves off onto a sidetrack. A hot lieutenant colonel who wants one or two more years where he is so that his daughter can graduate from high school with her friends may tell the Army's personnel people that he will gladly go anywhere and do anything thereafter, returning to the rat race for all he is worth. But if he really insists, and stays, he will have made himself uncompetitive. Thereafter, the only career question he will likely have to answer is whether to retire on twenty years, twenty-two years, or twenty-four years—as a lieutenant colonel. Most officers in such a position—and there are many—know full well that chances for a second career are greater the sooner they seek it; they leave as soon as they are eligible for their twenty-year retirement.

In the long term, improvements in retention will require much more extensive and effective adaptation of military personnel policy to the fact that the military is by and large married. What does this mean?

First, the military should sharply reduce the rate and volume of personnel reassignments, ensuring that for every move there is a reason other than the traditions and shortcomings of the military personnel system itself. A peacetime military will not, and should not have to, endure the stresses imposed by an unjustifiable and expensive tradition or system of personnel rotation.

Second, the regulations governing military moves should be redrafted to ensure that military personnel moving under orders, presumably for the good of the service, do not lose money by having to pay substantial portions of moving costs out of their own pockets. The government should pay the full and actual costs of moving military families and their households, including reasonable costs for house-hunting trips and family travel from one duty station to the next. Present travel regulations are designed to protect the government against petty chiseling, at which they are at best ineffectual; they are not designed at all to give military families a fair chance of having their actual and legitimate expenses met.

Third, the military and the Congress together should devise and provide bonus or premium payments to people in certain career and service specializations that require more frequent than average family relocations. Such a system could perhaps be linked to service in the combat arms, in which moves are justifiably more frequent than the average, in which the most frequent and extended hardship tours usually fall, and in which the all-volunteer force has so far fallen short of finding adequate numbers of enlistees and officers.

Increasingly, American military professionals are finding that their work guarantees not only an unsatisfactory family life but an unsatisfactory professional life. The military is marked by a loss of leadership, a loss of confidence, a loss of pride, and lowering expectations of the future.

There is something of a vicious circle in operation here. Pay and other problems cause people to leave the service; their loss draws down both the leadership and the work force of the military; those remaining find their burdens increased, but not their rewards, and so they think too about leaving at the next opportunity.

In the officer corps, the leadership problem is insidious, because in its most important respects it is hidden now, waiting to emerge clearly only when it has become virtually insoluble. Shortages of officers in the lower and middle ranks encourage the military's already pronounced tendency to apply the Peter Principle, that is, to promote people beyond their abilities. In one variety of this practice, the military may recruit and commission officers from among inappropriate candidates. During the Vietnam War, for instance, shortages of junior officers led for a time to numerous promotions of experienced sergeants to lieutenancies; the Army, as one seasoned veteran described it to me, was "passing out commissions like fucking buttercups." In the short term, this device created overage lieutenants and captains, men who in some cases had lost the brashness and confidence necessary to lead boldly if not recklessly in war. Over a longer term, this maneuver prevented the military from retiring people who had outlived their usefulness. In another version of Peterism, really a sort of inversion, shortages of skilled operators at lower officer levels now are causing lieutenant commanders and majors to perform jobs that lieutenants and captains should be doing—flying aircraft, repeating tours as junior staff officers and department heads, and more. In years to come, such practices will intensify the more traditional effects of the Peter principle. As noted above, the Air Force has forthrightly if bureaucratically recognized that this practice is certain to diminish the ability of officers so employed to equip themselves with the experience, skills, and perspective of senior managers and administrators. They will arrive at higher ranks and levels of responsibility for which their overlong stays in cockpits, squadrons, and the like will have prepared them not at all. If there is a better way to wind up with the top jobs being held by people who really believe in bombing people back to the stone age, or making the rubble bounce, who really think that complex social and political problems have simple, available, and often violent answers, it has yet to be discovered.

In the enlisted ranks, the costs of losing experienced professionals, though different in detail, are similarly damaging to the organization and to the nation. The problems show in morale, and they are paid for in competence. The skilled people who are leaving the enlisted corps are essential both for their on-the-job work in training, supervising, and leading the ratings and for their expertise in caring for the weapons and systems of a modern, high-technology military.

Admiral Crawford A. Easterling late in 1980 told the *Wall Street Journal* about some of the on-the-job costs of losing enlisted professionals: "In many positions aboard ship we have one man—and only one man—assigned to do a job.... We have many ships where we have nobody trained to repair delicate electrical systems—navigation, fire control, radar."[52] When systems go down, the Navy must either fly a technician out to the ship, which is cumbersome in peace and problematic in war, or instead bring the ship back to port for repairs. At the end of 1980, the Department of Defense admitted publicly that seven of America's thirteen aircraft carriers were not ready for combat. Five were in overhaul, and the *Independence* and the *Kitty Hawk* both had shortages of skilled personnel too serious to permit them to go into action. "Most of the other six carriers," reported the *Wall Street Journal* on October 30, 1980, "are ... rated only barely fit for combat."

THE PEOPLE | 91

The loss of supervision that results from the exodus of skilled and senior enlisted personnel is also costly in terms of morale and development of new enlistees. "After a while, you lose your ambition," one young woman enlistee told me. "I was trained to repair electronic equipment; I can fix circuit boards and other stuff. But I mostly get told to take care of the coffeepot and sell doughnuts. I would like to get more training; right now I am supposed to be learning on the job. But no one wants to teach me anything."

The loss of good supervisors also means that, at least to some extent, they are replaced by bad supervisors. Again the results for those with good intentions are distressing. Another first-term enlistee left me with this view: "Sometimes I wish the military was more military. Right now it's the same as working with a bunch of civilians. The guys steal tools and take them home, so you can never find what you need. Everybody flirts on the job. People are mostly trying to skate out [loaf] as much as possible. You can never find anybody when you need them, because they're hiding or off sleeping. It's hard to have respect for your chief [noncommissioned officer] when he says, 'Hey, would you do me a favor,' instead of telling you what you're supposed to do."

Late in 1980, in his column of November 22, Jack Anderson raised another disturbing aspect of the morale problem. "The Navy loses hundreds of thousands of dollars a year to suspected sabotage," he wrote. "One disgruntled sailor threw a wrench into his aircraft carrier's reduction gear, delaying its sailing for months. Several shipboard fires have been attributed to arson."

Inevitably, people lose confidence in their equipment because they have less confidence in the people maintaining that equipment. A number of news reports in 1980—true ones—indicated that American military aviators were becoming uneasy about the quality of maintenance work being done on many of the advanced and extremely complex aircraft and weapons of the American military.

Again the vicious circle: as an Air Force general noted in 1980 in the guardedly neutral language of officialdom, "Low equipment readiness has also had a negative effect on the retention of our maintenance and flying crews."[53] Put more bluntly, many in the American military have begun to feel that they are working for a second-class outfit. In a superior military, a first-class operation, pride might compel many officers and enlisted men and women to stay in; now, pride compels many of them to leave. Also, the hope for advancement, critical to professional commitment over a long term, suffers in a military with the kinds of people problems now rooted in the American military.

"What do young enlisted men and women have to look forward to?" one Navy commander asked me. "They look at their noncommissioned officers now and see that their lives are marked by the same economic marginality and hard work as those of their subordinates. The enlistees know that if they stay in and do well, after a few years they will be able to work a noncom's eighteen-hour day instead of a sailor's or soldier's twelve-hour day—and still qualify for food stamps. In all, it's not much to hope for."

In a similar vein, a prominent sociologist and political commentator, Irving Kristol, wrote an open letter to Secretary of Defense Caspar Weinberger in the pages of the *Wall Street Journal* in February 1981: "Today, as before, all the emphasis seems to be on the *management* of men and matériel, not on military leadership, and certainly not on military pride and morale." More pointedly, one woman observed to me that a nation could scarcely hope to revive morale and instill pride in a military whose uniforms neither impressed nor attracted the young ladies.

Some people would like to believe that in the long run it will not be necessary to resolve such issues of personnel and manning directly. After the 11.7 percent pay increase of October 1980, for instance, the Navy led the services in asserting that manpower problems had essentially been solved. But this solution—if one can call it that—involved no more than an increased intake of raw recruits and new officers. Retention figures continued to slip.

There is also the thought that American technological developments will render these difficulties either obsolete or trivial. Both novels and supersensitive secret projections have been written to describe the wars of the future in which a few people would fight by remote control, pushing buttons to engage powerful enemies with wonder weapons across vast distances. And one of the most significant attractions of advanced technology, at least for the United States, has been its contribution to enhancing military capability without necessarily calling for large increments in manpower. The idea that, through technology, the United States must—and can—make each soldier as "productive" as possible, as mobile as possible, and as lethal as possible largely inspires defense thinking and programming for the future.

Unfortunately, the same limitations on manpower that encourage emphasis on high-technology warfare also militate against it. Rising levels of technological sophistication put a premium on the very people now leaving the military: those with training and experience. High technology increases the burden of training; it raises maintenance difficulties; it makes the problem of casualties and replacements still more critical than it already is in American politics.

Further, as one Marine colonel pointed out to me, the more valuable people become, the more it takes to care for them. People who are educated enough and smart enough to man and maintain a high-technology military are also smart enough to seek and to obtain personal and legal rights comparable to those in civilian society and, in addition, to demand satisfying work and professional development. In the late 1960s and 1970s, military justice and military personnel administration both adopted practices and standards incorporating the kinds of personal and legal rights the courts were extending to the civilian population. This was a necessary adjunct, if not actually a precondition, for any attempt to recruit an all-volunteer force. But it has greatly raised the administrative overhead of the services.

In short, early experience suggests that movement toward a higher-technology military may as easily accentuate as reduce manpower requirements. Even in a high-technology military, the American military, people problems count heavily. Although improved retention is the key to easing present manpower problems, for all the reasons discussed the necessary improvements will be difficult to bring about.

"The guys are cynical," one Air Force colonel told me in summing up the attitude of the enlisted corps. "Since Vietnam, cynicism seems to be built into the system. It's even worse among those deployed overseas. You don't have to have a high IQ or a college education to have high anxiety."

This attitude means that gestures, marginal changes, incremental changes, good intentions, and good wishes will not reverse present retention trends. These can be reversed only by fundamental and extensive alterations in the way the American military compensates people, uses people, and shows regard for their families and family life.

Pay, pride, and opportunity: these words sum up what America's military manpower needs. Sharp increases in pay are absolutely necessary—for the enlisted ranks, to lift them above poverty levels; and for the officers, because they have choices even in the present job market. People want, and need, to have pride in their work and their organization; they cannot be expected to accept the strains of military life in anything less than a first-class military. People want to have opportunity, and not simply the opportunity for promotion, which now, ironically, is sharply on the rise as experienced people depart the services. Rather, people need the opportunity to better themselves, and if they cannot see that opportunity in the military, they will, as they are now demonstrating, seek it elsewhere.

IV THE WEAPONS:
TECHNOLOGICAL DREAMS,
STRATEGIC VISIONS,
ORGANIZATIONAL RITUALS

*There is something about preparing for destruction that causes
men to be more careless in spending money than they would be
if they were building for constructive purposes.*

SENATOR RICHARD RUSSELL

AMERICA'S ADVANCED TECHNOLOGY, once the source of military
advantage, is becoming a root of military malaise. On the battlefield, Soviet and Warsaw Pact forces outnumber those of the
United States and its allies. It is conventional wisdom, enshrined
in the official Army field manual on operations, FM-105, that
"the US Army must prepare its units to fight outnumbered, and to
win. . . . Above all else, [it must] prepare to win the first battle of
the next war."[1] In the 1950s and 1960s, the United States counted
on superior weapons, logistics, and mobility to multiply the effectiveness of its numerically inferior forces. Technical advantages
were to ease the requirement for military manpower and to save
money. Now, in the 1980s, such "force multipliers" derived from
the superior technology and quality of arms and equipment have
become vital not just to diminish expenditures and manpower
needs but to avoid crushing political and military disaster in areas
of primary importance to American national interests.

The American military has an estimated $1.5 *trillion* in assets.
But size is not the only—or best—measure of modern military
competence. America's weaponry is aging, its material readiness is
low, and its lead in technologies critical to military competence—

95

metallurgy, high-energy physics, is diminishing. In part, problems in these areas have resulted from the manpower difficulties addressed earlier. In part, they have reflected genuine lack of funding, at least in certain critical areas. But bigger defense budgets in coming years will not alone remove all the stumbling blocks. For, in addition to shortages of money, aspects of military bureaucracy, budgetary politicking, and conceptual cloudiness have widened the distance between America's military needs and America's military capabilities. In important respects, the American military compromises its potential, so that improvements in capability require not only more investment but fundamental change in organizational practices and thought.

Events in Afghanistan and Iran in 1979 and 1980 brought attention to equipment problems in the American military. By obstructing SALT, the Soviet invasion of Afghanistan brought a new measure of public attention to the obsolescence of America's strategic nuclear forces, the triad. The bombers, B-52s in use since the middle 1950s, had an average age of nineteen years, ten months; 291 out of 349 still in service actually had been in operation for more than twenty years. If the aircraft had been people, one general observed, most would have been eligible for retirement. As it was, some of the aircraft were older than some of the crew members flying them. The Navy's fleet ballistic missile boats, the nuclear submarines carrying long-range nuclear missiles, similarly were approaching the end of their useful life. Their replacements, the new *Ohio*-class Trident submarines, were being built too slowly to keep pace. The land-based missile force, the Minutemen and Titans, were less antiquated but perhaps more vulnerable than either the sea-based missiles or the old bombers. Indeed, the expected vulnerability of the Minuteman force had, by 1980, become the unrivaled centerpiece of America's nuclear concerns.

The Iran rescue attempt also increased concern over the readiness and reliability of America's non-nuclear military equipment. Three of eight helicopters on the mission failed to reach the intermediate checkpoint on the way to Tehran, all because of mechanical failure. Ironically—and confusingly—the craft that failed were not even the ones with the highest number of engine hours and presumably, therefore, with most wear and tear.

Later in the spring of 1980, America's system for warning of nuclear attack delivered two false alarms about two weeks apart. No damage was done. The spurious alarms were traced to an overheated forty-six-cent microchip. But the triviality of the electronic malfunction little allayed worries about the reliability of the system. Later in 1980, a Senate report concluded that the early warning system had produced 147 false alerts of Soviet missile attacks in a period of eighteen months. This finding led Jack Anderson to comment that "the generals might profitably turn their attention to upgrading the strategic system already in existence before they lavish billions on fancy gadgets like the MX missile-shuttle program."

In June 1980, an operational readiness inspection at Langley Air Force Base was halted prematurely because only a third of the sixty-six F-15 fighter aircraft there could be made ready for simulated missions. Shortages of spare parts as well as of maintenance personnel simply prevented the prompt remedying of conditions disqualifying the planes for operational assignments. In fact, reports indicated that it had become necessary to use emergency war reserve stocks of parts to keep the F-15s in Europe and the United States going in routine peacetime operation.

In October 1980, a secret Pentagon budget document was leaked to the press. It predicted that America's ground forces could not catch up in quality to the best Soviet arms and forces deployed in Europe, at least not in the next five years. It had been the administration's goal to match Soviet ground forces in quality by 1985 and to surpass them by 1990. The commanding general of the U.S. Army forces in Europe, General Frederick J. Kroesen, was quoted in *Time* magazine: "If we go to war tomorrow morning, we go with an obsolescent Army," with some equipment, including artillery, "not much improved over what we had in World War II."[2] Another expert, William S. Lind, formerly on the staff of Senator Robert Taft, had argued as early as 1976 that foot infantry—which still made up half the American Army, was obsolete in Europe.[3] Of the 166 divisions then in the Soviet order of battle, 159 were motorized or mechanized; the remaining seven were airborne.

In the early 1980s, America at last is confronting the price of its military policies of the 1960s and 1970s. The Department of

Defense, wrote Lawrence J. Korb (then at the American Enterprise Institute, he is now Assistant Secretary of Defense for Manpower, Reserve Affairs, and Logistics), "is encountering bloc obsolescence. The procurement account has been underfunded for a decade. In the last half of the 1960s, funds were diverted from new weapon systems to support the American effort in Vietnam. In the immediate postwar period, many programs were deferred or stretched out so that increasing personnel costs could be absorbed within a fixed defense total."[4]

There were other signs, small indications, of a military somewhat short of peak condition. In 1980, ammunition for small arms as well as for naval ordnance was in such short supply that throughout the Army and Marine Corps, training was severely restricted. Infantry units were unable to practice live firings of some weapons, and .45 caliber ammunition was virtually unobtainable. Overseas, in deployments of high political and military importance, American troops stood on the very margin of adequacy. In Korea, for instance, ammunition supplies would have limited each rifleman to a mere twenty rounds per day in the early days of a quick-arising war, an amount so trivial as to make effectiveness extremely doubtful. The high cost of air-to-air and air-to-ground munitions has made it normal, not exceptional, for an American pilot to go through a twenty-year flying career never having launched more than, say, one such weapon.

As one Marine colonel told me: "We used to train according to criteria of readiness and competence; now we train according to the limitations of the budget, which is far inadequate to produce the levels of capability formerly considered minimally essential. Eight-inch mortar rounds used to cost $17; now they cost $92. The result is that the number of rounds available for training has been cut 80 percent. TOW and Dragon teams° fire one round per year on a weapons range. We call it a qualification round; you have to call it something, and Congress would scream if you said your

°TOW and Dragon are wire-guided, optically tracked missiles fired from tubes. Dragon missiles weigh about 25 pounds, and the launchers are small enough to be fired by a single soldier. In fiscal 1978, the launcher cost $6,099, the missile $2,935. TOW is older, heavier, and larger than Dragon—with a missile weighing 54 pounds and a launcher weighing 172 pounds. It is fired from a tripod, or mounted on a helicopter or vehicle. TOW cost, in fiscal 1978, $44,194 for the launcher and $3,903 for each missile.

THE WEAPONS | 99

teams were not qualified. But one round a year doesn't qualify those guys to scratch their asses."

One thread unites the foregoing concerns of obsolescence and readiness: American military equipment has become so costly and so complex that training is difficult, maintenance demanding, and reliability doubtful. The inevitable result is a lack of readiness for war or crisis.

Such harmful—or at least unwelcome—effects of the technological revolution in modern defense have not gone unnoticed in the American defense establishment, nor even in the popular press. Former Chief of Naval Operations Elmo R. Zumwalt commented on the Navy's high-performance fighter-bomber, the F-14, that "It is a rare piece of military hardware indeed that is as easy to develop as either the contractor or the Pentagon hopes it will be, given that each such weapon system presses the state of the art."[5]

In October 1979, James Fallows—formerly chief speech writer for Jimmy Carter, now the Washington editor of *The Atlantic*—published a long article discussing the ways in which modern management techniques, higher and higher technology, and the metaphysics of nuclear strategy had driven the American defense establishment away from a focus on "real defense." "As I spoke with soldiers, analysts, and politicians," he wrote, "I was most impressed by those who understood that the nature of the Pentagon's internal machinery is far more important than the amount of money that is poured in. . . . If Congress decides to spend more money on defense without paying attention to *how*, [then ideas now guiding our defense effort] will guarantee that we create nothing more than larger versions of our strengths and weaknesses."[6] According to Fallows, and in this he was surely correct, the weaknesses included a managerial style emphasizing rational analysis while overlooking the brute realities of combat; a nuclear strategy so dominated by theoretical preoccupations that it has lost touch with technical and political realities; and commitment to a level of technology that, over time, is making the American military less capable rather than more so.

The costs of new military equipment have risen to staggering heights. Between 1945 and 1971, the costs of Army tanks increased ten times over, the cost of combat aircraft by 100 times, that of antiair weapons (which involved the transition from guns to missiles) by 2,000 times. But between 1954 and 1971, the defense budget increased only by about 15 percent after adjustment for inflation.

Two Air Force officers, Lieutenant Colonel Dino Lorenzini and Major Chuck Fox, described part of the cost problem in an important article in the March–April 1980 issue of the *Naval War College Review*. "The F-16, which represents the low-cost end of the present Air Force fighter modernization effort, costs almost $11 million each and the F-15 is approaching $20 million. These prices can be compared with an F-4 unit cost in the mid-1960s of $2.4 million. . . . The F-4 that sold for $2.4 million in 1965 would cost about $6.6 million in FY 1980 dollars. But even after adjustments for inflation, today's F-16 costs nearly twice as much as the F-4, and the F-15 is roughly three times more expensive. Most of these after-inflation cost increases can be attributed to the modern avionics subsystems that give current fighters much of their presumed qualitative combat superiority. . . . [Avionics] costs 1,000 times as much as in World War II; engines cost 50 times as much, all in constant dollars."[7] Of course, repairs and other improvements become more expensive as well. The cost of the overhaul of Navy ships, for example, has multiplied five times in the past twelve years.

This trend toward increasing cost is widespread, not centered on one or two lines of weapons development. The B-1 bomber canceled in 1977 would have cost about twelve times as much as the B-52s it was intended to replace. The Trident submarine is costing at present more than five times what the Polaris submarines of the early 1960s cost. The MX missile now under discussion, if built in its present planned form, will be some ten times as expensive as the Minuteman III. The XM-1 tank, originally expected to cost $1.1 million apiece, now seems likely to cost $2.7 million each; this is somewhat more than three times the cost of the M-60 tank. According to Lawrence Korb, as of fiscal 1978 the forty-seven major weapons being purchased by the Department of Defense had doubled in cost over their original estimates. Inflation, of course, in part accounts for this. But Korb points out that "modern weaponry is entering a new technological age."[8] It is, clearly, an expensive age.

Because of cost, discussions about replacements for current weapons and systems invariably contemplate not only higher technology but lower numbers. America's aging 1,000 Minutemen are, so it seems, to be superseded by only 200 MX missiles. The proposed replacement for the B-52, the B-1 bomber, would have cost about $100 million each in the middle 1970s; the Air Force had asked to buy only 244 of them as compared to the 770 B-52s purchased in earlier years.

Despite rising military budgets, the increasing cost of military technology means that there are simply not enough weapons to do all that military planners think war would require of the United States, even if war could be restricted to just one of the world's regions. Also, their small numbers make American forces highly sensitive to losses: "Our naval aviation is based on 12 large platforms," congressional staff expert Jeffrey Record told James Fallows, "and they're all so expensive that we can't afford to lose a single one."[9] In the Navy's war games, an unwritten rule prohibits the sinking of any American aircraft carrier. The carriers are so few in number and the Navy's tasks in war so great that to do without one is literally inconceivable. In more than five years of experience as an umpire and adviser in high-level naval war games, I have witnessed the unwillingness of senior naval officers to permit carriers to be sunk, even when taken under overwhelming attack. On some occasions, indeed, it has been impossible to obtain the agreement of the senior officer in the game merely to put the carrier—or carriers—out of action for a few hours, to simulate lesser damage. The carrier's sacrosanct role in modern naval thought prevents, in many if not all cases, the realistic assessment of possible results of combat even in the Navy's own internal games and analyses.

It is a vicious circle: fewer weapons necessitate greater sophistication, and greater sophistication, because of its cost, implies fewer weapons.

This circular relationship of cost and sophistication and numbers has given special point to the question of whether, or to what extent, the United States still possesses a lead in weapons technology. President Carter's Secretary of State, Edmund Muskie, in a speech to the Pittsburgh World Affairs Council on September 18, 1980, unhesitatingly claimed that "Technology is another American advantage. 'Faster,' 'more accurate,' 'more advanced'—these generally are terms that apply to American weapons and American systems. Soviet technology has lagged behind."[10] In the course of the October 1980 preparedness controversy, then Secretary of Defense Harold Brown likewise asserted that America's military lead "rests on a scientific ability and technology ability and an industrial base that is spread across the U.S. economy." While able to match the United States on some individual items of military equipment, he said, the Soviets "still don't have the broad capability in their industries that are provided to us by our computer and data processing capabilities."[11]

But in my opinion, the picture was, and is, not as clear as Secretaries Muskie and Brown suggested. America's much-vaunted military computer edge loses some of its keenness in the face of January 1980 reports that 77 percent of the people who operate computer and automated systems in the field failed their skill qualification test in 1978—this before the Army's record influx of 46 percent mental category IV enlistees in 1979.[12] Further casting doubt on America's computer-based advantages, one Army colonel told the Los Angeles *Times* late in 1980 that in his view, "all this stuff about battlefield computers is never-never land. You just know that when the balloon goes up, it is going to be binoculars and eyeballs, and grease pencils on overlay sheets."[13]

Moreover, some of the nation's most respected military analysts were unwilling to express confidence in America's technical advantages in any wide-reaching sense. John M. Collins, a defense expert on the staff of the Congressional Research Service, and a respected analyst in his own right, concluded in fall 1980 that "The day has passed when the United States could be smugly sure of unquestioned scientific and technological superiority, which has sustained this country in the past and is the key to future capabilities."[14] The consensus of defense experts was much nearer to the views summed up by Collins than to those of Secretaries Muskie and Brown.

Diminishing technical advantage is likely to force changes in America's approach to weapons decisions in the 1980s. No less a figure than the Chief of Staff of the Air Force, General Lew Al-

len, Jr., has said it in so many words: "As our margin of technological superiority erodes, it is *no longer sensible to try to overcome* increased numbers with increased sophistication." In
summing up the results from many air combat evaluation tests,
another officer put the issue somewhat less elegantly but a good
deal more bluntly: "The reason that numbers predominate in the
long run is that people aren't perfect, and they make mistakes
with the tendency to goof it about as often as they do something
brilliant."[15]

For many reasons, numbers count in war, and this realization,
while never really absent from American defense planning, is
again becoming a theme of defense analysis and decisions. Recent
tactical evaluations of possible battles in Europe, or in other areas
where the United States could expect to face well-armed enemies,
have reminded planners that in large engagements, confusion and
disorder rule. Exotic weapons confer less and less advantage. Some
analysts have concluded that outnumbered American forces might
have to avoid rather than accept combat in war even in areas of
the highest national interest, such as NATO Europe. "You can
buy three F-5s for the price of one F-15," one defense consultant
told *Newsweek* in October 1980. "The Air Force doesn't like to
admit this, but in tests they themselves have run under simulated
combat conditions, three F-5s will shoot down an F-15."[16] It is
these calculations that give such point to observations like those of
Drew Middleton of *The New York Times*, who reminded his
readers on September 21, 1980, that "The question of operational
readiness is critical because the allied air forces, outnumbered by
three to two, must count on putting as many of their qualitatively
superior aircraft into action as possible to meet any threat by the
Soviet Union."[17]

It has long been assumed, for instance, in considering the battle for air superiority in a non-nuclear NATO war, that American
pilots would face odds of four to one in some portions of the front.
Soviet and Warsaw Pact pilots are known to be improving. American aircrews may very well be declining in ability, in large part
because of the retention trends among officers with six to eleven
years of service. "This trend is dangerous in the most literal
sense," wrote Lieutenant Colonel Lorenzini and Major Fox in
their *Naval War College Review* article, "because their replace-

ments often turn out to be very junior crew members not far re-
moved from undergraduate pilot and navigator training. . . . the
Air Force has gradually redefined its concept of an experienced
fighter pilot by scaling down the standards used to confer this
designation. . . . Whereas all the evidence is still not in either to
support or debunk the relevancy of NATO aircrew quality advantage, the reliance on this factor to achieve air superiority while
being outnumbered raises some very serious concerns."

Similar calculations pervade virtually every aspect of American defense planning. The Warsaw Pact now fields upward of
27,000 tanks in Europe; NATO possesses about 11,000, of which
only 7,000 are American. At sea, if one assumes that over time the
bulk of the enemy's forces would come into play rather than being withheld, the Navy would have to obtain something better
than a three-to-one exchange ratio in submarines; the Russians
have 254 attack submarines to 74 for the United States (this does
not include the strategic-missile-firing boats).

Another consequence of dependence on the increasing exoti-
cism of military technology is greater susceptibility to failure, disruption, and breakdown. Put forthrightly, there is a widespread
failure of American military equipment to perform to specification. Worse, much military equipment often does not perform in
any real relation to advertised test results. In one example, the A-
7, an attack aircraft purchased early in the 1970s, proved seven
times less reliable in service in the fleet than it had tested in the
laboratory and in its performance demonstrations prior to purchase.

Because information on Soviet equipment is so hard to obtain,
it is not clear whether Soviets or Americans experience more difficulty in regard to the reliability of military equipment. But I
think one distinction is of interest. American shortcomings in
equipment and performance come mostly from flaws of design or
engineering. Soviet equipment deficiencies seem to be the consequence more of poor or uneven manufacture than of design inadequacies. This does not mean that Soviet weapons engineers are
better than their American counterparts. Soviet weapons technology, while advanced, reflects a conservative penchant for relying
on proven technology rather than seeking always to advance the
state of the art. This has become known as the "bite-back" phe-

nomenon. Soviet weapon engineers "bite back" into technologies previously proven and used, while American weaponeers reach ahead, with obvious risk.

Some equipment shortcomings are colossal without being catastrophic. The new Trident submarine, with its 90,000-horsepower nuclear power plant, is the second most expensive weapon system in the American inventory, and thus in the world (nuclear aircraft carriers still cost more). Yet in early trials, the propulsion plant did not meet speed specifications. In the long run, one or two knots difference in top speed may not make any difference to the effectiveness and usability of the Trident. But it is disconcerting to realize that, even by spending more than one and a half billion dollars, the government and the military—and the taxpayer—still cannot get what they are paying for, what the military and civilian engineers think is possible, and what the contracts call for.

Other shortcomings in military equipment have important consequences for the reliability and usability of weapons and equipment. The new XM-1 tank was designed and developed with a gas turbine engine that, unfortunately, proved supersensitive to dust. In addition, under trial conditions—almost certainly better than real battlefield conditions—the XM-1 averaged only 93.97 miles between major breakdowns, by one calculation, and a shocking 34 mean miles between failures in another design goal. This figure is no better, and possibly worse, than that attributed to older Soviet tanks, long ridiculed by American armor experts. Even a more reliable engine would not correct still another notable shortcoming of the tank: its weight. The 59-ton tank is so heavy that only the giant C-5A aircraft can carry it.

With the need for the C-5A as an airlift vehicle, the XM-1 tank entered on a further complication: of the seventy-seven C-5As in the active fleet, only about 45 percent could be expected to be available for use at any one time. The rest would be casualties of routine parts and maintenance problems. Worse still, the C-5As proved to have "weak wings." Under pressure to reduce the weight of the plane, Lockheed's engineers ordered the shaving down of structural wing supports, a design failing that left the C-5As unable to carry their full nominal load. (A program is now under way to correct this defect.)

In view of these and other difficulties with the XM-1 tank and

its associated combat systems, the General Accounting Office rec-
ommended early in 1980 that "production be held to a low rate"
pending improvements.[18] On February 28, 1980, the first of these
dubiously useful tanks (except for prototypes) was nevertheless
produced on the Chrysler line in Lima, Ohio. The unattractive
choices: to proceed with production of a tank that might prove
unreliable in combat, and impossible to get where you need it; or
to redesign the engine, accepting both long delay and enormous
additional costs.

There is another drawback to weapons depending on highly
advanced systems, as Lorenzini and Fox wrote in their *Naval War
College Review* article: "their tendency either to work 100 percent or not at all. In the F-16, for example, if the computer associated with the Stores Management System (SMS) is programmed
incorrectly or malfunctions, then no weapons release is possible.
Naturally this computer is designed to be so redundant that it can
never fail. Nevertheless, one . . . pilot who recently spent a week
fighting F-16s in mock air combat reports that on two occasions
during that week F-16s were unable to 'fire' missiles at him because their SMS computers had failed . . . 'and thence would not
provide them with ANY form of gunsight or release capability
(except jettison).' "[19]

All-or-nothing operation of essential systems in aircraft is understandably unsettling in prospect. In peace it is bad enough; in
war it would be intolerable. In peace, failure of a critical system
can cost the service a pilot's life and a $25 million airplane; in war
the costs can run much, much higher. The F-14s now deployed
aboard the Navy's carriers have, according to Vice Admiral E. R.
Seymour, Chief of Naval Air Systems Command, about six hours
mean time between failures at present. "The idea," Seymour told
Aviation Week in an intriguing formula, "is to design it to fail
gracefully. If something fails, you don't lose the whole thing, in
other words."[20]

Missile electronics are if anything as complex and sensitive as
aircraft electronics. Sparrow missiles have been in use for more
than a decade. Intended to be a major fleet air defense weapon,
Sparrow proved impossible to maintain in carrier operations during the Vietnam War. "After 100 traps [carrier landings], a Sparrow seldom works," one technician explained.[21] It is not widely

realized that when ships fire off test missiles in peacetime, there are almost always technical representatives of the manufacturer aboard to oversee the test firings, help with preparations, and the like. An article in the *Wall Street Journal* late in 1980 pointed to the technical representative aboard the carrier *Kennedy*, who was making more money than the sailors but doing similar work, and who in fact had been a sailor not long before. That was one point to make, and a good one in the manpower context. But it was equally important that, because of the complexity of modern military equipment, and the difficulty of making it work even under peacetime conditions, manufacturers' technicians must go to sea to operate and maintain vital systems and weapons.

In the same vein, the Los Angeles *Times* reported in its September 14, 1980, defense survey that the United States had never successfully launched a Minuteman missile from a regular operational silo. All successful launches had been specially prepared missiles from special test silos. After four failed attempts to launch a deployed Minuteman in the late 1970s, the Air Force stopped trying, to avoid further embarrassment.

American military equipment is, simply, too sophisticated for its own good. In the Pratt and Whitney–built F-100 engine of the F-15, the Air Force has its own version of the engine problems encountered in the XM-1 tank. In an effort to achieve the utmost in performance, designers produced an engine with operating temperatures so high that the engine proved unmaintainable. In effect, the engine burns itself up, wearing out at a very rapid rate. According to Senator Howard Cannon, who has long experience on the Senate Armed Services Committee, it will take more than $1.1 billion to mend the mistakes. One official from the President's Office of Management and the Budget told *Aviation Week & Space Technology* in the fall of 1980: "We joke that it takes $800 million to develop an engine and $2 billion to improve it."[22]

No area of advancing military technology has either mattered more or suffered more than communications. The much-publicized ability of Presidents and chiefs of staff to talk with on-scene operational commanders in such instances as the Iran rescue, the *Mayaguez* operation, or the Cuban Missile Crisis has contributed to a public impression that military communications embrace the world quickly, reliably, and securely. But, to the chagrin if not embarrassment of those responsible, the World Wide Military Command and Control System, a computer-assisted, highly advanced communications network built at enormous cost, simply does not work very well. In 1977, tests of the system led to breakdowns or failures in 62 percent of the trials; the Tactical Air Command had computer communications failures 70 percent of the time; and in a forerunner to the false alarms of 1979 and 1980, the Readiness Command, on alert for Soviet attacks, showed an 85 percent failure or error rate.

These things are bad enough in peacetime; in war they could be immeasurably worse. For the military, in an excess of enthusiasm for new communications technology, has come to rely more and more on satellite relays for command and control. As a result, the military faces an increasing likelihood that, in war or crisis, it might be genuinely unable to communicate rapidly and accurately with local commanders. For example, by 1980 the high cost of sophisticated satellite communications for the military, together with congressional parsimony, resulted in there being only two satellites to carry America's entire worldwide military communications traffic. Both were of a type conceded to be vulnerable to already proven Soviet antisatellite weapons. In addition, the Soviet military has avoided overreliance on space communications. Soviet military satellites are in use, to be sure, and ever increasing in number. But the Soviet military also maintains secure land-line communications, underground cables which, though slower than satellite relays, are also more durable in war.

There is also the "EMP" problem. Nuclear weapons, upon detonation, emit a powerful electromagnetic pulse—EMP. Gradually scientists have realized that very large warheads detonated high above the earth will produce a burst of electromagnetic energy that has the potential to wipe out the solid-state electronics of every device in Western Europe and North America that has not been hardened against it. NATO's communications, the electronics of advanced weapons, the communication systems of naval and air forces, even the transistor radios stockpiled for use in civil or military emergency—all could be destroyed by a nuclear explosion high above, say, the territory of the Soviet Union itself. Such a step might not even be an act of war in any traditional sense; but its consequences in crisis, emergency, or early in war could be incalculable. The good news is that Western scientists believe it possible to build protection into the electronics of new systems. The bad news, as always, is that it will vastly increase costs.

The complexity, unreliability, and sensitivity of much modern military equipment means that it takes more maintenance and more complex maintenance to keep American weapons operating. Much of the recent attention to reliability in military equipment has come as the Air Force and Navy have recognized that an enlarging portion of their budgets was going to manpower for maintenance and for "spare block boxes." Here the outright shortage of skilled maintenance personnel, and not only the cost thereof, becomes truly critical. Together with the cost of new weapons, maintenance-related difficulties have prejudiced our military readiness.

From the military side, the budgetary logic on weapons is simple and convincing: if funds are going to be limited, and new weapons cost so much that it is impossible to obtain enough of them, then it is best to acquire as many aircraft or ships as possible in each budget year. Once bought, such equipment will simply have to be supported and maintained. The obvious need to do so will, so the military hopes, inspire Congress to make up in subsequent years the shortcomings in initial purchases of spare parts, maintenance equipment, and contractor-provided services for support and upkeep of weapons and platforms. In 1976, for instance, when President Carter was running for election, he promised to cut the defense budget by $5 billion to $7 billion. When he came into office, he found that it was easier to propose than to make such cuts. But at least in his first year in office, there was strong pressure to follow through on the pledge. Required to trim their budgets, senior military leaders chose to chop moneys for parts, fuel, ammunition, and the like rather than to forgo acquisition of ships, planes, and other high-visibility items.

Unfortunately, this logic has not proved as effective in Congress as it has proved attractive to the military. Year after year, the Navy, Air Force, Army, and Marines buy as many weapons and systems as their appropriations will permit, trusting to the future for the money to buy parts and other support apparatus. But that future never comes, and thus the usability of what the military owns actually declines. The effects of such cuts in spare parts, maintenance moneys, and supplies continue to be felt, although they may not show up until exposed by war. In war, the ability to keep machines operating is often more a matter of quantity than of quality—the quantity of spare parts. *Aviation Week & Space Technology* quoted one officer on this point: "If a unit knows it will have to replace a certain number of UHF radios per 1,000 sorties, and that quantity is not available, then 1,000 sorties is just a goal, not a reality." It is that simple.

A few brief examples may help to establish this point. In the early 1970s, the Navy's Material Command attempted to reduce its reliability and maintenance problems, already grown beyond tolerable levels. The Navy's approach was to hire reliability specialists from the National Aeronautics and Space Administration (NASA), men who had worked on the Saturn-Apollo moon projects, on which no serious failures during the mission could have been tolerated. W. J. Willoughby, Jr., a high NASA official, became deputy chief of Naval Material. After surveying the operational status of major weapons in the fleet, he concluded that most of them failed to meet minimum reliability standards, *even though they had passed the Navy's reliability tests before being put into service*.

Another example, alluded to already in another context: The Air Force's new F-15, at more than $19 million apiece, spends more than 40 percent of its time down for repairs.

Example: The Navy's new F-18 now looks as though it may cost more than $25 million per plane. More than five years in development already, it is still not ready. Meanwhile its cost has risen at least *$10 million per plane over initial estimates*.

Item: Military aircraft radios operate from five to ten hours, on the average, without failing. The radios in commercial airliners, many times cheaper, normally work for more than 800 hours before similar breakdown. Many other aspects of aviation performance as between military and commercial equipment favor commercial equipment in terms of reliability and durability, yet the military specifications result in aircraft and equipment that cost much, much more than commercial counterparts. *Aviation Week & Space Technology* reported on October 6, 1980, that some aircraft manufacturers now boast that their equipment is "not military specification," an assurance of quality to their customers.[23]

In what may be the understatement of the year, at least in this field, *Aviation Week* reported in that same issue that "Field commanders have noticed a decline in the ability of the maintenance personnel to keep up with the demands of more complicated aircraft."[24]

It can be difficult, in describing the problems of reliability, to distinguish precisely between failures due to inappropriate complexity and failures resulting from cost pressures on maintenance and spare parts. There is no doubt, as former Assistant Secretary of the Army J. Ronald Fox has written, that "When the military gets new weapons, the most sophisticated components usually are specified." He quotes another defense official as saying: "A major problem that we have in the acquisition process is that when we have to design a system as a total gestalt, all the guys down in the buying organization specify all the latest components from the brochures. The system then has all the 'razmataz' and each one of these components ends up still having a number of problems that must be worked out."[25]

Ironically, the same occasions that bring to light shortcomings in readiness and reliability make those problems worse. In the first six months after the seizure of hostages in Iran, the increased operating tempo in the Indian Ocean had already cost more than $500 million in Navy operating costs, not to mention the longer-term costs of additional wear and tear on people and equipment. This figure climbed to about $1 billion by the end of fiscal year 1980. For a time there was talk of charging such costs against the Iranian assets frozen in the United States by presidential order. But no action followed, and so the Navy continued to "pay" those costs "out of its hide," that is, out of moneys appropriated for the current fiscal year but earmarked for other uses. Inevitably, this meant that once again, and throughout the Navy, money for spare parts, equipment, and stores dried up; acquisition of ships and planes programmed and contracted for proceeded; problems of maintenance, reliability, and sustainability increased.

The problems of reliability and maintenance, as well as their implications for American military competence, are painfully obvious to the professionals of the military establishment. But the proper responses to such difficulties, and to the technological pressures producing them, are a good deal less clear. In something of a miscarriage of the determination to improve material readiness, for instance, the military has created inspection and evaluation systems that are onerous, annoying, and possibly detrimental to capability.

This is what it looks like from the fleet, as Navy Lieutenant Commander Bernard D. Cole wrote in the Naval Institute *Proceedings*: "If we consider the first year of the five-year operating cycle for a guided missile destroyer in the Atlantic Fleet, we find that it is theoretically possible for that ship to be scheduled for as many as 39 inspections and assist visits. This means that an outside activity could descend upon the ship on an average of once every nine days. [The figure for the] Pacific Fleet is somewhat better: once every 12 days."[26] He was, however, speaking only of engineering inspections, as another Navy commander pointed out to me. If he had included all the others, on everything from human relations to gunnery, the total would have been 138 inspections, or one every two and a half days.

The full panoply of possible inspections and visits is unlikely to occur. Yet enough come along to prevent the officers and crew from performing all the maintenance, study, training, and other preparation necessary to put themselves into first-class shape for deployment and, more, for potential combat. Each such inspection or visit calls for painstaking preparation—but it is the preparation of paperwork, of elaborate showpiece performances of selected drills, operations, and maneuvers, not the accumulation of skill and confidence and coordination that an operating unit needs to do well when and where it counts.

Various inspection teams and their heads acquire reputations among the commanders of ships, squadrons, and other units. Their quirks become known. Hence the captain of a naval vessel preparing for inspection might ensure that all its grease fittings on all its machinery have been freshly anointed, even though the time might be better spent trying to repair a broken mount that prevents the ship's only gun—a single five-inch piece—from being trained. With luck, the inspection team will follow its reputed practice, construing well-greased machinery as evidence of a vessel conditioned to the peak, even the smallest details of good maintenance well in hand.

Why the charade? Why not simply report the malfunction and schedule repairs? Despite its inspection and maintenance emphases, the military penalizes honesty in its responsible officers. When a ship or an aircraft squadron—or any operating unit—is not up to operational standard, it is taken as a direct reflection of the current commanding officer's fitness for command and promotion potential. The captain of the *Canisteo*, mentioned in an earlier chapter, in declaring his ship unfit for deployment in April 1980, was putting his future and his reputation at risk *even though the crippling manpower shortages could not conceivably have been his fault*.

Penalties for honesty are not unique to the United States Navy, or even to the American military. Yet the results of such a climate, such a system, necessarily fall far short of needs. "Maybe," Lieutenant Commander Cole suggested in his *Proceedings* article, "the only thing the ships are being prepared for is to pass inspections and battle problems." Ships occasionally pass the first battle problem (set by a visiting inspection team), "and some occasionally fail the final exercise. Far more common is what might be called the '45–65–85' syndrome: the ship fails the first battle problem, barely passes or fails the second, then passes the final exercise. Thus the training group demonstrates the effectiveness of its own efforts. . . ." Under these conditions, "deploying is no longer considered the hardship it once was; it is now a relief from the shore establishment's onslaught. . . . The inspection system must cease being an end in itself."[27]

Here I must interject an aside. I showed the foregoing passage to a Navy captain whom I have known for some time, a man who has held important posts in naval aviation in the field and in Washington on various staffs. He asked, "Where did you get this? It's true, every word. And it's much worse than this. The inspectors are usually people who aren't terribly good at being naval officers. If they were better than they are, the Navy couldn't afford to put them on inspection teams for a couple of years or more. Instead they would be commanding ships or squadrons, or working closer to the seats of power. These inspectors know they have been sidetracked, and they are usually bitter about it, determined to prove that they are better professionals than those whose units and equipment they inspect. It is terribly hard on the morale of a ship that only months before has won the E [an award for excellence] to have one of these teams come on board and tell them they're doing everything wrong—and score them at 45 or even 60. A good commander gets his troops together before inspections and tells them the truth—that the inspectors must play a game for their own reasons, and that the crew's best interests lie in polite cooperation until the inspectors are, once again, gone."

In another important response to the problems of reliability, cost, and numbers in advancing military technology, defense experts have argued the relative merits of what is called "high mix" versus "low mix" investment. Simply put, proponents of a high mix, of continued investment in the most advanced technologies, point to the increasing sophistication of America's adversaries, to the possibility of falling into obsolescence, to uncertainties about likely future uses of American forces. They argue that only the most advanced technology will be (1) adequate to deal with the most worrisome enemies, and (2) flexible enough to make American forces effective in the variety of political-military contexts the nation might face. Advocates of the "low mix" contend that the costs of advanced technologies make it impossible to buy necessary numbers of weapons and to maintain them properly; that numbers matter; that in places such as Europe, where Soviet military power is greatest, the United States has no choice but to deploy more and cheaper planes and tanks even if they are individually less capable. There are also, as one might expect, advocates of a middle course, a "high-low mix." It should be possible, they suggest, to analyze expected uses of weapons to determine which of them require the ultimate in technological sophistication and, in contrast, which might be adequate even though less than the best.

"High mix" and "low mix" are, of course, relative terms. Nearly all weapons are very expensive indeed. But some cost enough more than others to make a difference in basic choices about force size and composition. Consider a high-mix versus low-mix issue that has been at the heart of naval force planning for the last decade: whether to build a small number of very large nuclear aircraft carriers, such as the *Nimitz*, carrying about one hundred warplanes each; or a larger number of smaller aircraft carriers, possibly conventionally powered, carrying forty to sixty aircraft each. The larger ones cost more than $2 billion apiece, and with the cost of their aircraft and associated equipment, more than $4 billion each. The low-mix carrier's costs have been a matter of dispute, but usually they are estimated at between $1.2 and $1.6 billion, plus planes, for a total cost of about $3 billion, or slightly more.

From issue to issue, each position—high mix, low mix, and high-low mix—has merit. But political uncertainties and analytic difficulties have prevented overall consensus within the military on high-low mix issues. From year to year, budget to budget, and administration to administration, the direction pursued in military modernization varies. Yet in general, with a few notable exceptions, the military leadership of recent years has tended to favor high-mix systems; nonuniformed military experts in the Congressional Budget Office, in the Office of Management and the Budget, and on congressional staffs more often favor low mix or high-low mix compromises. Decisions on major weapons and systems thereafter reflect the prevailing bureaucratic and political balances, and not their military merits, a fact that also contributes to long-term inconsistency in the character of American military forces.

As it now thinks and operates, the American military is virtually certain to produce inferior answers to the problems of modernizing an aging force in ways that will meet the nation's requirements. Years ago, in 1969, the Deputy Secretary of Defense, David Packard, told the Aerospace Industries Association: "I have reached the firm conclusion that we are designing and building weapons that are too complex, and therefore too costly. We further compound the problem by trying to produce hardware before it is fully developed. . . . A computerized fire control may increase the accuracy of tank gunnery, but so far it does not give evidence of increasing the reliability of gunnery. A tank with its gun out of order is no tank at all."[28] In the years since Secretary Packard's absolutely correct observation, things have gotten worse, not better. James Fallows, after leaving the Carter White House, said very simply: "What can be built, will be, even at the cost of bad military sense."[29]

The question is: Why? Why does the military pursue complexity at the expense of competence? For this there are a number of reasons, all deserving of discussion.

One large pressure for more—and more complex—weapons grows out of military thought and military politics: the American military has a tendency to look for, and to propound, quick fixes for deep-seated political and strategic problems. As an abstract proposition, the search for quick fixes is a close cousin to the age-old military search for, and belief in, decisive weapons—devices that could confer such advantages on their possessors that no adversary could hope to stand against them. From the slingshot through the crossbow through the atomic bomb, military professionals have sought and simultaneously feared truly decisive weapons. That such concerns can cause as much fear as hope is one of the most troubling aspects of contemporary interest in military breakthroughs or technical revolutions.

The current interest of both the Soviet Union and the United States in solving the strategic antisubmarine warfare problem illustrates this dilemma. The most secure portions of the strategic forces of both countries are their submarine-carried-and-launched strategic nuclear missiles. No single technical breakthrough could do more to destabilize the strategic relationship between the superpowers than the discovery of means to detect and locate missile-carrying nuclear submarines. Both powers have committed large resources and energies to pursuing such a capability.

The dilemma is this: in view of American need to have a secure second-strike nuclear force, such a breakthrough would be extremely unwelcome. If the United States solves the strategic antisubmarine warfare (ASW) problem, it will enjoy the momentary satisfaction of having untied a technical knot of the highest complexity; it will also enjoy the temporary advantages that may flow from an improved ability to counter Soviet nuclear submarines. But it will also know that if American scientists have found the answer to the detection and location problem, those of the Soviet Union will not be far behind. In most important areas of military technology, the two superpowers are working in the same generation of technical sophistication. The real interests of the United States are in forestalling any breakthrough in strategic ASW for as long as possible. But the United States cannot afford to be second if such a breakthrough is to come. So it must pursue with all its vigor a solution that, when attained, will hold almost as much threat as promise.

As a bureaucratic concern, the search for quick fixes to profound political-strategic difficulties also has contradictory, and therefore not entirely helpful, aspects. The military's interests are not well served by equipment so complicated that it is unreliable, so costly that it cannot be acquired in adequate numbers, so inadequately designed or tested that it does not have a long enough life or good enough performance to have been worthwhile in the first place. The military's leaders, men of intelligence and considerable professional attainment, know this full well. But they know also how rarely the public mood, congressional attitudes, presidential policies, and program suggestions together permit major force improvements.

In bureaucratic terms, and for practical political reasons, the military's best hopes of replacements for obsolescent forces lie in emphasizing the immediacy and urgency of needs. The military, as its leaders see it, must seize opportunities to get programs and acquisitions authorized whether or not the programs are in ideal form. The moments in which large moneys for modernization become available are few; the times in which inadequacies can be corrected are long. Or so, at least, it seems to military bureaucrats.

Further, American politics hold a political imperative for the military. A military that does not respond when called, that has no answers when the President or the public ask for them, can expect little sympathy when it next seeks political and budgetary support. Political conditions, domestic and foreign, do not always permit time for leisurely, idealized military reactions. But a military that cannot on a moment's notice protect endangered citizens and national interests cannot expect public favor.

Together, the conceptual, organizational, and political aspects of the quick-fix approach have caused America's political and military leaders to deal more and more in symbolism, less and less in reality. The ascendence of the representational over the real is not entirely new in American defense, but it is getting worse as pressures for quick fixes to basic problems continue to grow.

One early example of the quick fix at work occurred in the early 1960s. In 1963, President John F. Kennedy directed the military, and in particular the officers corps, to master counterinsurgency warfare; the Vietnam problem clearly promised both to enlarge and to become a prototype war. Many if not most military installations and bases had no counterinsurgency experts in residence then, but in response to the presidential directive they had counterinsurgency courses and instruction anyway. Virtually every officer on active duty received some form of instruction, with, as might be imagined, considerable variation in the quality of that instruction. The fact of such instruction was duly and solemnly noted in the service jackets of all the officers, in a bland paragraph signed by some faceless military bureaucrat. How effective all this was may be inferred, at least in part, from the war's results.

A more recent example of the quick fix, with its symbolic rather than real consequences, came in fall 1979. The Carter administration "discovered" a Soviet combat brigade deployed in Cuba. The administration, as was well known, pronounced this unacceptable, but within weeks had recognized that it could not force the brigade out. The answer was to establish a new Key West–based task force for the Caribbean area. The task "force" got, in actuality, no forces, few people, and little money. But it was a fix, a response. By January of 1981, this particular quick fix had so faded in importance that it received only two sentences—three lines—in Secretary of Defense Harold Brown's annual posture statement.

Not all quick fixes are total failures, as another example from the Vietnam War demonstrates. In 1966, the Air Force shot up a Coast Guard cutter, the *Point Welcome*, while the cutter was on patrol duty off the coast of Vietnam. This unfortunate incident took place despite the elaborate radio and other electronic recognition procedures and mechanisms in use in American forces off Vietnam. The crew abandoned ship but, embarrassingly, the ship did not sink, so after a somewhat unpleasant swim the crew went back aboard and took the cutter into port. The fix: American ships in the war zone painted huge white stars on their fantails, and mounted floodlights over them. When officers on the bridge heard aircraft overhead, they raced for the switch to illuminate their white star, hoping to avoid what had befallen the *Point Welcome*. As it happened, and because of American undisputed air superiority over seas adjacent to Vietnam, this fix worked quite well, despite its primitiveness in comparison with all the electronic recognition devices supposedly available to meet this need.

Another example of grand, expensive, and dubiously effective political-military symbolism showed in the NATO context so prominent in the Carter administration's strategic perspective: the POMCUS program. POMCUS is the acronym for positioning large amounts of military equipment abroad, in this case in NATO Europe: *Prepositioned Overseas Matériel Configured in Unit Sets.* The idea is that in crisis, or early in war, American troops could be lifted to Europe to "marry up" with their equipment. The equipment is too heavy and bulky to move quickly in emergency. To ship troops and equipment would take time, possibly too much time. Such shipments early in war would also risk the loss of substantial portions of men and equipment to submarines.

Despite its clear rationale, the POMCUS program is vulnerable to criticism. It is costing the United States a great deal of money—each division set of equipment in FY 1980 dollars cost $1.2 billion just to buy, and more, of course, to move, store, and maintain.[30] Equipment put into Europe in advance of need cannot be used meanwhile by troops in their training and exercises; in effect, the United States has to buy double what it needs for those divisions earmarked for early wartime use in Europe. Since current plans call for the stockpiling of equipment for five or six divisions by 1982, this is no small matter. The entire American Army boasts only sixteen divisions; hence POMCUS amounts to dual-equipping 37.5 percent of the whole U.S. Army.

Further, military equipment is both expensive and difficult to maintain in storage, even though NATO allies are sharing some costs of constructing depots and shelters for vehicles and supplies. In the latter 1970s, surveys of military vehicles stored in Europe—tanks, trucks, jeeps—showed that only 42 percent were in usable condition. There were, of course, no guarantees that the next large-scale military involvement for the United States would be in NATO Europe. But there was high likelihood that POMCUS sites would be well up on Russian priorities for chemical, tactical nuclear, or even airborne assault in the event of war. There was one more concern, little mentioned in the public discussion of POMCUS and NATO. Some of the most important equipment and supplies belonging to a division simply cannot be bought and stored in POMCUS without undue deterioration. Helicopters are one such essential but unstorable item. Air defense weapons, vital on the modern battlefield, similarly are not included in POMCUS. Ammunition, for the most part, also remains outside the POM-CUS program. This has two important implications. In one, the costs of POMCUS are certain to understate the actual costs of equipping a division for combat in Europe. In a related and even more important point, even if everything works, POMCUS would produce somewhat less than full, and fully effective, American divisions in Europe in the event of crisis or war.

The gap between symbolism and reality remains very wide, very obvious, and very disturbing.

The military's quick-fix approach, with its symbolic and inadequate answers to modernization dilemmas, is encouraged by present budgetary rituals. In defense, everything is colored by the marginal nature of year-to-year programs, decisions, and budgets. Past investment—in equipment, in organization, in bases and facilities, in training, in some technologies but not in others—places military management decisions into the context of marginality because of the extremely low ratio of annual military expenditures to sunk cost.

In an economic sense, as glamorized in the McNamara management revolution of the 1960s, marginality means that change is slow, that year by year developments will bring incremental alterations of capability, but not revolutionary, order-of-magnitude changes. In a political sense, the principle of marginality means that the United States will meet its choices for war or peace ten years from now, twenty years from now, and even in some cases thirty years from now with forces that are already on hand or in development. It takes a very long time to design, develop, and procure modern weapons; as technology becomes more esoteric, this time extends.

In 1980, Edward Hidalgo, then Secretary of the Navy, tried to explain the dimensions of this problem: "In order to substantially affect our forces in the year 2000, immediate action is required. . . . suppose that, for whatever reason, the fleet should be a modest 10 percent, or roughly 50 ships, larger at the beginning of the 21st century. To accomplish this, we would have to add three ships a year, every year, to our building plan, starting now and continuing at least through 1996. . . . If a critical incremental need is not identified until it is within the mid-term planning period, five to

10 years hence, it can be redressed only by drastic or heroic measures."[31] The same, of course, is true not only for numbers of ships or other systems but for the specific technological capabilities they must possess, and it is even more true of totally new weapons or technologies.

There is a certain momentum that creeps readily into military logic, and for this there is a reason, if not always a good reason. The need to deal with the planners and programmers in each budget cycle encourages the military to put means before ends. Ideas about military needs, strategies, and programs must be shaped with an eye to what is feasible, to what is after all "doable," not over time but on time. No military service can serve its interests, or for that matter any broader interests, by failing to produce its strategic concepts, program decisions, and budget submissions when due.

The schedule is a tyrant. In 1978, the Chairman of the Joint Chiefs of Staff, General George Brown, denounced the tendency to make policy and strategy "secondary to programming and fiscal considerations." *Time* magazine repeated the charges of Navy staff officers who believed that strategy had become a product of budget requirements, a reversal of the theoretical ideal.[32] Long experience made former Chief of Naval Operations Elmo Zumwalt tolerant, if cynical. There are, he wrote in his mid-1970s memoir, "two sets of 'budgeteers,' the 'scrubbers' who . . . comb budgets for non-essential details to cut and the 'systems analysts' who hope against hope that budgets will make sense. The Chiefs, on the whole, are on the side of the scrubbers, who do not, as the analysts do, make assumptions about enemy actions, a prerogative the Chiefs tend to believe is theirs. Moreover, scrubbers do not have any illusions that under present procedures budgets can make sense. They just want them to add up right. The Chiefs find this, if not helpful, at least reasonably honest."[33]

It is true that budgetary business has begun to fall behind the supposedly immutable budget process deadlines established in the mid-1970s. But everyone is falling behind together. A service that moves more slowly than the rest risks having its decisions made by someone else, its own budget a patchwork of what may be left over. In military matters, this means that for all practical purposes, weapons tend to drive strategy. Instead of building weapons that permit pursuit of previously determined interests, the military has capabilities searching for missions, weapons and forces in need of justification. Rather than reflecting on the question of what the American nation needs most from its Navy, for instance, the naval establishment has promulgated a series of strategies designed to preserve the large-decked aircraft carrier as the mainstay of naval thought and hence of naval forces. After the Second World War, as each service scrambled to win a role in the nuclear weapons business, aircraft carriers became ungainly and in some respects unsafe platforms for aircraft scheduled to deliver nuclear weapons against the Soviet Union. As time and technology deprived the carriers of that role, the new naval strategy of the late 1960s and early 1970s exalted the carrier as the most powerful naval weapon in the world, a flexible instrument for bringing American power to bear on land or sea virtually anywhere in the world. As military, technical, and political developments of the 1970s diminished the carrier's usefulness against targets on shore, the Navy once again produced a new carrier-centered naval strategy: a strategy of sea lane protection amid threats to lines of communication in a resource-starved era.

When all was said and done, its carrier fixation undoubtedly had slowed Navy exploitation of crucial new technologies—surface-to-surface missiles, vertical and short takeoff aircraft. Yet it remained likely that between 1980 and the end of the century, further naval strategies would affirm the carrier's continuing dominance in American naval thought.

Weapons in development can drive strategy almost as successfully as weapons already in use. In August 1980, the Carter administration announced a new nuclear strategy emphasizing the ability to attack hardened military targets and other difficult-to-attack installations. Tom Wicker, writing in *The New York Times*, shrewdly recognized that momentum for a new nuclear strategy flowed in part from the need to justify construction of the MX missile and basing system to which the Carter administration was already committed.[34]

The weight of forces on hand, and the vested interests associated with them, press the military relentlessly toward short-term thoughts, solutions, efforts. The military's leaders are reduced to fighting *this year's* fiscal fray, leaving what comes later for another day, another struggle. But by doing what is possible instead of what may be wise, the military thus equips itself better for the annual budget battles of peacetime than for the decisive engagements of war.

Quick-fix thinking and marginality in military investment help explain the military's inability to resolve the issues of modernizing a high-technology force. In addition, the American military tary depends for much of its sophistication and all of its equipment on an ailing economy. This, together with the military's business practices, results in a widespread failure of American military equipment to perform up to specification and to stay within budget.

Many shortcomings of present military posture reflect the poor performance of the American economy through the 1970s. One defense contractor, R. A. Fuhrman, president of Lockheed Missiles and Space Co., frankly told *Aviation Week* late in 1980 that as regards defense, America's industrial base was weak to nonexistent, "not healthy."[35] The often-remarked problems of an obsolescing industrial plant, insufficient capital investment, energy-related disruptions of long-term financial planning and growth, slowdown in basic research and related losses of relative advantage in basic physics and electronics, delays and other costs associated with environmental regulations, the generalized effects of severe and unaccustomed inflation—all have had serious effects on the military condition of the United States. The same companies that build America's front-line defenses—Ford and Chrysler—are building cars that cost them millions of dollars in recalls, repairs, and lawsuits. The companies that design and develop America's most advanced military technology, gazing a generation or more into the future, have lost hundreds of millions of dollars in the last few years because of inadequate vision in their primary concern, the American automobile market.

Further, a considerable amount of the equipment bought by the military does not do the job. One reason for this was advanced long ago, by Congressman George P. Miller. J. Ronald Fox, former Assistant Secretary of the Army, quoted the congressman's 1963 observation: "The best qualified scientists and engineers are engaged in writing proposals and, when the proposals are successfully sold to the Government, the scientists are put on a new proposal. Then second-rate scientists are given the job of performing work while the more highly regarded people scout for new business."[36] This still is true. After the attempted Iran rescue mission, a Senate staff member told *Aviation Week & Space Technology:* "The problem I have with readiness, which was made into a catchword by the American mission into Iran, is that discussions of it never include one word about the manufacturers putting out deficient systems. We are not getting what we pay for. We need to focus on American industry. They should be ashamed."[37]

Every time U.S. Steel raises the price of steel by a dollar a ton, it means that current military procurement budgets will buy fewer tanks, ships, and aircraft. When Lockheed gets into financial trouble, the United States Government has to bail it out—that is, if it still wants to obtain C-130s, the workhorse cargo and troop transport planes; or S-3s, the country's foremost carrier-based anti-submarine aircraft; or P-3s, the long-distance maritime patrol and anti-submarine warfare aircraft. When Chyrsler Corporation verges on financial disaster, again the government must find a way to help—that is, if it wants to buy tanks from a domestic supplier. Chrysler is the only remaining manufacturer of tanks in the United States. The Army's hopes for modernized ground forces, the nation's hopes for a credible military position in Central Europe—both depend on the ability of Chrysler to develop and build the new XM-1 main battle tank and its successors.

The financial disasters of contemporary American business are doubly costly to the government. Not only does the government of necessity provide short-term help, but through the military budget it also pays the increased costs these companies meet through massive borrowings in an expensive money market. Later, these businessess try to recoup in current and future earnings the huge losses that brought them near to collapse in the first place. The government, the military, pays again.

The result of government assistance to ailing industries is not cheap military equipment but expensive military equipment.

The military's way of doing business worsens the effect on defense posture of economic sluggishness. There is, for one thing, virtually a conflict of interest embedded in defense management itself. This was explained in the 1974 book by J. Ronald Fox, which we have quoted earlier. In *Arming America,* Fox wrote:

"Every Assistant Secretary . . . wants to acquire the weapons and equipment needed by the services, on schedule and for the lowest reasonable cost. At the same time, each is directed to build and/or maintain an industrial base that will meet tomorrow's uncertain defense needs. Lowering contractors' costs means reducing the number of employees in a contractor's plant. This supports the first objective but endangers the second."[38]

Since World War II, it has become inappropriate to think of the government business relationship in terms of the classic distinction between public and private sectors. As long ago as 1968, John Kenneth Galbraith, the liberal economist, suggested nationalization of major defense contractors. He argued that they were already in effect public, not private enterprise, because the government provided a goodly share of their working capital, because much defense procurement was not price competitive, and because the contractors were sustained by the government even when they failed to perform as promised.

The practical complications of business/government relations encourage the misrepresentation of new weapons programs while they discourage effective control of rising costs. The complexities that bedevil America's weapons also hinder wide public understanding of some unpleasant truths. Much of this problem has been set out in *Arming America*. Few people, as the author correctly argues, really can grasp either the costs or the technical merits of a weapons proposal. As one senior defense official put it years ago, "appraising the reasonableness of a cost estimate for a new complex program is like estimating the number of fleas on Manhattan Island. You know the number is high, but you don't have any idea how high. This is the condition in which most people find themselves—Congressmen, Senators, many senior military and civilian personnel in the Pentagon, the press, and the average citizen."[39]

Both business and the military have an interest in increasing complexity. For one thing, technology—and hence research and development—seem to possess their own momentum. "R & D specialists," as one officer told J. Ronald Fox, "want to acquire the best possible weapons and equipment that American technology can devise, whether or not there is actually any foreseeable military threat." For the military, there is in addition the formidable task of trying to prepare for threats yet unknown. "To cope with the uncertainty inherent in the situation, those who define requirements 'hedge their bets.' They recommend the acquisition of the most sophisticated systems attainable. Cost is, at best, a secondary consideration."[40]

In an even more interesting reason for increasing complexity of weapons, and hence for rising costs, Mr. Fox quoted the president of a firm that handles defense contracts, who said: "If we build something that is well within the state of the art, we don't sell many of them. The things we sell lots of are those that are advanced right up to the state of the art, or 20% beyond—and, of course, these are often the programs that get into trouble during the development phase."[41] It is small wonder that, as Mr. Fox indicates, defense contractors routinely—and informally—"assist" Pentagon officials in drafting the government's requests to industry for new weapons proposals. Often the companies know a good deal more about what is possible and desirable than the military does.

Because of this complexity, weapons issues routinely become collaborations in which business, the military, and the Congress all seek to further their individual interests without making anyone look bad to the public. In effect, defense acquisition becomes a game with its rules and ethics. "The over-riding concern of each military service," Mr. Fox has explained, "is to win approval for programs that will enhance its prestige and will allow it to continue its traditional functions."[42] He quotes from a November 1969 article by General David M. Shoup, former Commandant of the Marine Corps: "At the senior command levels, parochial pride in the service, personal ambitions, and old Army-Navy game rivalries stemming back to academy loyalties can influence strategic planning far more than most civilians would care to believe. The game is to be ready for deployment sooner than the other elements of the joint task force and to be so disposed as to be the 'first to fight.' "[43]

With this outlook—and I believe that the ethics described by General Shoup are alive and flourishing in the military—it is small wonder that the military looks on its job in regard to weapons programs as one of "marketing." The essential device in marketing new weapons—both within the Department of Defense and in dealing with the Congress—is underestimation of costs. One program manager in the Department of Defense told Mr. Fox in the early 1970s: "If we told the truth to the Congress, we would never get our programs approved. So we have to understate the cost and overstate the performance. . . . Our military bias is to get as much as we can get—after all, we don't know who the future enemy is or what he will have in the way of weapons. . . . We are the ones who have to fight the wars, not the people in the Congress or the average taxpayer."[44]

Even within the Department of Defense itself, this tradition of concealing costs and other problems prevails. Another program manager told of filing a quarterly progress report in which he listed fourteen serious problems with his program. By the time the report reached the Office of the Secretary of Defense three days later, all fourteen of the subjects had been deleted. "Middle-level managers," concluded Mr. Fox, "fear that if higher-level officials in the Department or the Congress know what is really happening on some programs they will make the 'wrong decision'; that is, they will cut back or cancel programs. These middle-level managers are convinced that Pentagon and Congressional officials have neither the background nor the training to understand the need for additional funds."[45]

To complete the circle, Pentagon officials help congressmen and senators avoid embarrassment while going through the motions of overseeing defense. For every congressman or senator who has taken the trouble to master the intricacies of one or more defense issues, there are a dozen or more who have not. Recommendations of the House and Senate Armed Services Committees are by and large accepted on the floor of the House and Senate because they are too complicated for most legislators to debate seriously. It has long been standard practice for congressional staffers to ask Pentagon officials for lists of questions that congressmen and senators could ask at hearings on defense appropriations.

Thus the weapons acquisition process: business helping the Pentagon prepare requests for weapon proposals to which those same businesses will respond; the Pentagon helping congressmen prepare questions to ask about the Pentagon's own proposals; the Congress approving new weapons, making token budget cuts,

when times demand it, in such things as operations and maintenance moneys—but not in new weapons appropriations. These are
the features of a system marked not by evil intent, or even by
dishonesty, so much as by the neutral ethic of "marketing." In all,
this somewhat saddening process is probably best understood as a
flawed effort to accommodate politically to a complexity that is
unmanageable technically.

For men and organizations to be overwhelmed in a world of
complexity and risk is a theme of art as well as a fact of defense
politics. It would not do to get too abstract about this here. But it
was this, exactly, that gave such point to the 1970 comments of
Congressman Allard Lowenstein during the debate on the great
cost overrun scandal of the Lockheed C-5A. At those hearings, a
number of congressmen and senators had simply admitted that
they could not themselves judge the merits of many military aspects of the project. To his colleagues in the Congress, Representative Lowenstein said: "I speak with some sadness as this comes to
a conclusion. I love this place. To be elected to it is easily the
greatest honor I shall expect to attain. Yet much that happens
here leaves me feeling that we are not conducting ourselves as we
should. . . . we have greater obligations to the country than has
been shown by our behavior today."[46]

Weapons acquisition falls short of preventing undue complexity and controlling costs for mundane reasons as well as for lofty
ones. Much military procurement, for instance, is done on the basis of "cost-plus" contracts. Contracting companies estimate their
costs of production; they and the government negotiate a figure
that is supposed to take into account those costs, the expected inflation rate over the life of the contract, and a negotiated percentage of profit.

In the last fifteen years, the results of this business style have
not been particularly good. Late in the 1970s, Sears, Roebuck
publicly announced that it would no longer bid on government
supply contracts. For a time in the latter 1970s, the leading American shipbuilders refused to accept any new work and threatened
to discontinue work on nuclear submarines and other ships in
progress if their claims were not settled.

Increasingly, business and government have taken each other
to court to win changes in contract terms. Businesses have

charged, with some justification, that the government has not allowed adequately for inflation. Through the middle and latter 1970s, inflation estimates as represented in procurement contracts consistently ran about three percentage points behind the actual annual rate. Industry has further charged, and congressional studies have confirmed, that many defense contracts become unreasonably burdensome because of changes in specifications demanded after work has begun. Reductions or slowdowns in procurement after contracts are signed are commonplace in defense. Whether mandated by the Congress or by the White House, or even by the office of the Secretary of Defense, these changes inevitably cause costs to rise. For this, too, industry expects the government to pay. And pay it does. Walter Guzzardi, writing in *Fortune* in September 1980, quoted a congressional staffer on the Army's new infantry fighting vehicle, long in development, whose cost had doubled before it even entered production. "At that rate," said the staffer, "we could double the amount we spent on defense and get nothing back at all." [47]

On its side, the government claims that guaranteed profit percentages encourage bad management. Companies may carelessly fail to control costs, then turn around and attempt in court to force the government to pay not only the higher-than-expected costs but a profit percentage based on the adjusted cost figure. The government has also demonstrated that many defense contractors pad costs by adding disproportionate amounts of corporate overhead to cost-plus defense contracts.

One Marine colonel with experience in overseeing development contracts summed up the dilemma for me in these terms: "Cost-plus is the only fair way to do business if the company has integrity. If the government ends up doing business with a crooked firm, it will get raped. As a military man," he continued, "you sometimes have to think that your profession is essentially amoral; but after six months supervising a contract with_____, let me tell you, the ethics and morals of the service look pretty good. Business with the government is not run amorally; it is run immorally, and it's cutthroat besides."

The results of all this are difficult to calculate, but small indications give reason for concern. Between 1968 and 1975, so *Newsweek* reported on October 27, 1980, the number of aerospace contractors fell from more than 6,000 to fewer than 4,000. Only three large foundries, *Newsweek* continued, can still supply large forgings for very large equipment. Some metal castings for the new XM-1 tank have to be ordered up to twenty months before they are needed for assembly. This peacetime attrition in defense industries, according to Walter Guzzardi, "destroys the U.S.'s ability to mobilize industry quickly in the event of war."[48]

In all, it is a sobering picture: a military baffled by technological complexity, trying to arm itself in a turgid economy by means of dubious business methods. It is a wonder that the overall results are not worse.

Another facet of business/government relations contributes to difficulties in resolving the technological quandaries of modernization. This is the military's heavy dependence on private industry for ideas about future military problems, tactics, and equipment. Things were not always this way. In the 1950s and early 1960s, vigorous funding for military research and development, particularly that of the space program, produced new plastics, cheap and sophisticated electronics, synthetic fibers, even exotic medical equipment and techniques as "spin-off" benefits for the consumer. These developments were celebrated as a serendipitous dividend for assiduous and proper attention to the nation's military needs. But the costs of the Vietnam War and the human needs of a Great Society grew prohibitively expensive as the 1960s progressed. I talked about this with Steve Teel, an executive in the United States Department of Transportation, formerly with the Department of Defense, and a specialist in the development of advanced technology in the United States. As he explained it to me, it began to seem shrewd late in the 1960s in effect to transfer a portion of the enlarging cost and burden of research and development from government to private industry. Then, of course, American industry led the world in productivity, innovation, and efficiency.*

---

* Between 1964 and 1980, the Research and Development budget just about kept pace with inflation. But the competition from Soviet science and the growing complexity of weapons rendered this level of expenditure completely inadequate to maintain American supremacy in numerous critical technologies.

Through the 1970s, inadequate military R & D budgets, sharp reductions in space programs, and the natural momentum of American salesmanship reversed the earlier relation between military research and American business. Now major corporations— General Dynamics, Westinghouse, LTV, General Electric, Litton, and more—form high-level planning groups of scientists, engineers, retired generals and admirals, and a sprinkling of futurologists. Their task: to anticipate the nation's technical military needs. This permits the long-term direction of huge corporate research programs. It also lays the foundation for aggressive attempts to sell ideas and obtain commitments from the services for expensive, long-lead-time weapon development projects.

In short, the American military has come to depend on private industry to suggest to the military what it is going to need in the distant future; to carry out the basic scientific research, to work out the engineering applications of this research, and to produce the final weapon, system, or device. Like the use of cost-plus contracts, this development would likely have proved advantageous in a healthier economy. Gradually, however, government experts in technology development are concluding that the present situation retards military modernization. There is an obvious danger of incoherence in a decentralized, profit-motivated military R & D enterprise. It is equally clear that in some cases salesmanship will triumph over science, that companies will succeed in selling ideas, weapons, and systems that do not prove out. Up to a point, this is not worrisome from the perspective of defense. Any basic research, and much advanced engineering, involves wrong turns as well as right ones, errors and not only successes.

Here lies the importance of the test and evaluation effort that complements research and development. In recent years, as we have seen, the military's test and evaluation organizations have not performed an adequate job. In fairness, difficulties of assessing complex new weapons are now so great that it may be unreasonable to expect better results from testing and evaluation. One of the most disturbing aspects of increasing technological sophistication is that it is now possible to conceive and to build devices that literally defy thorough testing. In computers there are virtually no means completely to check out programs. In the summer of 1980, in the important flyoff tests between cruise missiles built by Boeing and General Dynamics, twelve of twenty flights were successful. But the most significant problems in the flyoffs came from errors in the computer programs that controlled the missiles in flight. "It is impossible and it would be prohibitively expensive," said then Senator John C. Culver, "to wring out those programs to cover every possible situation. This is something we are just beginning to see, and something which guarantees problems in the future."[49] The senator also observed that Raytheon's new Patriot missile involved thousands, perhaps millions, of lines of computer instructions. It was a virtual certainty that there would be combinations of instructions and directions impossible to anticipate or to test.

In silicon chips, technology is developing so fast that theoretical design work is being carried directly into drafting and from there into production. Some chips even apart from their programs are so complex that only a few companies possess the technology to test them for unintended circuit paths. This "sneak circuit" testing, as it is called, is again quite expensive. Because so few companies actually can do such work, a requirement for more such testing in defense would mean not only increased expense but new delays.

A certain vulnerability to surprise and error, therefore, inevitably remains in the new advanced electronics. Thus the reliance of most advanced military technology on microprocessors and other sophisticated electronics means that most advanced military equipment shares this resistance to thoroughgoing evaluation.

In another problem, many weapons have either physical or political characteristics that make them impossible to test adequately—nuclear, chemical, and biological weapons come to mind. Still others are so expensive that they cannot be sufficiently proved; most missiles and aircraft show at least some limitations here. Finally, of course, most weapons and military systems will be employed under conditions that cannot be truly duplicated in peacetime. There remains a residual uncertainty on that score.

By relying to a greater extent on proven technologies, the Soviet military avoids or minimizes some of these problems. Certainly any advanced military, the Soviet military included, will face serious problems of equipment reliability. Some of America's problems are bound to show up in Soviet equipment by virtue of the fact that Soviet industrial espionage numbers among its chief duties the theft and/or duplication of advanced American microprocessor chips. But because this factor cannot be predicted with confidence or in detail, American military planners cannot realistically engage in some automatic discounting of Soviet military power.

The foregoing conditions affecting equipment testing are, of course, handicaps rather than excuses for test and evaluation shortcomings. In the early 1970s, the Navy put its new A-7 fighter-bomber into service. But the A-7s that had met maintenance and reliability tests *under test conditions* performed far worse in the fleet. A-7Ds and A-7Es passed tests proving that they would require no more than 9.6 maintenance man-hours per flight hour; but in service this figure doubled, to about eighteen hours. Overall, the A-7 was about seven times less reliable in service than it had been in tests.[50] This was the more sobering because the A-7 was a program in which, in contrast to so many other weapons, reliability and maintainability were stressed from the very beginning of development, and testing was considerably more rigorous than was customary.

What accounts for the failings of weapons testing?

In evaluating new weapons—missiles, aircraft, fire-control systems, and the like—judgments are often based on test engagements between a single U.S. system and a single enemy system— say, one U.S. fighter against one enemy fighter. Such one-to-one tests tend to reinforce the conclusion that the plane with qualitative and technical advantages is greatly superior. It is difficult to go beyond such a test result in view of the extent to which the military and industry are predisposed to favor high-mix, complex weapons in the first place.

Further, a Lockheed engineer told *Aviation Week:* "If the manufacturer doesn't have absolute control over maintenance, he can't take all of the responsibility for failures . . . If you look at a piece of equipment after two or three cycles of Navy or Air Force maintenance, you can find a lot of unspecified parts inside, [with differences so large that they don't] even appear to be the same in form, fit, or function. . . . The lower bid [for system support] gets the contract. Anything goes. But it's not the military's fault—the edicts have been laid down by the GAO [General Accounting Office], Congress, and ASPRS [Armed Services Procurement Regulations]."[51]

Beyond this, when the General Accounting Office produced a study in 1979 arguing that a substantial portion of military cost overruns were the consequence of inadequate testing, it appeared that in some cases flaws were known to the military, revealed in test and development, but concealed from Congress in order to get the weapons and systems funded, then fixed, rather than rejected or delayed.

In addition, an intricate but important problem of weapons acquisition deserves brief mention: production decisions are often made on new weapons before development testing is complete. For this there are several reasons. Sometimes the need seems urgent; the program really can't wait. Sometimes, as with metal castings for the XM-1 tank, components for production require long lead time, so that a delayed production decision must mean still more delay when a decision finally comes. Further, in most cases the development contractor will also be the production contractor; if a decision is delayed he may have to lay off employees critical to the project, or commit them to another job. Hence the practice of "concurrency"—jargon for making production decisions before development is complete.

Fox advanced one more reason for this practice: "If commitment to production is not made before the end of R & D, cost growth in R & D is harder to conceal."[52] If the production decision comes before development has to be finally accounted for, it may be possible to merge enlarging development costs into early production costs, a more satisfactory solution for all those concerned with saving the taxpayer unnecessary worry about his government's spending and defenses.

Of course, such a practice also means that flaws, mistakes, and low performance can be concealed—perhaps to be fixed later, perhaps not. The Navy's F-14 fighter-attack plane is a case in point. At the time the Navy committed itself to buy the F-14, the program manager bought only airframes—no spare parts, no support packages. The airframes themselves had defects known to him and a few associates. However, their action reflected their judgment that the Navy needed the plane; that it could be made right; and that it was critical to make the price look attractive to the Congress. In later years, so I am told by Navy colleagues, the program manager bragged about his maneuver, considering it a model of bureaucratic tactics.

Business has an interest in selling; the military has an interest in buying; both will always hope to get the Congress to pay later, if necessary, for refit, redesign, or repair of faults. Thus the military acquires ever more complex and expensive weapons without real regard for either the nation's needs or the weapons' merits.

Ideally, the military should be able to reject a defective weapon today in the confidence that it will be able to acquire it tomorrow, when the weapon has been put right. But the military rarely sees its choices in such terms, tending rather to believe that it must get what it can when it can, flawed or not, because the opportunity to get it at all will probably be gone tomorrow.

In another hindrance to orderly and successful modernization in a high-technology era, the perpetuation of service rivalries ensures less than ideal results. The American military ended World War II only to encounter a serious prospect of service unification. In part the service unification drive drew momentum from the wartime success of the Joint Chiefs of Staff. General George C. Marshall sent a unification proposal to the Joint Chiefs in 1943, and two other Army generals—Joseph T. McNarney and Lawton Collins—submitted similar plans to Congress in the following year. Army officials broadly favored the proposals; Army Air Force (one service then, not two) and Navy leaders, however, opposed them for obvious reasons. After the war, civilian experts on government organization were virtually unanimous in judging that a single military service would eliminate the competition, overlap, duplication, and waste evident in wartime experience. But the Congress in drafting the National Security Act of 1947 showed a bent for compromise. It created a new National Military Establishment, presided over by a Secretary of Defense whose duties included a mandate to unite the planning, procurement, and other policies of the services as a substitute for unifying their organizations.

For many years after World War II, the Joint Chiefs of Staff quarreled among themselves, seeking maximum budget shares, important missions, and increasing technical sophistication at each other's expense. Divided, they were often overruled. In time, the service leaders recognized that their interests would be better served by collaboration than by conflict. By the mid-1960s, in Vietnam-aggravated contentions with Robert S. McNamara's managers, the Joint Chiefs had developed a system of genteel co-operation. Disputes were settled in intimate discussions in "the tank," a windowless room in the "E" ring of the Pentagon. In public, and especially in dealing with the Congress and the President, the Chiefs of Staff enhanced their influence by presenting unanimous judgments and recommendations.

There is no point more vital to the new tactics of the Joint Chiefs of Staff than the principle of respect for each service's vital modernization programs. Each service can expect its interests, its budgetary needs, to receive support in turn. Any service chief who undercuts another service's modernization program must anticipate that his own program will meet potentially crippling opposition. Hence the Joint Chiefs of Staff, as it now functions, produces consensus, not wisdom, at the top. It results in JCS support for the Army's acquisition of the XM-1 tank, the Navy's of another large-deck nuclear carrier, the Air Force's of the MX missile. If the Marine Corps can ever make up its mind what destiny holds for it, its next generation of weapons will receive JCS support in due course. This system, as several of the service chiefs reiterated in the months following the Iran rescue attempt, produced the unanimous JCS conclusion, prior to the operation, that the rescue effort had a good chance of success.

The military's inability to solve modernization dilemmas stems in part from overdependence on nuclear weapons. Since the late 1940s, nuclear weapons have exerted a pervasive and on the whole deleterious effect on American military thinking and military forces. This problem can be properly appreciated only in modest historical perspective.

Directly following World War II, American authorities took decisions that established the nation's reliance on fission and fusion weapons for years to come. Use of the atomic bomb against Japan did not lead to an immediate conviction that atomic weapons would remain paramount—or even prominent—in American forces and strategy. For several years, American political/military thinkers cautiously avoided concluding that this new weapon had by itself brought World War II to a close; after all, these men had lived through that war, and fought it. They knew, I believe, how big a war it was and how small those two atomic bombs seemed in the larger context of a great and destructive war. For the first three to five years after World War II, thinking about the importance and possible uses of the atomic bomb was very tentative, even speculative. It was important, therefore, that in 1948 high government officials formally declined to rule out the possibility that the United States would use nuclear weapons in future wars. This decision, as W. Walton Butterworth of the State Department noted at the time, was tantamount to admitting that the United States would build and rely on such devices.

In January 1950, when President Harry S. Truman decided to approve development of a hydrogen bomb, it was evident that the Joint Chiefs of Staff were hoping to find the military's Holy Grail: a truly decisive weapon. This latter concern led diplomat George F. Kennan to an ominous conclusion in what he later considered his most important state paper. In opposing the decision to proceed with the hydrogen bomb, Kennan wrote: "I fear that the atomic weapon, with its vague and highly dangerous promise of 'decisive' results, of people 'signing on dotted lines,' of easy solutions to profound human problems, will impede understanding of the things that are important to a clean, clear policy and will carry us toward the misuse and dissipation of our national strength." [53]

In the absence of Russian capability to conduct nuclear war against the United States—that is, from about 1945 to 1956—decisions to rely on atomic weapons and to build fusion weapons were relatively easy to make. Though expressed in terms more befitting the exalted status of senior government officials, the prevailing philosophy was not materially different, in my view, from that of Captain Robert Lewis, copilot of the *Enola Gay*, who addressed the crew before the Hiroshima bombing run: "You guys, this bomb cost more than an aircraft carrier. We've got it made, we're gonna win the war, just don't screw it up. Let's do this really great." [54]

In one of the paradoxes of nuclear strategy, Soviet acquisition of significant nuclear forces only heightened the mystique attaching to such weapons within the American military. The logic of deterrence, emphasizing the interest of the United States in never using such weapons, might have been expected to promote an aversion to such weapons within the military. After all, what kind of a soldier wants to be armed with unusable weapons? Rarely in the annals of military history, I would venture, has there been such a conversion to the pursuit of inutility as in the American military in the nuclear era.

And the price of the American military's conversion to the doctrines of deterrence has been high, now that deterrence has become simply another name for thoroughgoing reliance on weapons of mass destruction and on the most complex technology imaginable.

Reliance on nuclear weapons has distorted not only America's military thought but its military establishment in ways that make ideal response to technological change difficult to achieve. For dubious reasons, it has forced every service to seek a mission in nuclear war, one that reflects its individual and distinct traditions, weapons, and tactics and hence could belong to no other service.

The Navy, as mentioned, after World War II used the aircraft carrier as a platform for nuclear-bomb-carrying planes, and by the early 1960s it had begun to operate nuclear-missile-armed submarines. The Air Force made its long-range bombers the mainstay of 1950s strategic nuclear war plans, moving steadily, like the Navy, toward missile technology. The Army competed with the Air Force for many years, trying to obtain the lead in missile technology, and in that way to establish a fundamental role in strategic nuclear matters. In the late 1960s, Army responsibility for anti-ballistic missiles (ABMs) was its best hope of retaining a significant role in general nuclear strategy. In the early 1970s, however, the Army settled for a second-echelon role, more closely allied to its basic operational responsibilities—a role involving theater nuclear weapons and so-called tactical nuclear war. The revival, in 1980, of discussions about deploying ABMs was particularly important, and divisive, for the Army. Some Army leaders welcomed the possibility that the Army could recover this important responsibility. Others feared that revival of the ABM would force the Army to split its attention and its resources, and diminish the Army's ability to acquire all the tanks, helicopters, and battlefield air defense weapons it had been seeking since the Vietnam War.

The strategic triad—bombers, intercontinental ballistic missiles, and ballistic missile submarines—is the organizational expression of a stake all the services have in retaining an important role in nuclear war. Changes in political conditions, and developments in technology that threaten to invalidate one or another portion of the triad, cannot be accommodated without threatening vital organizational interests of one or more services. Because the interests of all the services cannot be fully expressed within the triad, doctrines both about the usability of tactical nuclear weapons and about their clear link to strategic forces carry a similar institutional significance.

Let me put this important point very plainly: ideal nuclear forces cannot be designed or acquired by the United States. Political, technical, and philosophical influences on weapon design and acquisition are, in practice, a good deal less important than parochial service interests and bureaucratic politics. *Force modernization in nuclear weapons is not a process for making forces as right as they can be in view of current politics and technology; rather, it is a process of replacing obsolescing weapons type for type in ways that do not disturb the hard-won internal balance of the military establishment.*

In the 1970s, the services cooperated in emphasizing the importance of small-scale, theater-level, or even at-sea nuclear war. They developed elaborate theories and plans that enhanced the importance of tactical nuclear weapons by stressing the risks of escalation implied in the acquisition and deployment of lesser nuclear weapons. In this, to be sure, the services had the unstinting help of an academic community fascinated by the implications of nuclear weapons for political theory and political relations.

Nuclear weapons, and the possibility of nuclear war, have enlarged some of the military's worst inherent tendencies. The delivery of nuclear weapons has become the most important of any service's many potential missions; a very large proportion of research, development, and procurement funding in each service goes to enhance that service's ability to deliver nuclear weapons in a variety of ways. At the same time, because American nuclear strategy—so far, at least—revolves more around deterring war than fighting—it presses service strategies and service abilities toward the theoretical rather than the practical aspects of warfighting and combat readiness. In this sense, the addiction of

America's military to nuclear habits has contributed much to bringing about a "defense department which has subordinated war-fighting priorities to engineering ambitions and bureaucratic priorities." Strategic consultant Edward Luttwak went on to note that "ideas about cost efficiency have replaced those about military effectiveness; modern military management has become more important than combat leadership in America's present peacetime military."[55] Unfortunately, he was more than correct. Nuclear weapons have fostered not reality in American defense forces and defense thinking but unreality, abstraction.

It is in this context as well that the Carter administration's nuclear strategy, announced in August 1980, must be assessed. That strategy, still in use, calls for increased targeting of Soviet missile silos, command facilities, and shelters for the Soviet leadership. It is a worrisome strategy, however, in the context elaborated here. It is, for one thing, really *a recipe for fighting, not avoiding, nuclear war*, albeit of a "limited" sort. It also reflects the growing predominance in nuclear strategy of very traditional principles of military operations, such as disruption of enemy communications, command, and control, although there was in the nuclear age an early and correct realization that some classic military principles were inappropriate to the new weapons. There have been good reasons why such principles have long remained outside the realm of nuclear strategy. It has been difficult to reconcile the demands of deterrence, of war avoidance, with operational principles developed in conjunction with weapons whose chief importance was in their battlefield use. In use, the new weapons could threaten their users almost as much as their intended victims.

The tendency to introduce classic operational concepts into nuclear strategy suggests to me that America's military is now a less reliable convert to the deterrence doctrines of this nuclear age than it was ten years ago and more. This, clearly, is something about which to think long and hard.

New doctrines about fighting rather than avoiding nuclear war may relieve some of the intellectual dilemmas of America's military, but the price in reliability has yet to be honestly assessed. The price in potential catastrophe—wars fought that should have been avoided—may make other costs of complexity pale into insignificance.

In summary, the American military buys equipment that does not work and deploys it in ways that limit its usefulness. Even the best informed and most carefully considered attempts to come to terms with these deficiencies generally lead to one of two recommendations: the United States should either buy more of everything, the solution most often advanced by military professionals, or the military should do everything right, advice commonly put forward among civilian critics of military institutions and military actions.

But to be fair, there are real, and realistic, limits on the possibilities for improvement, whether immediate or gradual. Intellectual, structural, and organizational factors virtually ensure that if left to its own devices, the military cannot resolve the problems it has encountered in the postwar era of high technology. To buy more of everything is, in the long run, not likely to be possible. To do everything right is an even less viable injunction. By seeking thoroughgoing solutions, academic and journalistic commentators on national security affairs often reduce their recommendations to irrelevance.

Regrettably, office-holders often are too preoccupied with day-to-day concerns to attempt basic reforms. In 1979, at Newport, Rhode Island, Chief of Naval Operations Thomas B. Hayward told the annual meeting of the United States Naval Institute that he received far too much advice from armchair strategists, and that he wished they would all be quiet so he could get on with the real problems of running the Navy. Henry Kissinger, in his recent memoir, *The White House Years* (1979), similarly criticizes the irrelevance of the ideas and prescriptions of those not steeped in the government's secret information and even more secret ways. The scorn that practitioners evince toward professors in matters of public policy manifests the disdain of the operators for those who do not recognize the real limits of choice, and hence of potential change or improvement.

To be even remotely usable, recommendations must reflect a healthy regard for conditions and traditions that lie beyond immediate modification. By that test, most suggestions are doomed to fall short. And yet the question remains: What to do?

It would be good, I think, explicitly to adopt the principle that in the American military, good is better than big, reliable preferable to sophisticated. This is not a veiled argument for low- rather than high-mix weapons. Rather, it reflects the judgment that America's first attempts to right present wrongs should center on equipping, maintaining; and training the forces now available. "Many defense analysts," as *Newsweek* reported in October 1980, "think all three branches could make much better use of technology if they weren't convinced that bigger is automatically better."[56] Together with a proper regard for the virtue of simplicity even in this "technetronic" age, such perspective is the starting point for military improvement. Years ago, the Mayo brothers observed that men of great achievement do not work or think more complexly than the average man, but more simply. I suspect that something like this is true as well for large organizations.

Present budget projections show much larger increases for procurement over the next two or three years than for operations and maintenance. This is not surprising; given the high costs of new weapons, particularly the planned MX missile, it may be only natural. But it is all too reminiscent of the way in which Congress and the military over the past decade have chosen new, complex, and costly weapons over adequate maintenance and training whenever budgetary restrictions have required hard choices.

It is also essential to contend against the quick-fix philosophy both in military budgets and in arguments for or against particular programs. One way in which to start would be to devise and to follow out genuine mid-to-long-term defense plans. At present, the Department of Defense plans on a five-year basis; but each year budgetary and political winds topple the plans based on best hopes, good intentions, and solid analysis. The military understandably feels that it cannot count on the White House, the Congress, or the public to introduce any reliability into defense planning; inevitably that planning remains a year-to-year and hence ad hoc affair. This encourages the quick-fix philosophy, a certain opportunism, and the tendency we have noted to deceive or manipulate the nonmilitary "players" in national security and budgetary matters.

In the fall of 1980, Senator Sam Nunn endorsed the idea of practical defense planning for intervals longer than one year at a time. This is an idea whose time has come. Reliable medium-term funding for weapons procurement would be a boon to military planners; it would save money; and in the long run it would produce more nearly optimal forces. A high-technology military simply cannot be rationalized on a year-to-year basis. In 1980, the American Enterprise Institute began studying the laws and procedures that would have to be changed to permit multi-year defense budgeting. Congressional practices make these formidable indeed, for a congressman's right to propose amendments to legislation is almost unlimited; it is difficult to conceive of a legal way in which members of Congress could be barred from offering amendments to budgets passed months or even years earlier. Still, America's defenses demand a more structured, reliable, and consistent approach.

In recognition of this, the Reagan administration's fiscal year 1982 budget proposals included a call for trial multiple-year weapons procurement contracts on KC-10 refueling aircraft, SM-2 missiles for the Navy, and reconnaissance aircraft. By 1985, Reagan officials estimated, such contracts on these three programs could save $1 billion; eventually, so it was said, extended financial commitments to weapons programs could bring savings of $10 billion per year. But congressional opposition was certain, and in some respects well-founded. "If it [long-term contracting] were widespread," one analyst told *The New York Times*, "the Defense Department would, in effect, have a lock on future Federal funds. Defense would have a special place in the Federal budget that food stamps or other concerns wouldn't have." A congressional staff expert added this thought: "You would only want to try this with weapons systems that have had the bugs worked out of them, and with systems for which there is certain and fixed demand." Yet the possible benefits of extending defense budgeting and planning in coordinated fashion are too great to ignore.

Further, the military should—and indeed must—eliminate penalties for honesty in reporting shortcomings of equipment and readiness. The current elaborate reporting system, recently revised, permits the Joint Chiefs of Staff to know at a glance the personnel, matériel, and training status of any American unit— but only to the extent that information fed into the system is sound. Finding the faults of equipment, units, programs—even ideas—should be at least legitimate; fixing them should be rewarded.

In addition, to deal with the widespread failure of military equipment to perform up to specification or as advertised, the United States Government should establish an independent agency for testing military equipment. This agency should be independent of any government organization or private business responsible for the design, production, or procurement of weapons and systems. Such an agency could be created from scratch; or it could be developed within the framework of organizations such as the General Accounting Office, the Office of Management and the Budget, or the Office of Technology Assessment. The purpose is not to acquire weapons at bargain prices; rather, it is to introduce more reliability into American military equipment. This is essential to ensure not only that the government gets what it pays for but, more simply, that it knows what it has gotten before war reveals it. As a secondary responsibility, such an agency might sponsor research, development, and evaluation of promising technologies that either run counter to traditional force structure or languish outside the purview of one or another of the military's established interest groups.

Some will say this proposal is unwise, unnecessary, or both. In the last several years, there have been real advances in performance of some aircraft. The Defense Department has also issued its one hundredth draft of directive 5000.40, which among other things provides for independent reliability testing to verify contractor findings—independent, that is, of the contractors, but not of the military customers. The services have, in addition, recognized that maintenance and reliability are the problems not only of the logistics people, who must deal with what is bought after it is bought, but of development and procurement people, who must ensure that what is bought will work. And there is the view of Colonel Ben H. Swett, one of the officers who drafted the new reliability directive 5000.40: "Testing does not improve reliability; fixing is what improves reliability."[57]

But these steps and views are not enough to overcome misgivings about the durability of past practices. New weapons still have more "sex appeal" than do maintenance, spare parts, simplicity, reliability. As long as this is true, there is going to be a reliability problem. As one senior official in the Air Force Systems Command recently told *Aviation Week:* "We did an in-house study that showed we have the tools to do the [reliability and maintainability] job, but when the budget crunches come, that's the first activity to be cut."[58]

In October 1980, *Aviation Week & Space Technology* dedicated almost an entire issue to the theme of reliability and preparedness. After many articles surveying both the shortcomings and the improvements of the military in those areas, *Aviation Week* summed up the remaining concern in language the more distressing for its very blandness: "Reliability specialists at major West Coast aerospace firms foresee no revolutionary changes to the industry's approach to reliability, despite the apparent intensification of concern within the Defense Department over reliability of military systems."[59] That, I fear, is indeed the definitive word—unless the public requires something more and something different from the military, from industry, from Congress.

Finally, as the single most important step toward easing technology-induced military problems, the United States should, to the maximum extent possible, meet its military needs without resort to nuclear weapons. In the short run, such an approach might impose severe intellectual, political, and organizational strains. In the long run, it is the only answer to the paradox of impotence in power, the only wide-ranging remedy for the technological ills of the military establishment that embodies this paradox. The United States will derive the most utility from its nuclear weapons when it limits, rather than generalizes, their effects. The principal and most reliable function of nuclear weapons is to inhibit the use of such weapons against states that possess them. That may be enough to hope for in the way of consequences. Every effort to derive broader military and political effects from such weapons increases both the risks of their use and the irrational complications of politics, strategy, and military technology. The surest way to bring the United States to the brink of nuclear war is to become unable to fight and win any other form of conflict.

V THE NUCLEAR ISSUES:
MORE BANG, MORE BUCKS

I didn't want to shout, "The Russians are coming!" I wanted to say, "Look what you've done to yourself. Is this really what you want?"

JOHN M. COLLINS, 1980

THE PRESENT ADEQUACY and future development of nuclear forces stand among the most important defense issues of the 1980s. Expanding Soviet nuclear power, worsening Soviet-American relations, and aging American missiles and bombers have brought great urgency to the routines of force modernization. The design, size, and strategy of America's next-generation nuclear forces must all be decided early in the 1980s. These decisions cannot wait for long, in part because such decisions take time to carry out, in part because trends in Soviet-American nuclear power ratios have become a popular index of political will and future influence. It is politically unwise—and it may be militarily risky—to countenance continued public perception in America and outside it that the United States is indifferent to climbing Soviet strategic forces.

Nuclear weapons and nuclear power raise intensely political, sometimes emotional considerations. For that reason, and before entering into details about the nuclear issues of the 1980s, I want to make several explicit observations. I believe that nuclear war with the Soviet Union in the coming decade is extremely unlikely. Although the prospect of nuclear war must be foremost among the nation's strategic concerns, these concerns must also recognize that nuclear war is not now in sight. Further, in my opinion, our present nuclear forces are adequate to deter Soviet attack, to prevent Soviet nuclear blackmail, and to fight nuclear war if necessary.

But American nuclear forces are not ideal, either for deterrence or for war-fighting. For one thing, deterrence and war-fighting pose contradictory technical requirements, and in consequence, to obtain adequate forces is difficult; to design ideal forces may be impossible. Yet as present forces age, technology advances, and Soviet power increases, replacement of present forces becomes necessary, and scientists and military men naturally endeavor to produce significantly improved forces.

The complexities of nuclear issues, and of the jargon in which they are customarily discussed, makes it advisable to set a perspective on nuclear strategy. A former Deputy Secretary of Defense, Robert Leider, in June 1977 testified to his distress over the flood of tired terminologies as SALT II negotiations proceeded. On the Op-Ed page of *The New York Times*, he called for not arms limitation but word limitation. In his tongue-in-cheek draft agreement with the Russians, Leider proposed:

> 1. Each side agrees to phase out defense intellectuals by attrition. As a start, only those with 100,000 published words or more to their credit will be permitted to continue to produce and publish analyses.
> 2. When the number of defense intellectuals allowed to perform analyses declines to 50, each side will immediately apply output restrictions, limiting each intellectual to an annual production of 5,000 words or less.
> 3. A final restriction applies to vocabulary. The permitted 5,000 words per year must be expressed within the confines of an authorized vocabulary that is not to exceed 1,000 units. Correlative conjunctions will be prohibited entirely.[1]

Yet at heart, nuclear strategy reflects an unambiguous, if unsettling, fact: nuclear weapons mated with present-day delivery systems, especially missiles, confer overwhelming advantage on the attacker. Against nuclear weapons, defense in any traditional sense is not possible. In theory, therefore, the appearance of nuclear weapons in World War II and their prominence thereafter have produced something of a revolution. Classically, strategy was defined as the art of fighting on favorable terms, of combining battles to win wars. After World War II, the late Bernard Brodie, who was for many years America's most distinguished commentator on political-military affairs, argued that nuclear weapons had changed the very meaning of strategy. In the nuclear age, strategy would be the art of avoiding battle, of deterring injury or challenge to national interests.

Periods in which tactics and technology favor the offense are usually periods of widespread and severe political and psychological instability. The late 1930s were such a period. The new blitzkrieg tactics involving the combined use of tanks, infantry, and close air support upset the military balance of Europe and thus its already precarious political stability. In 1914, similar advantages accrued to states that could mobilize more quickly than their neighbors, and this factor raised the risks of the July Crisis. As World War I opened, that same concern with rapid mobilization encouraged the widening, rather than the confining, of the war.

The advantages that nuclear weapons confer on attackers have literally transformed America's strategic circumstances. In the latter 1950s, the Soviet Union acquired not only nuclear weapons but delivery vehicles capable of reaching the United States. In consequence, the traditional invulnerability of the American homeland evaporated. This change has received much attention from scholars and policymakers alike. Henry Kissinger addressed it in his landmark 1957 book, *Nuclear Weapons and Foreign Policy*. Because geographical isolation no longer secured the nation, he suggested, American leaders would have to analyze and respond to threats more quickly—and with more foresight—than in the past. Henceforward the United States, thought Kissinger, would have to conduct a more "precautionary policy. It cannot permit a significant change in the balance of forces."[2]

Interestingly, this change in America's circumstances has impressed Soviet leaders as well. The foremost Soviet expert on the United States, Georgy A. Arbatov, director of the Soviet Institute for the study of the U.S.A. and Canada, discussed this with Craig Whitney of *The New York Times* in an interview published October 5, 1980. To Whitney's comment that "There is a feeling of strategic inferiority in the United States," Arbatov responded in a way that revealed the significance of America's new vulnerability from the Soviet perspective:

These feelings were encouraged by the difficulty of psychological adjustment to a new situation. Americans lived for many years behind two oceans, with a feeling of 100 percent security. Then they lived a couple of decades after World War II with a feeling of overwhelming strategic superiority. Now they have become just as vulnerable as we are, as all Europeans. . . . The Americans have become vulnerable for the first time, so there have been constant attempts to somehow reverse the situation. And there was the naive hope that more dollars and more military hardware could make you invulnerable again. Now there is parity. Whatever you do won't be able to change that.

America's loss of invulnerability has more than psychological effects. It bears on America's military adequacy in very practical ways. In its modern wars, the United States has usually won by slowly making ready to meet obvious threats, as in the years 1914 to 1917 before we entered the First World War, and again in 1939 to 1941 before we entered the Second World War. In both world wars in this century, after preparation against clear and present dangers the United States has allied itself with great European states—France, Britain, Russia. These European powers carried the brunt of early war efforts, giving the United States precious time to respond, and they contributed as well to the conduct of the war after American entry. Finally, in its own American way of war, the United States has simply outproduced its enemies, pouring forth tanks, ships, and planes, guns, ammunition, boots, and fuel in literally overwhelming volume.

In nuclear war, the United States will not enjoy past luxuries of leisurely preparation and undisturbed war-time production. America's allies may be rendered hors de combat rather early. The American homeland, with its resources and industries, may itself come under attack from the earliest moments. Dependence on foreign sources of energy and critical materials—chrome, tin, asbestos, titanium, and dozens of others—may cripple American industries in war even if our home territory is not subjected to early attack.

The advantages that nuclear weapons confer on attackers, coupled with the characteristics of modern delivery systems, make peacetime military choices, spending, and readiness more important than ever before. The United States may have to fight—win, lose, or draw—with the weapons and supplies on hand when war comes.

Hence the issues of nuclear strategy, and of America's military condition, are unaffected by the traditional foreign policy abstractions of internationalism or isolationism; they remain the same whether ideology or power dominates in relations with the Soviet Union. They do not involve the choice between power politics on one hand or a moral foreign policy on the other. The political and rhetorical devices customarily used to distinguish right from wrong, right from left, young from old, in American foreign policy debates have little to offer in thinking through the issues of nuclear weapons.

Whether Americans like it or not, and no matter what they think about rationality and risk in the nuclear era, thermonuclear weapons have altered the military and therefore the political position of the United States. And this situation cannot be remedied by an act of will or by a policy. It will endure until technical developments permit redress of the imbalance between offense and defense in nuclear war.

Weapons that confer advantages on the offense encourage the adoption of strategies for initiating surprise attacks. Like having the choice of weapons in an old-time duel, or hitting first in a dirty street fight, taking the initiative with nuclear weapons may seem virtually to ensure the outcome of war. In the latter 1970s, hypothetical wars played on America's defense computers consistently demonstrated important benefits from shooting first rather than second in nuclear exchange. Such exercises confirmed that the side initiating large-scale attack would suffer less overall damage and fewer casualties than the side that retaliated. A first strike, properly executed, would destroy a significant proportion of enemy nuclear weapons before they could be employed and would thus spare the attacker whatever damage might have come from their use.

According to the computer studies, there is another advantage to shooting first in nuclear war: the side that attacks probably will possess superior forces when war ends. At present, relative advantage after large nuclear exchange is measured in terms of superiority in residual—that is, left over—nuclear forces. The side that runs out of nuclear weapons first loses; the side that has some left, or more left, wins. At least, so this highly theoretical reasoning now goes.

This standard falls far short of political adequacy. What effect residual forces will have on the causes, consequences, and costs of such a war is difficult to see. And the magnitude of disaster envisaged in large-scale nuclear war makes victory and defeat hard to define. In all, this concern for residual forces simply confirms that the probable costs of nuclear war are too great to comprehend. Yet, however abstract, concern for residual forces in fact now drives planning for nuclear war, and hence planning for improved forces to replace obsolescent ones.

The extent to which nuclear weapons encourage adoption at first-strike strategies heightens the importance of comparing forces. Dissimilarity of Soviet and American nuclear weapons and delivery vehicles, however, makes this very difficult to judge. The Russians, for instance, have more launchers, that is, missiles and bombers. The United States has more warheads. The Russians have bigger warheads. America's warheads are more accurate. The bulk of Soviet forces are land-based, where they can presumably be made more accurate over time. Fully 50 percent of America's warheads are deployed in ballistic missile submarines, where they are undetectable at least for the foreseeable future.

Although in one sense nuclear forces are probably no more dissimilar than are conventional forces, in nuclear forces these differences matter more, because there is no body of operational experience with nuclear weapons corresponding to that involving conventional forces. Today's infantry and armor may be different and better than what has gone before, but the history of warfare provides sufficient perspective to permit military professionals to judge—within limits—the relative advantage even in differently composed forces. Nuclear forces have to be assessed without benefit of such perspective. This means that a high degree of uncertainty inevitably attends assessments of nuclear advantage and disadvantage. Even the professionals must guess a great deal, which does little to allay the fears that make assessment necessary in the first place. It also means that the professional military is in no position to claim exclusive competence in modern strategy on the basis of hard-won operational experience. Almost anyone can join in nuclear theorizing, and the many civilians who do so cause considerable annoyance to military professionals jealous of their prerogatives.

America's strategic requirements in the nuclear age have exhibited great consistency from the middle 1950s to the present. In his 1959 book, *Strategy in the Missile Age,* Bernard Brodie set out the essentials of what Americans in the Nixon years would call strategic sufficiency.[3] He correctly recognized that the United States would have to acquire nuclear retaliatory forces protected against destruction in surprise attack. The United States also needed a certain ability to protect essential elements of government, industry, and possibly part of the population—in a word, civil defense. Finally, the United States would require the technical capacity to use some nuclear forces without using them all— limited strategic options, in present jargon—so that the nation would not face the suicide-or-surrender choices seemingly inherent in the new weapons.

But consistency in requirements has not prevented revived doubts as to the adequacy of our present nuclear forces. And in this renewed doubt about nuclear sufficiency, there is a certain irony. For in the 1970s, growing public attention to Soviet-American nuclear force relations was due in no small measure to the strategic arms limitation negotiations of that decade. As national security adviser to President Richard M. Nixon, and then as Secretary of State, Henry A. Kissinger believed that without SALT to regulate the threats of superpower confrontation, there could be no easing of tensions, no détente. In Kissinger's policies, SALT had a dual use as an instrument for moderating Soviet behavior and as a mode of acquiring information about Soviet forces and strategy to guide America's own force decisions.

Unfortunately, the SALT negotiations focused public attention on Soviet-American relations just as Soviet forces were expanding and improving. SALT in fact functioned reasonably well as a process for exploring Soviet attitudes on the political significance and military uses of nuclear weapons. But much that American onlookers learned in this revealing negotiation created deep unease. Soviet political and military leaders shared the view that nuclear war would be disastrous. But the Soviets, it appeared, did not hold with the American conviction that in nuclear war there can be no winner. They were not, it seemed, resigned to mutual deterrence. Rather, they were determined to fight and win nuclear war should political conditions seem to require it. They regarded the resort to nuclear weapons as potentially decisive, not as certainly suicidal. Soviet military doctrine, as revealed in SALT talks and in Soviet military writings of the 1970s, stressed the advantages of tactical preemption, surprise, and offensive warfare.

Thanks to growing Soviet forces and the continuation of SALT negotiations, trends in relative strategic power received extraordinary publicity. Out of this evolved the great debates on SALT II, which began early in the Carter administration and continued until the Soviet invasion of Afghanistan late in 1979 put the SALT II treaty politically out of reach.

In 1977, in an unusual bureaucratic maneuver, then CIA director George Bush asked a number of civilian experts on the Soviet Union and on defense to work in parallel to the official intelligence community team preparing the National Intelligence Estimate for that year. This document, prepared annually, attempts to sum up in broad terms the economic, political, and military developments bearing most intimately on American security and interests. The nongovernmental group, led by Professor Richard Pipes of Harvard University, concluded that from 1965 to 1975, official intelligence estimates had regularly underrated important improvements in Soviet nuclear and conventional forces. George Bush accepted this outside report in lieu of the less alarming conclusions presented by the CIA's own professionals. Leaked to the press, this conclusion quickly encouraged both interest and criticism concerning negotiations for SALT II. Professor Pipes wrote Op-Ed pieces for *The New York Times* and the *Wall Street Journal* depicting a Soviet Union bent on limitless nuclear expansion to permit it either to mount a disarming first strike on the United States, to fight a nuclear war to a conclusion, or to force the United States to make concessions under threat of such actions.

Gradually there developed a perception within the United States as well as outside it that present American forces—the Titan IIs, Minuteman IIs and IIIs of the missile forces, the old, slow B-52s of the bomber forces, and even the submarine-launched ballistic missiles—were inadequate to deter Soviet nuclear attack or to fight a nuclear war if necessary.

In a parallel development, popular summaries of Soviet military doctrines reopened the question of just what American forces had to threaten to do in order to deter Soviet attack. In the 1960s, when Robert S. McNamara had been Secretary of Defense, American deterrent doctrine called for the "assured destruction" of at least 25 percent of the Soviet population and 50 percent of Soviet industrial capacity as a minimum standard for an American retaliatory strike (later, these figures were revised to 25 percent and 70 percent). Estimates of the time indicated that only about 400 nuclear warheads needed to be delivered to achieve those results. By the middle 1970s, in the administration of Gerald R. Ford, assured destruction had been redefined. It would be necessary not only to deter a Soviet strike by inflicting casualties and damage but to prevent Soviet recovery at any rate faster than American recovery was likely to progress. This new strategy required the targeting of most Soviet military installations, a task involving the use of some 8,500 warheads.[4]

Presumptions of inadequacy in American nuclear forces as the 1980s open are based on several distinct considerations. The most prominent has been the expansion of Soviet nuclear forces, particularly the proliferation of Soviet nuclear warheads of improved accuracy. Another factor of considerable, though more limited, importance has been the pace of improvement in Soviet civil defense. Still another factor has been the age and obsolescence of American weapons.

The growth of Soviet nuclear forces in the 1970s changed perspectives on America's own forces in several notable respects. One of these, to be sure, was largely psychological. The large number of completely new Soviet missiles deployed in the middle 1970s— five new ICBMs and three new SLBMs—gave an impression of great vigor in comparison with the single new American ICBM (the Minuteman III) and two new SLBMs (the Poseidon missiles deployed beginning in 1971, and in 1979 enough Trident I missiles to equip one submarine). Further, Soviet warheads more than doubled in number, from under 2,000 in 1970 to about 5,000 in 1979.

Soviet nuclear forces also improved in accuracy. In some respects this was the most worrisome development of all. Since the middle 1950s, when the missile race began, American scientists and engineers had enjoyed large advantages in accuracy of missile warheads, which permitted the United States to rely on rockets with much smaller load-carrying capacity than the larger rockets used by the Soviets. With cruder bomb designs, and with low accuracy, the Soviets needed missiles that could carry very large and heavy warheads of high explosive yield.

But Soviet scientists of the 1970s followed their American counterparts into the technology of warhead fractionation—dividing the load of an individual missile into independently targetable reentry vehicles (MIRVs). Once this technology has been mastered, as American scientists have discovered, the chief limit on the numbers of individual warheads it is possible to carry on a single missile is that missile's load-carrying capacity. The larger Soviet missiles, originally a compensation for inferior weapon technology, in the 1970s thus seemed likely to become the basis for virtually unlimited expansion of Soviet strategic forces.

Together, the 1970s increases in deliverable warheads and improvements in accuracy enabled the Soviet Union by the end of the decade to target for the first time all of America's land-based ICBMs, bomber bases, submarine facilities, and other important targets, civilian as well as military. As a rule of thumb in nuclear targeting, two warheads usually are allocated to each hard target or point target. However, missile silos are hardened, that is, reinforced with concrete and earth to withstand blast effects. Further, silos and some other protected military targets offer a very small area of vulnerability—literally only a few square feet. Hence such targets can be difficult to destroy, because the attacking weapons must be aimed very precisely, at specific points, and not simply at a wide or general area. Consequently, America's 1,053 land-based ICBMs, plus the hundreds of other military, urban, and industrial targets in the United States, could not really be subjected to comprehensive attack until Soviet nuclear forces grew to between 4,000 and 5,000 warheads.

But as Soviet forces continued to increase, reaching some 6,000 warheads in 1980, calculations indicated that by the middle 1980s, the Soviet Union would be able to destroy between two-thirds and three-quarters of America's land-based missiles in a surprise attack. In retaliation, the United States might be able to destroy no more than 57 percent of Soviet silos, some of which would already be empty. With further expansion expected, predictions were revised to indicate that the Soviets might be able to attack as early as 1982.

By itself, expansion of Soviet forces might not have seemed immediately worrying. After all, even one fourth of the American land-based missile force, together with surviving bombers and missile submarines, would pose a huge threat to Soviet population and industry, as well as to some military targets. But from 1976 onward, Soviet force improvements were linked to Soviet civil defense programs. The Soviet Union, so the argument went, might start a nuclear war by attacking the United States, then ride out the reduced retaliation inflicted by America's damaged nuclear forces, and then deal a final blow to the United States with its remaining nuclear weapons.

Leon Gouré, a faculty member at the University of Miami's Center for Advanced International Studies, published a monograph in 1976 entitled *War Survival in Soviet Strategy*. His exposition of Soviet civil defense programs stimulated several years of intense debate. Seconded by writers in defense-related periodicals such as *Air Force Magazine*, Gouré argued that the Soviet government was training a great many of its people in civil defense techniques. In the Soviet military there were, it appeared, special "civil defense troops"; there was also a special military academy given over to the study of defense against nuclear attack. Programs to disperse and harden industrial and military sites were under way.

According to report, the Soviets were storing grain as a hedge against nuclear holocaust. Increased protection for Soviet officials and workers with critical skills was being provided through construction of shelters and through evacuation planning. Soviet maps, according to the civil defense literature, contained naive attempts at strategic deception such as the introduction of ten-to-twenty-mile errors into the published locations of cities, transportation routes, and other potentially significant military targets—an interesting anachronism in an age of advanced overhead photography and mapping.

For several successive years after 1976, articles on Soviet civil defense were read into the *Congressional Record* by defense-minded legislators such as Senator Orrin G. Hatch of Utah. Sandia Laboratories, a government-operated nuclear research facility in New Mexico, conducted a lengthy and, presumably, expensive study of the significance of Soviet civil defense activities.

The conclusions of those fearing Soviet civil defense efforts remained for the most part unchallenged. The editors of *Air Force Magazine* asserted in February 1977 that in a large-scale nuclear war, only 4 percent of the Soviet population would die from the initial effects of blast, fire, and radiation, as compared to about 40 percent of the American population. They further argued that the Soviet Union might be able to recover from such a war in two to four years; it would, they thought, take the United States something like twenty years to do the same.

In his fiscal 1981 posture statement, presented to the Congress in January 1980, Secretary of Defense Harold Brown summarized then current Soviet civil defense capabilities. According to his report, the Soviets had prepared hardened underground shelters for 100,000 government and party leaders. Between 6 percent and 12 percent of the Soviet work force probably could be sheltered at industrial installations. Evacuation plans for the cities had been developed and even tested on a small scale. The Soviets could evacuate their largest cities in about a week, barring serious unexpected difficulties. About 1 percent of the Soviet defense budget, perhaps a little less, had been going for civil defense, compared to only 0.1 percent so spent in the United States.[5]

But in my opinion, expressed in *Air Force Magazine* in October 1977, Soviet civil defense efforts are both less threatening and less important than they have been made to seem. Plans for employing American strategic nuclear forces do not envision the kind of one-time strike usually used as the basis for calculating casualties, damage, and then recovery. Rather, these forces would conduct phased attacks, at intervals. "In succeeding strikes, due to reduced warning and political direction, depletion of emergency stocks, and damage to transportation and other facilities, the consequences of follow-on strikes would be severe. The more the Soviets concentrated their population to begin reconstruction in the aftermath of initial attack, the more effective further attacks would be. The more they dispersed to avoid such consequences, the slower recovery would go forward. In addition to the effects of concussion, firestorm, and radiation, there would be the incalculable tolls of disease, infirmity, and disruption of complex communal life. . . . In short, estimates of Soviet casualties and damage have been based on inadequate appreciation of American targeting doctrine and its implications."

If it really seems necessary to respond to the possibility that the Russians are preparing to shelter themselves while conducting a nuclear war, there are relatively simply technical ways to make them stay underground for a very long while. For example, there would be no technical difficulty in manufacturing a limited number of extremely dirty warheads; their use would severely restrict any Russian recovery from nuclear war. It would be even easier and quicker to reprogram the height of burst of some weapons now on hand to cause their detonation on the ground rather than at altitude. This would produce tons of radioactive dust and debris, pulverized into microscopic granules and lifted into the atmosphere. Both these techniques would hazard the environment in ways menacing to people and nations besides the Russians. But if it is necessary to fight large nuclear war, and there is concern that the adversary will recover on advantageous terms, such measures may well seem appropriate.

Together, the 1970s evolution of Soviet nuclear capabilities, coupled with their civil defense programs, raised the legitimate and important question of whether American forces could still deter a Soviet nuclear attack.

In my judgment, however, these concerns were, and have remained, excessive. Soviet nuclear developments have been discussed in an imbalanced fashion, without corresponding attention to developments in American forces. In addition, the real difficulties of executing a large-scale nuclear attack on American forces have remained relatively unexplored, and thus have not been sufficiently considered. Moreover, as I have argued, despite Soviet civil defense activities, defense against determined nuclear attack remains highly problematic.

Soviet forces were not the only ones showing improvement in the 1970s. Between 1970 and 1978, for example, the Soviet Union deployed 330 new ICBMs of various types. Only 122 of these went into new silos; the others were replacements for older missiles. But the United States deployed 550 of its new and improved ICBMs, the Minuteman III.[6] Moreover, the Minuteman III's accuracy—a Circular Error Probable of 0.2 nautical miles—may not yet be equaled by Soviet forces today.* With evidence from ground stations in Iran and from satellite observation, the Soviet SS-17s, SS-18s, and SS-19s deployed in 1974 and 1975 were judged to have accuracies of between 0.25 and 0.3 nautical miles.† The new Mark 12A warhead being backfitted into Minuteman between 1979 and 1982 promises to improve accuracy still more, to about 0.12 nautical miles. In another noteworthy improvement, the number of deliverable warheads in the American land-based missile force increased from 1,050 in 1967 to 2,100 (including MIRVs) in 1978.

In addition, as the 1970s drew to a close, the United States maintained in its ballistic missile submarines about 3,000 warheads at sea, off Soviet coasts, constantly targeted on military and other locations in the Soviet Union. The Soviets, by contrast, could keep only about 200 seaborne weapons near American shores, ready for quick use, although long-range missiles on Soviet Delta-class submarines could reach the United States even when the Delta boats remained in home waters.

In regard to the theoretical ability of Soviet forces to attack American land-based missiles, or vice versa, two large considerations enter: the problem of reliability and that of bias.

The problem of reliability is straightforward, but little discussed. As Robert Sherman, a staff expert for the House Armed Services Committee, wrote in *Air Force Magazine* in February 1977: "Because it is nonglamorous and difficult to predict, and because such predictions as are made are in general highly classified, reliability is not highly emphasized in public discussions of strategic strength."[7] Simply put, for a nuclear weapon really to do what it theoretically is capable of doing, its delivery system must be "on line" rather than down for maintenance; it must work

---

* Missile accuracy is usually measured in terms of Circular Error Probable (CEP). Strictly defined, this term refers to the radius of a circle within which half of the reentry vehicles aimed at a given point will fall. That is, it is equally probable that a given reentry vehicle will fall inside this circle or outside it.

† The International Institute for Strategic Studies, in London, credits the SS-18 with a CEP of 0.1 nautical miles.

when activated; and all the electronics of the weapon itself must function in sequence and as programmed to bring about specific weapons effects necessary. In addition, the bomb must arrive in the proper sequence and timing in relation to other weapons in use in the area if it is not to be blown off course or otherwise prevented from operating properly. Finally, the weapon must detonate at the proper altitude, to obtain the desired overpressure at the exact target area.

Here, then, is the practical significance of the problem of complexity and reliability discussed earlier. The Air Force claims 90 percent reliability for the Minuteman IIs and IIIs now deployed, as well as for the MX still to come. But our inability in past tests to launch Minutemen from operational silos casts some doubt on that figure. In a survey of American defense preparedness published by the Los Angeles *Times*, reporters noted that modern missiles were many times more complex than the torpedoes of World War II. The torpedoes on hand at the outbreak of the war had a 90 percent *failure* rate.[8] As war continued, torpedoes improved, but that is small comfort in the age of nuclear missiles. It is difficult to believe that there will be time or opportunity to make up for initial shortcomings. Failures in World War II torpedoes in fact stemmed from the same factor that undermines confidence in the present missile forces of the United States: the impossibility of adequate operational testing.

Despite the estimated level of accuracy cited earlier, the United States does not have satisfactory figures on the reliability of Soviet missiles. But we do know that more than half of the Soviet ICBMs are older, liquid-fuel types. In the American experience, liquid-fuel missiles take much more maintenance, are less reliable, and have a lower readiness rate than solid-fuel missiles, and there is no reason to think that the Soviets have not encountered similar problems with their older missiles.

In short, the theoretical possibilities of attack as calculated on the basis of warhead numbers and accuracy must be adjusted to reflect realistic reliability estimates. Since, as we have said, reliability percentages are extremely difficult to derive with confidence, large doubts must remain about how actual, rather than hypothetical, nuclear attack would progress. Mathematically speaking—and reliability figures are in fact produced through sta-

tistical and probability calculations—high reliability is very difficult to achieve. Here is a simple example: Let us say that there are
three discrete phases or actions necessary to achieve success with a
nuclear missile—launch, guidance to target, and proper detonation of warhead. The overall reliability figure is derived by multi-
plying the reliability quotients of each factor in the sequence. If
each phase is 95 percent reliable, that is, performs correctly 95 out
of 100 times, the overall reliability of the three-step system is 0.95
× 0.95 × 0.95, or 85.7 percent. If each step has a reliability of
only 90 percent, still very high, overall reliability falls to 72.9 percent. In reality, modern weapons systems involve many more than
three discrete, sequential functions or operations. The F-14 fighter, for instance, has fifty-two separate systems that must be operating before it can carry out any of its missions; for the plane to
do all it was designed to do, 109 systems have to be functioning
properly and in coordination. High overall reliability is thus extremely difficult to achieve—and in some cases, it is not achieved.
This matters most in weapons and technologies that do not permit
repeated use and test under operational conditions.

The problem of bias further diminishes the real prospects of
successful nuclear attack on opposing missile forces. As noted earlier, missile accuracy is measured in terms of CEP, the radius of a
circle within which half or more of the warheads aimed at a given
point, *and shot from the same launch point,* will fall. This accuracy measurement, though in common use, is not well understood
even within defense circles. We have seen that the Minuteman III
missile, for instance, at present the most advanced land-based missile the United States deploys, is said to have a CEP of 0.2 nautical
miles. This means that if ten warheads were targeted on a given
point, five of them would fall within a circle having a radius no
larger than 0.2 nautical miles. The other five would fall somewhere outside the circle—presumably not too far outside it. The
usual assumption is that the center of the 0.2-nautical-mile circle
is the intended target of the warheads. But in fact, because of
bias, the center of the 0.2-mile circle is very likely *not* to be the
target.

Bias is the term for the distance, or difference, between the
intended target and the center of the circle within which half the
reentry vehicles fall. Course deviations result from variations in

the electromagnetic spectrum and gravity fields around the earth. They may be caused as well by variations in atmospheric density, temperature, wind, and in large-scale nuclear war, perhaps also by the heat, dust, concussion, debris, and radiation caused by other nuclear devices.

The importance of the accuracy and bias problems taken together lies in this: at present, it is scientifically impossible to measure bias in advance. Bias can now be calculated only over routes that have actually been flown by test missiles. The electromagnetic and gravitational characteristics of the North Pole's regions have been more extensively studied than those anywhere else on earth—with the possible exception of the American missile range over the Pacific Ocean. Many American missiles are programmed to fly polar routes, and there have been serious efforts to calculate and correct for bias on the basis of what little now is known.

These considerations of reliability and bias go a long way to explain why former Secretary of Defense Harold Brown emphasized that a disarming first strike is not a good bet for either side. To succeed in destroying hardened missile silos, a nuclear weapon must come very close indeed. As Secretary of Defense, Brown correctly concluded that "a number of our ICBMs could be expected to survive even a well-executed Soviet surprise attack."[9]

Present-day missiles are approaching near perfect accuracy, that is, if bias and reliability concerns are set aside. The new American MX is supposed to have an accuracy, measured in terms of CEP, of only 300 feet—this over a course some 6,000 miles or more long, and for each of its ten to fourteen independently targeted warheads. But until overall force reliability either improves or becomes more readily calculable, and until scientific progress permits prediction of bias over untried courses, further refinements of accuracy will not, in my judgment, bring much usable military advantage.

Quite apart from the new capabilities of Soviet forces and the import of Soviet civil defense, our own nuclear missiles and bombers are aging. This understandably has raised concern about their present and future adequacy. On September 20, 1980, an armed Titan II missile blew up in its silo near Damascus, Arkansas. Leaking fuel exploded forcefully enough to dislodge the 750-ton blast doors atop the silo and to loft the Titan's 8,158-pound reentry vehicle several hundred yards from the silo. This accident underlined the fact that these weapons have already exceeded their designed service life. The Titans were expected to be in use for about ten years; their average age in 1980 was nearly sixteen years. Originally scheduled to be retired beginning in 1971, the Titans instead got new guidance systems in 1979, when their old mechanical gyroscopic guidance devices were finally replaced with modern, solid-state electronic systems in the expectation that the Titans would remain in service.

Air Force officials denied that the Titan blowup in Arkansas had in any way resulted from deterioration or aging of the missile. In the strictest sense, this may have been true. The Titans do not have a particularly good safety record, as is the case with most liquid-fuel missiles. According to *The New York Times*, in the five years before the 1980 accident, Titans had been pulled off alert because of accidents no fewer than 125 times.[10] In a force of only fifty-four units (now fifty-three units), this is a surprising figure.

But advancing age surely is taking a toll in additional maintenance if not in safety. Air Force missile officers have told me that the Titans are increasingly costly to keep up. They remain in service principally to match Russian heavy missiles, which Moscow would not negotiate away in SALT I or SALT II. Further, the fifty-three Titans, with their ten-megaton warheads, still carry more than 40 percent of the megatonnage in America's entire land-based missile force. As the Minuteman IIIs receive the Mark 12A warhead, this percentage is declining, but even when conversion to the Mark 12A is complete for the 300 missiles expected to undergo the switch, the Titans will carry a relatively large fraction of America's nuclear punch.

Retiring the Titans would have a very unfavorable effect on Soviet-American megatonnage ratios and would probably therefore be unwise at a time when public apprehension about defense is already high. But to speak practically rather than politically, I think these missiles ought to be retired—the sooner the better. Safety and maintenance issues aside, they are not accurate enough for use against hard targets, and for technical reasons, large single warheads are not as effective as numbers of smaller warheads, even against soft targets such as cities. It would be better to take the fissionable material from these large warheads and remanufacture it into smaller bombs for new Trident or other missiles than to leave it in the old Titans.

Not only the Titans but the bombers, the B-52s that have formed the core of America's nuclear forces since the middle 1950s, are near the end of their useful life. Like the Titans, the B-52s show signs of age. The spare parts once made in mass production, with the relative economies that produces, have long since been exhausted and are now special-order items. Thus costs per hour for replacement of spare parts are slowly rising. Furthermore, its size makes the B-52 expensive to operate. Designed in the 1940s and built in the 1950s, it was never intended to be economical of fuel. At present prices, a B-52 consumes about $6,000 worth of aviation gasoline per hour. One consolation is that most of the B-52s remaining on active service are being refitted to carry Air Launched Cruise Missiles (ALCMs), nuclear-tipped and highly accurate, with a range of up to 1,500 miles, and by the middle 1980s the B-52s will not have to penetrate Soviet air defense. This is good, because even with all the black boxes—the fancy electronics—they would have great trouble doing so.

There are other signs of trouble with the B-52s, indications that time is if not running out on them at least running against them. Early in 1978, a B-52 on alert, carrying nuclear weapons, was vandalized at Robins Air Force Base, Georgia. By itself this may not reflect on the aircraft, but it was a sign of a lack of tautness inconceivable in the Strategic Air Command at its peak. In September 1980, another B-52 loaded with its nuclear weapons caught fire at Grand Forks Air Force Base, North Dakota. That same month, on September 13, Staff Sergeant Charles Johnson ejected from his gunner's seat in a B-52 on routine flight over Arkansas. For reasons unexplained in the press, Sergeant Johnson, somehow believing himself the only crew member left on board a nosediving plane, punched out.

In all, according to figures collected by the Stockholm International Peace Research Institute, the American military has had about 125 accidents involving nuclear weapons between 1945 and 1976. Of these, the Defense Department classed 27 as "major" accidents.[11] In a force as large as that of the United States—nearly

10,000 strategic warheads, more than 20,000 tactical nuclear weapons, stored in more than 400 special sites in the United States and in ten countries overseas—accidents involving nuclear weapons are virtually certain to occur. With the large number of forces and weapons on alert around the clock day after day, the chances of accident also grow. But it is difficult not to believe that the hazards multiply when aging forces, weapons and systems are pushed to and beyond design limits to contend against defenses more formidable than they were ever meant to face.

In comparison to the Titans and the B-52s, the Minuteman IIs and IIIs of the land-based missile forces are virtually new, only about half the age of the older weapon systems. Between 1979 and 1982, as mentioned, 300 of the Minuteman IIIs now in service will convert to the Mark 12A warhead, improving their accuracy and raising their yield. Despite such improvements, the pace of change in weapons electronics is causing the Minuteman to become obsolescent somewhat faster than expected.

The adequacy—or, rather, inadequacy—of the Minuteman is also related to the changes under way in American strategic planning for nuclear war. As announced by President Carter in August 1980, American nuclear strategy is gravitating toward an emphasis on retaliation against military targets—silos, communications, command and control facilities—and the shelters for Soviet leaders. Secretary Brown more than hinted at this in his January 1980 posture statement to the Congress: "In our planning, we take full account of the fact that the things highly valued by the Soviet leadership appear to include not only the lives and prosperity of the peoples of the Soviet Union but the military, industrial and political sources of power for the regime itself."[12]

American nuclear strategy has always included plans to attack military targets in the event of war. In recent years, in fact, American nuclear weapons have been roughly divided in half between intended civilian or urban targets and potential military or protected industrial targets. The new strategy is a matter of degree, not of kind. Nevertheless, an enlarging emphasis on the ability to attack military targets makes the present Minuteman force seem less and less satisfactory because of the related issues of target hardness, warhead size, and warhead numbers in American ICBM forces.

The hardness of a target is, simply, its ability to resist the effects of blast, and hardness is measured in terms of the number of pounds per square inch of overpressure (psi) required to destroy a given target. According to Robert Sherman, aircraft sitting on runways are by this measure rather delicate: 2 psi is enough to damage them. People, interestingly, are "harder" than aircraft, rated at about 10 to 20 psi.[13] Factories, buildings, and other industrial plants range from a hardness in the tens of psi to one in the low hundreds. ICBM silos and military command centers may have a hardness of several hundred psi up to as much as two or three thousand psi. Yet there are outer limits on hardness. Concrete has an ultimate compressive strength of 3,000 psi, although proper design can increase the functional results of hardening with concrete up to about 10,000 psi.

As I have said, the ability of a warhead to destroy a target is a function of both the warhead's yield and its accuracy. The higher the yield and the lower the CEP, the more lethal the warhead will be. In nuclear weapons calculations, this factor, derived in calculations concerning yield and accuracy, is usually expressed as "K." The largest warheads in the American inventory, those on Titan missiles, possess less than 20K. The warheads on Minuteman III missiles exert about 8K; the new Mark 12A warheads being installed on 300 Minutemen have a lethal factor of 50K.[14] Because they are not accurate enough, the missiles from the strategic submarines are usually not considered for counter-silo use. Similarly, the weapons carried by the B-52 bombers, of which the cruise missiles are potentially accurate enough, arrive too late to prevent Soviet missile launches in the early hours of nuclear war.

The importance of these lethality figures is this: according to John M. Collins of the Congressional Research Service, more than 30K is necessary to destroy a silo hardened to 330 psi. This is about the weakest of any hardened installation, and as indicated, even some industrial sites have a hardness of about this level. Many silos are hardened to about 500 psi; it takes 50K to put such a silo out of action. A silo hardened to 1,000 psi can withstand about 80K, according to Collins.[15] And this is by no means as hard as silos get. At present, the United States Air Force is hardening many Minuteman silos to about 2,000 psi. Some Soviet silos also have been reinforced to about this extent.

At this point, the deficiencies of present forces become clearer. To attack hardened Soviet military targets would require a very large number of the relatively small warheads deployed on American weapons. Further, in a missile with an accuracy of 0.1 nautical mile, a variation away from the target of only 600 feet beyond that 0.1 nautical mile would cut its lethal impact in half. Thus, from the perspective of what is required to attack military targets, America's present ICBM force has warheads that are too few in number and too low in lethal effect.

There is also the matter of range. Most of the land-based missiles now in use have a range limitation that prevents them from being targeted against Chinese nuclear weapons and facilities. As China's nuclear forces grow, it will be only prudent for the United States to devote a modest portion of its strategic forces to hedging against a bad turn in Chinese-American political relations. In the fall of 1980, Jack Anderson reported that in the new nuclear strategy, about 100 launchers had been reserved for this purpose. Further, whereas American missiles must currently be programmed to fly the shortest—and often the most obvious—routes to reach targets in the Soviet Union, greater range would permit more flexible course programming. This in turn would make it more difficult for the Soviets to concentrate their resources for defense.

There is one more respect in which present American nuclear forces seem inadequate: between 1980 and 1986, American nuclear forces will actually be declining in number. In July 1980, the Navy began to dismantle two Polaris submarines, each with sixteen missiles carrying three 200-kiloton warheads apiece (the warheads on these older missiles fall in a cluster around a single target). Eight more submarines were scheduled for retirement by the end of 1981, making a total of 160 missiles and 480 warheads to be withdrawn from the force. As planned, these retirements were to have been offset by deployment of new Trident submarines and missiles. The first Trident submarine, with twenty-four missiles carrying up to about 240 independently targetable warheads, was to have been turned over to the Navy in 1978. But production delays postponed that delivery at least until June 1981. It would have been possible to keep some of the Polaris boats operating a little longer; but some of them were out of nuclear fuel and in need of other time-consuming and expensive repairs.

Delays in selecting and constructing a successor to the Minuteman force, Trident submarine delays, and the necessary retirement of older missile submarines are creating a new "missile gap." Therefore, in the context of growing Soviet forces, the years from 1981 to about 1985 or 1986, have seemed to present a period of maximum advantage to possible Soviet attackers. After the middle 1980s, as Trident submarines and possibly MX missiles come into the force, this "window" will close. But according to an Air Force study of 1979: "Our capability after a Soviet first strike to damage the full spectrum of his military targets is roughly one half of what it was in 1977 and will remain there until about 1985."[16]

The commanding general of the Strategic Air Command, General Richard Ellis, refers to the period from about 1977 to about 1986 as a "strategic bathtub," to describe a graph showing the inability of the United States in that period to respond to a Soviet attack with the same level of success it would have experienced earlier or later. Paul Nitze, former Secretary of the Navy, Admiral Zumwalt, and other members of the Committee on the Present Danger have argued since the middle 1970s that trends in Soviet and American forces posed an unprecedented and immediate danger in the early 1980s, one that could be met only by immediate enlargement and improvement of American forces. In more restrained terms, Secretary Brown continued to refer to the need, over time, to keep each portion of America's strategic triad—the bombers and cruise missiles, the submarines, and the ICBMs—"in good working order."[17]

In my opinion, neither the arguments critical of present weaknesses nor those defending present strengths are definitive. The case for considering America's present nuclear forces inadequate rests on a number of factors, some straightforward and relatively uncontentious, such as age and reliability, others more arguable, such as presumed vulnerabilities and new strategic needs.

Portions of the strategic forces are, in a sense, already beyond argument, because next-generation systems have been bought or selected. The Trident submarines that will replace older missile boats are under contract and in construction—the first six, at least, are at this point. The only questions are how fast the Navy will receive them, and how many it ultimately will obtain. Present plans call for fourteen of the leviathans—they displace 18,700 tons each, somewhat more than a World War II destroyer. Carrying twenty-four MIRVed missiles apiece, these submarines will, by the end of the decade, keep about 3,000 relatively accurate warheads deployed under the seas.

As for bombers and cruise missiles, Congress has ordered the executive branch to present a new manned bomber proposal by 1987 at the latest. It is safe to say that the B-52 will have a successor in the 1980s, and that it will be more than a cruise missile carrier. In the meantime, the Department of Defense is purchasing 3,000 Air Launched Cruise Missiles, at a cost of $1.4 million each; 700 Ground Launched Cruise Missiles (@ $2.4 million); and 1,082 Tomahawk Sea Launched Cruise Missiles (also $2.4 million per copy; figures in fiscal 1978 dollars).

The importance of current arguments about the adequacy of present strategic forces, therefore, lies principally in their influence on decisions about weapons to replace or supplement the Minuteman and Titan land-based missiles. New forces, if they are to be better than the weapons they succeed, must have more numerous, larger, and more accurate warheads. They need improved penetration aids, to get past defenses. And for all the foregoing reasons, new missiles must have greater throw-weight. They also need greater range. And finally, they must seem more likely to survive nuclear attack in good working order.

The Missile Experimental now planned and under development, together with its basing system, embodies a complicated and controversial compromise. For the improvement criteria established by present weapons inadequacies have had to be met with forces that would not disturb either the bureaucratic arrangements of the American military or the prospects for renewed arms limitation. Sizable issues remain in contention: cost, basing method, urgency of deployment. These controversies as well as the intrinsic importance of strategic nuclear forces in American security virtually ensure that MX will hold a central position in defense discussions throughout the 1980s.

Preliminary work on a successor to the Minuteman force began about 1973. Originally, planners expected a new missile to go into production in 1978 and to be deployed by 1984. Late in the administration of President Gerald R. Ford, this timetable was accelerated. President Ford had been much impressed by evidence that Soviet forces would pose a threat to America's land-based missiles in the early and middle 1980s. He therefore wanted to start production of a new missile in October 1977, to permit deployment by 1983.

In its first year in office, the Carter administration reduced the money budgeted for the MX development in fiscal 1978. This put MX back on a schedule that would have resulted in a 1984 deployment. After further delays, Carter administration officials decided late in calendar 1978 to request more money for MX in fiscal 1979. In June 1979, President Carter resolved to put the MX into full-scale engineering development. Later, in September 1979, he announced his choice of a basing method—on which more later.

In the 1980 budget decisions, Congress appropriated $1.6 billion to continue development, a sum of money that at last put MX on the road to production and deployment. But the schedule had slipped still further: an "initial operational capability (IOC)" of only ten missiles would not be obtainable until 1986. For this, construction would have to begin in 1982, and test flights in 1983. Production decisions for the remainder of the planned force were being deferred, possibly until mid-1983. If the decision was to proceed toward the full system, that system could not be completed before 1989.

As planned in 1980, the MX missile was to be seventy-one feet long and eight feet in diameter, and weigh 190,000 pounds, approximately twice the weight of a Minuteman III. With a nominal range of 6,000 miles, MX was to have a throw weight of approximately 8,000 pounds, about four times that of the Minuteman III. It was expected to carry ten MIRVs, Mark 12A warheads of 350 kilotons yield, with a CEP between 300 and 500 feet. The 300 Minutemen being backfitted with the Mark 12A warhead can carry only three of them, and are less accurate than the MX. The MX system then in development was to deploy 200 MX missiles, each in a closed system of twenty-three shelters, one mile apart, linked by spurs to a straight gravel roadway called a "drag strip," in the trade jargon. Plans called for the purchase of 310 MX missiles, of which 110 were to be used in tests or held in stockpile. This is standard practice; as of 1980, there were about 140 Minuteman

III missiles similarly held in reserve for tests and to replace those that wear out or in other ways suffer damage.

In 1980, estimates of the cost of the MX missiles alone were running to about $10 billion in 1980 constant dollars. Construction of the shelter system, twenty-three shelters per missile for a total of 4,600 shelters, was expected to cost about $19 billion (again, in 1980 constant dollars). Maintenance costs through 1990, or barely into the system's first year of full-scale operations, were estimated at $5 billion (1980 dollars). Official cost estimates thus approximated $34 billion.

But there was a wide agreement that costs could run much more. Dr. Donald Snow, of the University of Alabama, writing in the July–August 1980 *Air University Review*, said that the $34 billion figure could safely be doubled in real dollars before the system would be completed.[18] Walter Guzzardi, Jr., writing in *Fortune* magazine on September 8, 1980, put it more bluntly still. "The MX," he wrote, "is going to be the most expensive weapon in history; it will cost by some estimates $60 billion, and by the estimate of SALT negotiator Paul Warnke, $100 billion."[19] A Townes Committee appointed by President Reagan in 1981 to reevaluate the MX assessed the cost of the 1980 scheme at some $80 billion.

As with most large, complicated, and costly weapon systems, over time there have been notable changes in MX particulars. Originally, the missile was to carry up to fifteen MIRVs, with a CEP of 300 feet. But to hold open the door for arms control negotiations in the future, the Carter administration directed that the number of MIRVs be held to ten per missile, the limit established in the SALT II treaty. Although the treaty was stalled in the Senate in 1979, and nearly withdrawn when the Soviets invaded Afghanistan, the Carter administration ostentatiously adhered to its limitations in the hope that the Soviets would do likewise. Presumably, the missile payload not used by the five MIRVs dropped from the plan would be used either in enlarging the warheads of the ten remaining MIRVs, in adding decoys and other penetration aids to the payload, or in extending the range and/or "footprint" of the missiles.°

° The footprint of a MIRVed missile is the area, usually roughly oval in shape, within which all the warheads from that missile must be deposited.

Interestingly—and this is really only a sidelight, not a matter of controversy—the figure of 200 MX missiles for the system was politically, not analytically, determined. An Air Force officer familiar with the MX's murky bureaucratic background told me that when the Carter administration finally decided to proceed with MX, it directed the Air Force to make the program work with 200 launchers. By no coincidence, this was a figure President Carter had advanced when, as a candidate, he called for reduced nuclear arms.

Concerns for survivability, politically the most important justification for MX, ensured that the basing mode of the new missile would be central to system design, cost, and deployment. It has also been the most controversial and technically difficult aspect of the program.

The basing problem results from several conflicting requirements: the concern for survivability, the question of cost, the aspect of environmental impact, and the preservation of arms control possibilities for the future. Apart from a number of basing schemes discarded early in the 1970s because of unfeasibility, only three basing methods seem still to offer any hope of meeting most of the criteria. One is a proposal to put new and improved missiles to sea, called SUM, for Shallow Underwater Mobile system.* The second is the Multiple Protective Shelter system actually adopted by the Carter administration—MPS for short. The third, which Secretary of Defense Weinberger considered at length in 1981 after the Townes Committee had finished its work, called for MX missiles to be ferried about—and launched from—large, long-endurance aircraft.

In MPS, the missiles when deployed were to be made survivable by a combination of mobility, concealment, protection, and dispersion. Each missile, mounted on a self-propelled Transporter-Erector-Launcher (TEL), was to traverse its own system of roads linking its twenty-three protective shelters. Movement and concealment will allegedly make it impossible for the Soviet Union to

---

* Physicists Sidney Drell and Richard Garwin sometimes also refer to this idea as the Smallsub Underwater Mobile system. Thus the SUM acronym is applied to a category of ideas, within which there are varying thoughts on the ideal size of the submarines involved, the preferred operating areas, the number of missiles each should carry, and so on.

target each missile, and the missile systems were to be far enough apart so that Soviet warheads aimed at one missile would not destroy an adjacent one; the number of shelters—4,600, as we have seen—was supposed to discourage the Soviet Union from targeting them all. (Applying the two-warheads-per-target rule, it would take 9,200 warheads to attack this MX system—before discounting for system reliability, bias, and other possible performance-degrading factors.)

The MPS plan would permit arms control because the protective shelters would be constructed in ways that would permit their roofs to be opened for inspection by Soviet satellites. At specified intervals, Soviet officials would be permitted to designate one twenty-three shelter system for inspection. All twenty-three shelter tops would be opened to prove that only one MX missile was deployed in the system. To provide further safeguards against cheating, each MX missile would go through final assembly only at the entrance to its own road and shelter system; once each missile is inside its road and shelter system, cumbersome barricades would be put in place, so that quick additions of forces would be impossible.

But the MPS basing plan called forth strenuous objections because of cost, environmental impact, and possible technical invalidity.

The issues of cost seemed if not peripheral at least a matter of perspective. One of MX's most ardent supporters, Lawrence J. Korb then still with the American Enterprise Institute, had this to say about the claim that MX was unduly expensive:

> . . . when adjusted for inflation, the MX will cost no more than the Polaris program, which was started in 1955 and completed a decade later at a cost of $13.5 billion. . . . in FY 1980 dollars, that program would have cost $38.5 billion, 16 percent more than the price of the MX in FY 1980 dollars. . . . Even at a cost of $50 billion, MX will not pose a severe burden on the . . . economy. . . . it will add less than one-tenth of 1 percent to our projected inflation rate [over the next decade] . . . and will increase defense-related employment by only 6 percent.[20]

Whether MX will come in at $35 billion, $50 billion, $60 billion, $100 billion, or more remains the question, and to this no one yet has the answer.

The scale of the MPS project also raised politically important environmental concerns. In 1978 and 1979, the Air Force selected areas in the Great Basin of western Utah and eastern Nevada as preferred deployment areas for the system. A final basing decision was deferred; an alternative area remained the Southern High Plains of Texas and New Mexico. There was also a possibility of split basing, some in the Great Basin and some in the plains. (The Air Force opposed the split basing scheme because it would make operation and command and control more complicated and expensive.) In aggregate, the system as planned would cover 11,500 acres plus another 11.5 square nautical miles for support bases and security. It would remove only 25 square miles of government-owned land from public use, but it would sprawl over some 5,000 square miles of government land formerly used for recreation, grazing, and mining.

The initial plan called for construction of the shelters in loops, quickly dubbed racetracks. In this form, the 200 missile sites would have required construction of 8,000 miles of roadway, plus the shelters themselves, command facilities, and control centers. According to construction industry spokesmen, this scale of building was enough to cause a nationwide cement shortage through most of the 1980s, a point contested by the Air Force. MPS construction called for 600,000 tons of cement, 32 to 48 million tons of sand, 210 million gallons of liquid asphalt, and 125 million gallons of fuel. Further, all this construction would require 17.9 billion gallons of water.[21] In a region where all known water is already allocated, this is no small matter. By Air Force estimates, this would amount to 12.5 percent of all available water in the region during construction phases, and 5.4 percent[22] of the annual water yield during routine operations thereafter. Even if the government drilled new, deep wells, which the Air Force has assured ranchers it will do, there is a possiblility that such water usage will significantly lower water tables for decades to come. In May 1980, in response to protests from environmentalists, ranchers, miners, and senators from Utah and Nevada, Secretary of Defense Harold Brown announced that the administration was abandoning the racetrack basing design for a linear shelter layout. This change would reduce roadway requirements by 20 percent, and presumably would therefore reduce water usage in construction, if not in operation.

But opposition to the deployment of MX in the Great Basin in the complicated and unwieldy MPS mode continued strong. Senator Paul Laxalt of Nevada, a strong prodefense legislator, was among those writing to oppose deployment of the MX as planned. Senator Jake Garn of Utah, similarly known for commitment to improved military posture, also made public his dissatisfaction with the MPS basing proposal. Moreover, on May 5, 1981, the Mormon church officially proclaimed its opposition to the construction of the MX in Utah. With such opposition, it was virtually certain that further refinements of the MPS scheme would have to precede final decisions to produce and deploy the MX.

In the context of the environmental concerns raised by MX's size and costs, it was more than a little amusing to read through the Air Force's official pamphlet of 117 questions and answers regarding what everyone wants to know about MX.[23] Question 54 asks: "Has there ever been a project of this magnitude in the United States?" Answer 54: "Yes, there have been several projects larger than MX. One is the Interstate Highway System." This question and answer, the product of the public relations staff of the Secretary of the Air Force, raised further questions and answers in my mind. Question: In the Interstate Highway System, were there large cost overruns? Answer: Yes. Question: Is the highway system finished, twenty years after its construction began? Answer: No. Question: Has the highway system been the source of contracting and other scandals and abuses? Answer: Yes. Question: Is the highway system well maintained? Answer: No. Question: Is it wise for the Air Force to try to sell its programs by simplistic analogies? Answer: No, not really.

More important, perhaps, than issues of cost and the environment, but less well understood, several aspects of weapons technology tended to invalidate the MPS scheme.

There is a question as to whether the concealment features of the shelter system would really prevent Soviet surveillance and location of missiles within each shelter system. I have been told by senior scientists familiar with the current state of the art in defense electronics and satellite systems that in the next ten years, it will be easier to defeat concealment measures for MX than to design secure, reliable communications, command, and control methods.

In the opinion of leading experts on this problem, better left unnamed here, it is entirely possible that by the time the United States can build and deploy the MX, the Soviets will be able to locate the missiles precisely, despite the planned concealment measures of the MPS system. This does not automatically mean that they will be able to attack them. Many of the obstacles to successful attack that I have discussed in relation to present forces will remain to hinder nuclear operations even in the 1990s. But if the concealment aspect of the MPS system is unsuccessful, a large portion of the system's justification falls away.

The MPS scheme is also threatened by the collapse of SALT II. Although the Carter administration made no secret of it, the extent to which present MX proposals depend on upholding several provisions negotiated in SALT II has not been widely appreciated. Two negotiated limitations are crucial to MX. In SALT II, the Soviet Union and the United States agreed to deploy no more than 820 MIRVed ICBMs. Further, they agreed to place no more than ten warheads on any single launcher. If the Soviet Union disregards either or both of these provisions, it could build enough MIRVs to saturate even the many targets presented by a multiple aim point basing system. This would be expensive. American experts estimate that it would cost the Soviets some $93 billion to deploy enough warheads to attack the 4,600-shelter MPS system.[24] But large Soviet missiles have enough throw weight to carry up to twenty MIRVs apiece if they are not prohibited from doing so by SALT II.

One additional possibility, unrelated to SALT restrictions, threatens the Multiple Protective Shelter scheme. Improvements in the accuracy of Soviet warheads in coming years may give the Soviets enough confidence to allocate only one warhead per hard target. Using the two-warheads-per-silo ratio now prevalent on both sides, this would have the same effect as doubling their number of warheads. This is an especially disturbing prospect, because in the MX itself, American technicians believe they have achieved a 90 percent probability of single-shot kill, as the jargon goes. It is certain that Soviet warheads will equal that accuracy in time. The question is whether 90 percent assurance will be good enough, and political relations bad enough, to make the risks of retaliation from remaining forces acceptable.

The possibility that the MX will not fundamentally improve

America's nuclear posture in the 1990s and that land-based ICBMs may be just as vulnerable then as now has prevented controversy over MX basing from simply dying away. Alternative basing schemes continue to attract both discussion and adherents.

Several of the feasible alternatives to MPS were quickly discarded because they failed to meet important criteria for improved weapons. The suggestion of a road mobile system, for instance, in which missiles on transporters would move at random around the nation's highways and roads, failed to meet several important needs. Missiles are heavy. A transporter carrying a missile large enough to have improved throw weight, more warheads, and other improvements simply could not be accommodated on the road systems of the United States. Further, the accuracy necessary to missiles targeted against enemy military targets could not be assured with a fully mobile system.

Another suggestion, the use of improved Minuteman IIIs or MX missiles in silos with defensive weapons protecting them, also seemed unattractive. Adequate defenses really do not yet exist. The possibility that increasing numbers of Soviet warheads would simply saturate meager defenses is not a real improvement over the possibility that they might saturate the MPS shelter scheme. Further, the anti-ballistic missile restriction negotiated in SALT I remains the only real achievement of modern arms control. Its reversal would have adverse significance reaching far beyond the immediate issue.

One of the most intriguing alternative basing ideas came from physicist Sidney Drell of Stanford University. He has suggested the deployment of MX missiles on fifty small, conventionally powered submarines operating relatively close to American shores. The missiles would be secure because the submarines would be undetectable. The variant of this proposal, already alluded to as the Shallow Underwater Mobile system, suggests putting improved Minuteman III missiles on up to 138 such submarines. Defense Department studies have shown that the SUM idea is feasible and its advocates claim that it would be substantially cheaper than MX—perhaps as low as $12 billion in cost. They point out as well that forces deployed at sea have the great advantage of posing no invitation to attack the American homeland. Further, by deploying fewer missiles and warheads than MX—the proposal is for two MX missiles on each of fifty submarines, or three Minuteman missiles on each of 138 submarines—SUM would reassure the Soviets of America's peaceful, defensive intentions. By putting the new missiles underwater, where the forces are difficult to coordinate, SUM would also, according to its advocates, demonstrate that the United States was not seeking a first-strike capability.

Opponents of SUM argue that additional antisubmarine forces would have to be purchased to protect the deployed submarines. This would raise costs to a figure very similar to that originally advanced for MX, something on the order of $35 billion. In addition, SUM would cost four times as much to maintain as would MX, and it would not be able to maintain as high an alert rate as land-based forces. The MX is supposed to have a ready rate of 90 percent, the same as that claimed for the Minuteman force. America's ballistic missile submarines, due to normal maintenance, crew rotation, and time spent traveling to and from patrol areas, have a ready rate of between 50 percent and 60 percent, although it can be made higher for short periods of time.

Critics of SUM also raise two other important considerations. Sea-based missiles cannot be made as accurate as land-based missiles. If American strategy calls for attack on large numbers of hard targets, accuracy is essential; with present technology, that in effect means that land-based forces are essential. In a related point, opponents of SUM note that the problem of rapid communication with sea-based forces, a sign of defensive intentions in the view of SUM advocates, could be a serious liability in war. This consideration also makes preservation of land-based forces attractive.

Further, the SUM basing scheme has its own special vulnerability. According to Edgar Ulsamer, the highly respected senior editor of *Air Force Magazine*, small submarines operating in shallow water would be "highly vulnerable to tidal waves, known as the Van Dorn effect, that could be induced by a Soviet barrage bombing of the Continental Shelf area. This tidal wave in shallow water would crush any sub in its path." Dr. Donald Snow, commenting on this thesis, stated: "If the Soviets are willing to invest the number of warheads necessary to induce the Van Dorn effect, SUM could possibly be overpowered in the same way as MPS."[25]

Sidney Drell disputes this danger, but neither side can, at present, prove its case.

As a last consideration, whatever its technical merits, SUM flies in the face of present alignments of bureaucratic forces in the American defense establishment. Any program that calls for one of the services to surrender a share of the strategic nuclear mission to another service—in this case, the Air Force to give over the majority of the missile business to the Navy—is doomed from the outset.

In other words, the case for SUM is no better, and in some respects worse, than that for MPS. Advocates of SUM cannot claim cost savings. They cannot make a convincing claim of superior security from attack, as long as they operate in shallow water with small submarines. They cannot hope to overturn the strategic triad or the defense bureaucracy without offering clear and overwhelming fiscal or technical advantages. Consequently, SUM does not, in my judgment, offer a reasonable alternative to Minuteman, much less to MX.

There is a final element of controversy about MX: the matter of its urgency. Within the Air Force, so officers of all ranks tell me, the word has been passed: Say nothing against MX unless you want trouble. The speeches of senior officers are studded with testimonials to the imminence of danger and to the elegance of MX as a technical solution to the conflicting demands of strategic and political concerns.

In June 1980, the Chairman of the Joint Chiefs of Staff, General David C. Jones, told the Boston University overseas commencement audience in Heidelberg, Germany: "We face a period of high risk as a result of the shift in the strategic balance. . . . We must be resolute in pursuing . . . the development and deployment of the M-X missile."[26] About the same time, General Richard Ellis, commander of the Strategic Air Command, remarked: "Positive and immediate action is needed to redress the deteriorating strategic balance and send a clear signal to the Soviets that this Nation intends to remain a strong, effective leader in the international community. . . . Heading the list of programs designed to redress the threat is the MX missile deployed in a mobile basing mode. This is our Nation's top military priority."[27]

In Washington, on September 16, 1980, the Air Force Chief of

Staff, General Lew Allen, Jr., told the Air Force Association convention: "I reemphasize that we must maintain and demonstrate firm determination to protect the free world's interest in [Southwest Asia]. In displaying that determination, it is important to remember that equally cogent in Soviet calculations of risk and gain in local conflict are judgements about the strategic nuclear blanace. Therefore, to preclude any possibility of disastrous miscalculation, we must, as a first priority, redress the impending disparity in the U.S.-Soviet strategic nuclear capability. . . . [The] answer is deployment of the M-X in a survivable, multiple-protective-shelters basing mode."[28]

And in Newport, Rhode Island, on August 20, 1980, as he unveiled the administration's new nuclear strategy, Secretary Brown observed: "Our most significant force deficiency in the next few years will be the vulnerability of our fixed-silo ICBMs. Observers saw this trend coming for many years, but no sound technical solution was found until the M-X multiple-protective-shelter concept was developed and selected in 1979." Earlier, in his annual posture statement, Brown had similarly stated that "Reducing the vulnerability of the land-based ICBM force is the highest priority strategic initiative in the five-year program."[30]

By the standards of American political rhetoric—for that is the proper category of the foregoing remarks—these statements are not notably exaggerated. But the earnestness with which they are made became evident in a story of October 5, 1980, by Richard Burt in *The New York Times*. According to the report, Secretary Brown admitted in a letter to the Chief of Naval Operations, Admiral Thomas B. Hayward, that "senior Pentagon aides, in an attempt to build political support for the proposed new MX mobile missile, may have exaggerated the vulnerability of the Navy's strategic submarines."

The MX, in my view, has become an example of the quick-fix philosophy at work. There is a good case for a new and better missile than the Minuteman III, not to speak of the old Titans and the relatively limited Minuteman IIs. But the Multiple Protective Shelter basing scheme does indeed have serious flaws, and so do the alternatives under discussion. Quick-fix philosophy and organizational jealousies are preventing a thorough canvassing of these shortcomings. The pressure is on: officers who value their careers will not speak out against MX now. Many tell me that they expect

MX to fall of its own weight, that it is madness, unworkable, ungainly.

But I fear that MX will be built unless the public demands more prudent and thoughtful attention to troubling aspects of present plans. In the absence of a compelling case for acting now rather than later—and I do not think there is such a compelling case at present—a decision on the basing method should be deferred while work on the missile goes forward. As I have set them out, the factors involved in assessing the adequacy of present forces do not support the conclusion that nuclear attack is likely or imminent. I know of no responsible official who will say flatly that such a danger now obtains. But many responsible officials and officers are contributing to an unwarranted public impression of urgency. Dr. Donald Snow addressing the MX basing problem in his article in the July–August issue of the *Air University Review*, concluded: "The extent and implications of solution to these monumental problems are of sufficient gravity that a rush to judgment is unwarranted."[31] I concur.

The Air Force understandably considers any possibility of MX being delayed or discarded to be highly alarming. Its 117-question catechism for the edification of the public is quite forthright. Question 101: "If the MX is critical to the maintenance of a nuclear balance with the Soviets, what will happen if the American public forces the cancellation of the MX program?" Answer 101: "The Minuteman and Titan missiles will be increasingly vulnerable to Soviet ICBM threat. As a result, the U.S. will lose military equivalence with the USSR. We would lose the extraordinary degree of nuclear deterrence provided by a strong, viable, survivable TRIAD of nuclear forces."

Then there was Question 30: "What will the Air Force do if the President decides not to build the M-X?" Answer 30: "The Air Force will continue to carry out its assigned mission to the best of its ability with the resources that are allocated." However artful, the business-as-usual humility of that latter answer is exactly right. The difficulty is to believe in the sincerity of the oh-so-proper catechism.

In the face of all the technicalities, a few commonsense principles will help in thinking through America's nuclear issues and interests in the 1980s.

To begin, it is essential for the public to avoid the quick-fix mentality, since the military apparently cannot. The key to this is perspective on Soviet-American relations in their largest dimensions.

The proliferation of measurements of the strategic relationship, of things to count or in other ways to evaluate numerically, lends an aura of false precision to arguments about relative strategic advantage. The truth, very simply, is that the Soviet-American nuclear relationship is exceedingly complex, and that the results of large war would be catastrophic for both nations, though not predictable in detail or in ultimate consequences. Overly precise arguments, laden with statistics and numbers and leading to specific conclusions about what the United States ought to buy, how much, and how soon, ought to be regarded with the same skepticism normally reserved for the assurances of used-car salesmen and real-estate agents.

To repeat, Soviet and American interests conflict; but there is no issue now in view so fundamental, urgent, and irremediable that nuclear war seems in the least possible, much less likely. Only ten or fifteen years ago, limited nuclear exchange was conceivable, at least in theory, in terms that might impose no more than 2 to 5 million casualties on each side. Now, even the most moderate scenarios for limited exchange involve calculations of death running into the tens of millions for Soviets and Americans alike.

In one sense, failures of American missile attack warning computers in 1979 and 1980 hold the key to perspective on this problem of nuclear war in Soviet-American relations. Three times over some six to seven months, indications of incoming nuclear attack alarmed those on duty to respond. Once, late in 1979, a test tape was mistakenly fed into the alert and warning system. Then, on June 3 and June 6, 1980, the nation's air defenses were alerted and SAC bombers started on their way to Soviet targets.

Faithfully reflecting the Defense Department's press releases, news reports made much of the fact that the false alarms were caught relatively quickly. The errors took three to six minutes to be identified as mistakes. In one case, it took about twenty minutes to recall SAC bomber crews.

But apart from their significance for America's overdependence on certain technologies, these alarms showed that the top national leadership has no hope of surviving an attack that comes while they are at their regular jobs. In the two cases in June 1980, the President and the Secretary of Defense were not even notified until everything was well in hand. Depending on launch points, some Soviet weapons could strike the United States in as little as ten minutes after launch, moments after being sighted by early warning systems. In practice, and as a matter of routine, the authority to conduct nuclear war is vested in relatively low-ranking officers—one- and two-star generals and admirals commanding air, missile, and naval forces. Missile submarines will be virtually impossible to communicate with in war; they regularly deploy under standing orders. The major with a black briefcase full of release codes for nuclear weapons reminds the President of his own heavy responsibilities. For the nation looking on, this is ordinarily reassuring, despite the sensationalism of stories about the "football"—the bag of codes—after the attempted assassination of President Ronald Reagan. But the symbolism of the code bag hardly reflects the brutal likelihood that nuclear war will deprive the warring nations of their leadership. If large-scale nuclear war ever comes, it will be conducted and concluded not by high political and military leaders but by survivors left by chance. The illusion of rational conduct of such a war is perhaps useful for the most abstract reasoning about nuclear war and nuclear weapons. But it lacks practical political importance and, if not treated with proper skepticism, may seriously distort public judgment about what is important and what is necessary in regard to nuclear weapons.

The reasons for caution, restraint, and war avoidance between the Soviet Union and the United States are growing much faster than any possible reasons for direct engagement. Americans must deal with the theoretical issues of nuclear balance and the coming issues of nuclear force development in a measured, intelligent, and serious way, not in a rush to score political points or to satisfy the military bureaucracies. As a case in point, consider the plans for the nuclear inventory in the 1980s. There are 22,000 or more tactical nuclear weapons and approximately 10,000 strategic nuclear warheads now on hand. But these are not enough, as such calculations go, to attack all Soviet targets (now numbering more than 11,000), to compensate for battle losses and system failures, and still to have adequate residual forces. Plans call for the manufacture of some 8,500 more strategic warheads in the 1980s. This in turn will require revival of plutonium manufacture. Ironically, in recent years the United States has led the world in opposing production of plutonium, and there is a further irony in the months of debate in 1980 over whether the United States should sell nuclear fuel to India, for fear that it would be turned into plutonium.

Huge increases in the inventory of warheads and the deployment of forces that exceed our ability to control under wartime conditions—these are questionable measures. Policies and strategies that require them ought to be reconsidered. It is ancient wisdom that a nation cannot serve its long-term interests by doing injury to its short-term interests.

In addition, the United States must remain committed to the pursuit of arms control and arms limitation. In the context of the SALT II treaty and the recent worsening of Soviet-American relations, this point is certain to be controversial. Whether SALT II was itself an ideal or adequate treaty is one question. Whether arms control can benefit the interests of the United States is another, more important question. I believe the answer to the latter query is clearly: Yes.

Since World War II, the Joint Chiefs of Staff have consistently opposed arms control negotiations and measures. In 1947, almost as soon as they were legally established, the Chiefs prepared a paper saying forthrightly that they considered American interests better served by a nuclear arms race than by imperfect control of atomic weapons.[32] In the middle 1970s, at the height of SALT negotiations, it was still JCS policy not to originate proposals for arms control. As a result—and the memoirs of then Chief of Naval Operations Elmo Zumwalt bear this out—senior military leaders were pushed to the sidelines of an important strategic endeavor. There, on the sidelines, they remain, at least as regards arms control.

Arms control is no substitute for force modernization and readiness. But in regard to strategic weapons, it has several important benefits that can be obtained no other way.

SALT negotiations have been the principal forum in which the

United States could explore Soviet ideas on nuclear weapons and, correspondingly, share American views. The point is not that what Americans learn is necessarily reassuring, only that American political and military leaders *do* need to learn their adversaries' minds as well as their weapons inventories.

SALT affords the United States its only opportunity to exert direct influence on the character and size of Soviet forces. It would be a mistake to exaggerate the results to date. But this opportunity may become more valuable with time. It is already too important to discard lightly.

SALT negotiations, by establishing certain limitations on force sizes and technical characteristics, have introduced modest predictability into force development on both sides. This is a major planning advantage. The most difficult aspect of defense planning is its pervasive uncertainty. To know that Soviet forces in 1981 or 1985 are going to be no larger than, say, 2,400 or 2,250 launchers, with no more than 820 MIRVed vehicles, helps very considerably in planning the size and capabilities of America's next generation of forces. SALT has not produced limitations on all that the United States would like to see limited, and the limitations that now obtain are not as low as Americans might prefer. But some limitations are better than none. American defense planning benefits even though it still is necessary to plan for defense against the implicit threats of Soviet forces.

The United States cannot expect SALT to render nuclear technology and Soviet arms completely manageable, no longer threatening. It can expect arms control negotiations to help in thinking through America's own force development issues.

Beyond the quick-fix fallacy and SALT, the United States has a large interest in redressing the balance between offense and defense in nuclear weapons. As President Nixon initiated serious arms control negotiations with the Soviet Union in 1969 and 1970, anti-ballistic missiles as protection for cities and forces seemed "destabilizing." Ballistic missile defense seemed a barrier to a situation of mutual vulnerability that would require nuclear restraint. Now, as the first-strike problem looms larger than ever, defense of strategic forces may aid rather than erode deterrence. Immediate construction of a ballistic missile defense system would be premature. But the time for benign neglect of missile defense is past, and with it the time when underfunding of research and development in this and other areas can be tolerated.

Perhaps most of all, nuclear dangers give the United States a fundamental interest in good relations with the Russians. Certainly our interests cannot be well served by prolonged bad relations with them. Since the invasion of Afghanistan at the end of 1979, this point has become less clear than it ought to be for constructive public attention to nuclear and other defense issues.

I am not suggesting appeasement of Soviet leaders, but the reaction to the Soviet invasion of Afghanistan has reminded me of wisdom expressed in the 1960 campaign. Adlai Stevenson, supporting the Democratic nominee for President, John F. Kennedy, said in one speech: "The real question is not who can stand up to talk back to the Russians. That's too easy. The real question is who can sit down with them at the bargaining table and negotiate with them from a position of strength and confidence. The real question is not who is tough and who is soft. The real question is who is wise and who is foolish, who likes to play with words and who likes to get things done."[33] Stevenson was right then; his advice is right now.

Individual conflicts of interest in Soviet-American relations must be handled in ways that restrain the paranoia induced on both sides by the contemporary primacy of the attack. In the United States, the illusion of the political right is that recovery of military supremacy, of nuclear superiority, will force the Soviets into amenability; the illusion of the left is that inadequate American defense will induce the Soviets to return to sanity, to give up their delusions of persecution. I see little reason to believe that either remedy will cure America's nuclear ailments.

Restraint in nuclear weapons development and in Soviet-American relations go hand in hand. These are the pillars of a proper program for American security. Some will say that these cannot serve without Soviet cooperation, and that such cooperation is unlikely. But to say that something is difficult is not to say that it is wrong. George F. Kennan, one of America's foremost modern diplomats, once wrote lines particularly appropriate to this concern. In January 1950, Kennan addressed the awesome decision to develop hydrogen weapons, a decision that he opposed.

. . . But St. Paul's observation that, "We know in part and we prophesy in part," was never truer than it is of the time ahead of us, particularly in respect to the development of the international situation, the meaning of war and the function of weapons. In such a time there is only one thing a nation can do which can have any really solid and dependable value: and that is to see that the initial lines of its policy are as close as possible to the principles dictated by its traditions and its nature, and that where it is necessary to depart from these lines, people are aware that this *is* a departure and understand why it is necessary. For this reason, there is value in a clean and straight beginning, even though the road ahead may be torturous and perhaps impassable.[34]

Both the management of nuclear weapons and the adjustment of Soviet-American relations are problems for the long run. To judge results in the short run, to justify actions on such judgments, is to invite failure at best, catastrophe at worst.

VI THE CONVENTIONAL ISSUES:
POLITICS AND PREPAREDNESS

Any amateur can shove tanks, planes, and infantry around a map. The real business of war is getting gas, ammunition, and spare parts to people when they need them, where they need them.

GENERAL WALTER BEDELL SMITH

WILL AMERICA'S PEACETIME military shortcomings become wartime disasters? It is one thing to describe the military's manpower and technology dilemmas; but it is quite another to gauge their potential significance in war. In September 1980, former Secretary of Defense Melvin Laird publicly concluded that "If our armed forces have to go into combat in the near future, there must be considerable doubt about their ability to perform adequately." A few weeks later, in October, then Secretary of Defense Harold Brown stated emphatically that America's military was "ready to go to war—if need be," and that any contrary conclusion would be "strongly misleading."[1] Although these two men were not alone in staking out positions on the readiness and competence of the nation's armed forces, their divergent views framed the issues of America's conventional forces for the 1980s.

Apart from its nuclear responsibilities, America's military must support and defend traditional and important allies in Europe and Asia. In addition, as underscored in Persian Gulf and Indian Ocean developments of 1979 and 1980, it is supposed to possess the capacity for prompt response to unpredictable provocations. But the growth of Soviet power, the changing character and costs of conventional war, and the unpredictability of contemporary politics have reduced the abilities even of defense experts to judge America's military adequacy or plan its military development. As

188

a result, the conventional force issues of the 1980s are as difficult and as urgent as those relating to nuclear forces.

Both analytical and political factors seriously disturb consensus on what America's next war—or wars—will demand of its military and, correspondingly, what may therefore be required in peacetime military investment and reform. The Department of Defense has often tried to prepare a comprehensive "net assessment," a summary analysis of how American forces would fare against Soviet forces in possible wars. Despite its obvious importance for sound defense planning, an overall assessment has never been completed. Individual services have analyzed portions of their potential problems, but a grand appreciation of military competence has eluded the analytic community to date.

One obstacle to thorough assessment arises from the pace of technological change, not only in American forces but in those of potential enemies. It takes time to find out about new weapons developed and put into service in Soviet forces, and the Russians do not make this easy. The exact capabilities, expected deployment patterns, and total acquisition programs of new weapons are not, as in the West, the subject of detailed public discussion. When new weapons appear, it can take several years—and millions of dollars—to acquire information about their capabilities. Usually gaps in information require guesswork despite the best efforts of intelligence and defense experts.

For about ten years, for instance, from the middle 1960s to the middle 1970s, CIA analysts consistently underestimated the number of ICBMs the Soviet Union would build and deploy. Errors occur just as easily in the other direction. According to some analysts, the Department of Defense overestimated by 60 percent the number of SS-9 ICBMs the Soviet Union would deploy in the early and middle 1970s, and reached, therefore, the erroneous conclusion that the Soviets were seeking a first-strike nuclear attack capability with that weapon.[2] In a less exotic vein, the appearance of new classes of Soviet warships regularly leads to years of Western speculation about the strategic and tactical concepts these may represent in Soviet thinking, the ways in which the new ships will be used, and how many more of the same the Soviets will likely build.

It is even more difficult to come to useful conclusions about the practical implications of breakthroughs on the margins of technology—our own as well as those of the Russians. It is easy to see that lasers, particle beams, and other high-energy technologies have major military potential. But it is impossible to know how soon they will become tactically and operationally significant. Yet given the long service life of many weapons, it is always possible that portions of present military investment will simply be rendered useless by technical evolution.

Similarly, the fluidity of the political environment prevents satisfactory military assessments. Considering the two years during which the Shah of Iran fell from power, American diplomatic personnel were held hostage, the Soviet Union invaded Afghanistan, President Tito of Yugoslavia died, Polish workers staged prolonged strikes, and Iran fought Iraq for Middle East predominance, it is unnecessary to belabor this point. It is impossible to predict the provocation or opportunity that next will elicit military initiative or compel military response in the United States, and equally impossible, therefore, to know how American forces will next fare in war.

Further, important factors that determine results in war remain incalculable. Even if everyone's assumptions about the occasion of conflict and the alignment of friends and enemies were identical, it would be impossible to predict outcomes in combat merely on the basis of known orders of battle. Many other considerations shape victory and defeat in war: initiative (who moves first); strategy (how forces are deployed, committed, and operated); tactics (the style and skill with which men and machines conduct actual engagements); morale (confidence, determination, and endurance in the fighting forces, the national leadership, and the nation as a whole); logistics (military competence in supply, distribution, and maintenance as well as national economic ability to support military effort); and luck.

This problem was recognized millennia ago. Sun Pin, the author of one of the Chinese military classics from the fifth century B.C., wrote that "In regard to war, there are no constant conditions which may be relied upon; this is a principle practiced and handed down from the earliest kings." In modern Western annals, Napoleon among other great commanders emphasized that in war, moral factors outweigh material factors "as three is to one." In other words, in war the things that can be measured or counted may very well have less to do with results than those that cannot. Of all the qualities that Napoleon sought and admired in his subordinate commanders, luck was first in importance.

In view of such considerations, judgments about military adequacy can be neither simple nor precise. This was a truth relearned at great price in Iraq late in 1980, as Iran's military forces and civilian population rallied to resist what should have been easy military gains for Iraq.

In the American military, present shortcomings and future requirements are usually assessed by means of contingency planning. Because of the obvious inadequacies of simple numerical comparisons of forces, planners analyze hypothetical conflicts and their results, attempting to think about wars in places, over issues, and against enemies that make sense in terms of the nation's interests and commitments. This is not regarded as wholly satisfactory. It is, simply, the best that the military bureaucracy now can do.

It is important to distinguish between contingency planning and crystal ball gazing. "Contingency planning," as Bayless Manning of the Council on Foreign Relations once correctly explained, "is not the same as prophesying. It is not necessary that United States foreign policy officials accurately *predict* what will in fact happen. But—as is well understood in military strategic analysis, and as large-scale American companies understand in the conduct of their business—it is necessary to invest hard intellectual work and research in a careful preconsideration of what we should do if certain important and possible events were to occur."[3] The problem is to maintain this distinction as carefully in practice as it is here set out in the abstract. In five years or so of experience with high-level war games, I have detected a certain tendency to think that what could happen will, and that what can be done should be done.

Despite the intimidating technical terms in which it goes forward, contingency planning is an intensely political affair. Planners must interpret the political and strategic intentions of other governments, make judgments about the import of developments in the international environment, and come to conclusions about large questions of resource allocation within the defense community. In every aspect, such planning can lead to vigorous disagreement.

The military services naturally tend to favor contingencies that yield the largest and most traditional force requirements. The Navy's contingency planning, for instance, consistently proves that at the very minimum, the Navy needs sixteen aircraft carrier battle groups—three more than it has now. The carrier's critics point out its potential vulnerability to cheap precision-guided munitions launched from airplanes and submarines. The Boston Study Group, composed of experts in science and defense, recently wrote: "Experience indicates that the fighting carrier is delicate; flight-deck accidents have put carriers out of commission for months. Every carrier hit in World War II by two or more kamikaze planes was forced to retire for repairs. Prolonged carrier defense seems doubtful; cheap antiship missiles are getting more sophisticated daily. They will fly low, fast and in large numbers against carrier task forces. A couple will surely get through."[4]

In the face of analytic contradictions such as these, civilian leaders avoid relying too much on the results of contingency planning. Political leaders, who must broker the competing claims on available fiscal resources of defense and domestic programs, more often stress that contingency planning is, after all, only planning, not the prediction of the future. It is not the business of preparing for every possible adversity. Rather, it is one among other instruments for arranging the inevitable compromises between what seems desirable and what is affordable, between what appears most dangerous and what most likely. This quality of defense planning permits—and perhaps it encourages—charges that defense budgets, decisions, and programs are as political as any other aspect of administration policy and performance.

John M. Collins of the Congressional Research Service is the single best-known, and possibly also the best, net assessment analyst now working on the Soviet-American military balance. He is honest enough to say, very simply, that net assessment remains "an uncertain art. No net assessment tells the truth, the whole truth, and nothing but the truth, no matter how hard its architects try."[5]

The practical analytical and political difficulties of contingency planning virtually ensure that everyone involved will be dissatisfied with the results. In recent years, the nation's military professionals have voiced particular discontent. In his 1975 memoir, for instance, former Chief of Naval Operations Elmo Zumwalt criticized the "intellectual dimness that characterizes most public pronouncements about Defense budgets" and about the fundamental question of how well the United States could do in war against likely enemies. "It is not the great difficulty of answering it correctly," he wrote; "rather it is the fear that the correct answer will be politically explosive." In 1978, another Chief of Naval Operations, James L. Holloway III, told *Time* magazine that if the American people didn't want to keep leadership in the world, then they could change national strategy. If the people did want such leadership, he argued, the Navy had to have a lot more ships.[6] Both statements reflected an attractive but outdated belief in the simplicity of the issues and choices of contemporary national security affairs.

Inside the government, the practical difficulties of contingency planning lead to a curious practice. Except with the nuclear forces, contingency planning is always done on the basis of future forces, usually those forces called for in the five-year defense plan. These forces are not on hand; they may never be on hand; the five-year plans are not binding. They are always revised, sometimes radically, so that from year to year the American military rarely if ever really acquires the forces called for in the plan. The five-year defense plans always show the military "getting well," finally overcoming fundamental problems of equipment, people, training, supplies—but always in the "out years," the last years of the plan. The near term, the first one or two years of the five-year plan, calls for austerity and patience to obtain the promised bonanzas of the out years. The out years, of course, never come, as year after year the plan is revised and extended once more.

There is no written down, fully fleshed out, strategy for conventional war based strictly on current forces, and any attempt to produce such a strategy would give birth to truly unmanageable political and fiscal dilemmas. In peacetime, it can take years, literally, to get clearances and concurrences of political and military bureaucracies even on vital concerns, and therefore a strategic plan of any scale based on current capabilities would be out of date by the time it could be completed. Further—and this is a problem endemic to America's military, because peacetime forces are unlikely to be fully up to war's demands—strategies based on forces on hand usually raise awkward questions of strategic priorities. Such questions, in turn, promise only trouble for alliance relations, interservice rivalries, and domestic politics.

Reflecting the political problems of net assessment and the practical problems of contingency planning, recent national security debates have failed to present America's military situation and needs in intelligible, sensible terms. This comment may seem inappropriate after a year in which defense issues loomed large in presidential and congressional elections, and in the last five years, after all, there have been extensive public discussions about strategic arms limitation, the B-1 bomber, cruise missiles, the Trident submarine and missile, the MX missile and basing system, civil defense, troop deployments in Korea and Europe, and the need for another nuclear aircraft carrier.

But as one jaundiced officer said to me in 1980, recent national security debates have tended to resemble pissing contests between skunks: by the time they're over, nothing smells very good. The debate on the SALT II treaty aptly exemplified the problem. Proponents and opponents of the treaty assailed each other's judgment, motives, and information so thoroughly that they left the public no reliable standards by which to judge the merits of the proposed treaty. After political and procedural delays in the White House and the Senate, late in 1979 the treaty was overtaken by events. The public was left with half-formed arguments and information on verification, cruise missile limitations, and other political and technical aspects of the arms control measure. Thus the relation between SALT and strategic modernization in the United States remained obscure.

The national security debates of the 1970s, because they have tended toward hysteria, have failed to aid the public in grasping the problems and solutions in national security affairs. Debaters have exaggerated the consequences of being right or wrong about trends in Soviet-American power relationships. In the past few years, virtually every decision on force development has called forth predictions of ultimate doom for America if the weapon was not bought, the forces not authorized. The Carter administration's announced intention to withdraw forces from Korea led Army Major General Karl Singlaub into open insubordination. Many senior military officers more discreetly criticized administration decisions on other issues. The B-1 bomber decision of 1977 brought predictions of defense disaster dire enough to ensure that bomber technology would remain an issue in the 1980 election. Hence the importance of news leaks concerning "stealth" technology in the months before the presidential election day. It has, in short, been impossible to dismiss or decide against any major weapon proposed in the past five years without stirring politically significant assertions that each and every weapon proposed was vital to America's security in the immediate future.

This current style of national security debate fails to meet public needs in important respects. The philosopher Alfred North Whitehead once was asked: "Which are more important, facts or ideas?" His answer: "Ideas about facts." In national security matters, it has been especially easy, in Roger Fisher's words, to "direct attention to 'hard' facts that are certain and to divert attention from matters that are less certain but more important." Debates on Soviet-American power ratios therefore gravitate inexorably toward aspects that can be counted—orders of battle, nuclear and conventional. But these discussions communicate little about how to judge the meanings of the figures and facts. Such "squishy" matters the strategists leave to academicians and others whose lack of current security clearances condemns them to deal in ideas rather than facts.

The military issues of the 1980s will be shaped by the military challenges the nation faces: not only the Soviet nuclear threat, but commitments to major allies and the fear of unpredictable injuries to the national interest. In each area those aspects of the problems most important to informed public discussion depend not on arcane scientific knowledge or on classified military secrets but on basic elements of politics and military affairs accessible to virtually any interested citizen.

The United States is committed to the defense of major states in Europe and Asia—not out of altruism but because their political independence and economic vitality are essential to America's well-being. This fact gives rise to a principal category of military concerns for the 1980s, which in practice centers on the defense of the North Atlantic Treaty Organization (NATO).

Since World War II, American policymakers have consistently placed Europe first among the world's regions in terms of importance for America's interests. The first serious disagreements between the United States and the Soviet Union after World War II arose over European issues, and this was no accident. Both the Soviet Union and the United States saw in Central and Western Europe more essential interests, higher political and economic stakes, than anywhere else on earth. Three of the first four planning papers originating in the new Policy Planning Staff of the State Department in 1947 concerned Europe. The first series of memoranda from the National Security Council, created that same year, also dealt with European problems.

To Europe, not Asia or South America or the Middle East, went $13 billion in post–World War II Marshall Plan aid. In the earliest strategic assessments of the Joint Chiefs of Staff in 1947, Europe stood first on the lists of the world's regions ranked in order of importance to American security. With the states of Europe, the United States signed the first peacetime military alliance in its 174-year history, on April 4, 1949. That alliance, the North Atlantic Treaty, pledged the United States to defend ten states in Western Europe.° The Carter administration's emphasis on American commitments to NATO Europe was thus no more than a slight accentuation of a political premise informing a generation of American statecraft.

War between East and West over Europe, in Europe, is no more likely at present than is Soviet-American nuclear exchange. But the ability of the American military to meet its commitments in Europe, even with the full cooperation of European allies, is not now adequate.

In part, this inadequacy is the consequence of traditional alliance defense difficulties. NATO has a large number of obstinate and durable military dilemmas around which there has grown up

---

° The original signers of the North Atlantic Treaty were the United States, Canada, Great Britain, France, Italy, Norway, Belgium, the Netherlands, Luxembourg, Iceland, Portugal, and Denmark. Greece and Turkey were admitted in 1952, and West Germany in 1955.

a very large and specialized literature. These have included stan-
dardization of equipment, burden sharing within the alliance,
command and control coordination, nuclear doctrine and strategy,
logistics, sea versus land strategies, and more. Indeed, as I have
written elsewhere, in NATO, strategic problems once created never seem to go away.[7]

Beyond such traditional defense issues, American inadequacy
in NATO terms results from the interplay between the growth of
Soviet power and America's commitment to European allies. For
growing Soviet forces have not only exerted direct effects on Soviet-American power politics and on the strategic environment;
they have so altered the NATO problem as to require changes in
American's conventional forces and strategy for the 1980s.

No military relationship in the world receives more frequent
discussion than that of NATO to its chief adversary, the Warsaw
Treaty Organization (WTO). Founded in 1955, the WTO is composed of the Soviet Union and its Eastern European satellite
states—Poland, Hungary, Czechoslovakia, East Germany, Bulgar-
ia, and Rumania (from 1955 to 1963, Albania as well). Interestingly, the Soviet Union organized its own alliance only after being
refused admission to NATO. In a note of March 31, 1954, the
Russians had asked their wartime allies—France, Britain, and the
United States—to let them join NATO. On May 7, 1954, in a
remarkably prompt reply, Russia's former friends denied that ap-
plication, a step that over the following months led to Europe's
formal division into opposing military camps.

Despite the subject's familiarity, it may be helpful to mention
here some of the force ratios now obtaining in Europe. In North-
ern and Central Europe, taken together, NATO fields some 27
division equivalents, the WTO 46 divisions. (WTO divisions usually have about two thirds to three quarters the manpower of Western divisions, but they have about as many tanks and guns, so that
combat power is nearly equivalent.) In Southern Europe, which is
virtually a separate theater of potential war, NATO owns some 44
division equivalents to 21 for the WTO, although the Greek and
Turkish divisions making up most of the NATO force are now
poorly armed. The WTO has vastly greater mobilization potential
than does NATO, possibly as much as 113⅔ divisions to NATO's

52⅓. WTO reserve forces could, the International Institute for Strategic Studies (IISS) suggests, also bring reserves into action faster than could the NATO countries.

Moreover, in Europe, NATO deploys about 11,000 tanks; the WTO operates more than 27,000. NATO's tactical aircraft number some 3,200, not counting some 400 French fighters, another 100 American aircraft dual-based between Europe and the United States, or American carrier-based planes. The Warsaw Treaty Organization—often called the Warsaw Pact—maintains tactical air forces nearly 5,800 strong. NATO air forces are generally said to hold a qualitative advantage, but it is difficult to know how much this will—or will not—help in war.

Tactical nuclear weapons are also important in calculating the strategic balance in Europe. Here there are large technical complications, some similar to those discussed in relation to strategic nuclear systems. Mere numbers, whether of warheads or delivery devices, do not tell the story. Numbers must be adjusted to take into account survivability, reliability, penetration likelihood, and other aspects of weapon use bearing on ultimate effects. In calculations reflecting such adjustments, the IISS concluded in its authoritative September 1980 assessment of the military balance that rough parity now exists between the tactical nuclear forces of NATO and the Warsaw Pact.

Thus the prospect in Europe does not immediately threaten war simply on the basis of military ratios. The IISS states, I believe correctly, "that the overall balance is still such as to make military aggression appear unattractive. NATO defences are of such a size and quality that any attempt to breach them would require a major attack."[8]

To bring matters fully into perspective, one more observation is essential: politically speaking, setting military balances aside for the moment, the issues of East-West relations have not reached an impasse that would justify either thoughts of war or talk of war on either side.

The real difficulty in regard to America's alliance obligations flows not from force numbers themselves but from the way military trends have altered American responsibilities for NATO defenses. Despite the post–World War II economic recovery and the pronounced political independence of America's principal European allies—Germany, France, Britain—America's responsibilities for NATO defense have increased, not diminished. To explain what has happened, and how it matters militarily, it is necessary to review the evolution of grand strategy in NATO from the 1950s to the 1980s in counterpoint to the growth of Soviet power set out in an earlier chapter.

Since NATO's founding in 1949, the organization's strategic requirements have remained remarkably consistent. They have separated into several broad categories: the requirement to deter Soviet military initiative against Western Europe; the requirement to retain a usable military position on the continent of Europe even in large-scale war; and the requirement to guarantee sea lanes of communication between North America and Western Europe. Over the thirty years of NATO's history, these requirements have one by one become harder to meet. The increasing difficulty of doing so in the 1980s is forcing a revision of military responsibilities assigned to the alliance's various members, particularly the United States.

In its first decade, from 1949 to about 1960, NATO strategy was neither complex nor strenuous. Today, it has largely been forgotten that NATO took shape at a time when Western European governments verged on internal economic or psychological collapse, and the probability of armed incursions by Soviet troops seemed very low—at least, such was the view of the American government. Furthermore, NATO's early strategy mirrored America's massive retaliation doctrine, resting on the fact that the United States held a monopoly on deliverable nuclear weapons and expected to maintain a decisive lead for some time.

Initial postwar advantages in atomic air power shaped the alliance's allocation of military responsibilities among its members. Despite Soviet acquisition of atomic and hydrogen weapons between 1949 and 1954, the United States—and the NATO allies— maintained their high confidence in the doctrines and weapons of air power epitomized in strategic bombers. According to an early agreement, DC 6/1, "A Strategic Concept for the Defense of the North Atlantic Area" (signed December 1, 1949), these strategic bombers plus naval forces were to constitute America's material contribution to NATO.

In those early postwar years, Britain's navy shared equally in the naval responsibilities of the alliance; France, too, contributed greatly to NATO's naval power. With World War II so recently over, France and Britain had no shortage of slightly used but still serviceable vessels. Similarly, and despite the war's great losses, there was a more than adequate supply of trained manpower on the Continent. No American troops were deployed in Europe in 1949 to give weight to the new alliance. After 1951, when such deployment began, they retained a symbolic quality: the Americans were in Europe in small numbers to ensure American intervention in larger numbers. Their purpose was to die in early hours of war, to make the American commitment to Europe irreversible.

The Russians did not come West in the middle 1950s, but they nevertheless did something of consequence for NATO strategy. In the middle 1950s, as discussed earlier, they acquired the ability to deliver nuclear weapons against the United States. And because the United States was NATO's only significant nuclear power, the new Soviet nuclear capabilities struck heavily at the basis of NATO's massive retaliation strategy, forcing the abandonment of earlier doctrines.

In its second decade, from the early 1960s through the early 1970s, NATO relied on a variety of flexible response strategy. NATO's version of flexible response was adopted in reaction to new Soviet nuclear power and to the Soviet threat to NATO's military position on the European continent. The Western allies had learned in World War II how difficult it could be to regain military effectiveness after having been thrown off the Continent. In their strategic planning, they were determined to avoid a reprise of the sorry saga from Dunkirk to Normandy. But, as American scholar Morton A. Kaplan has noted, the Soviet Union emerged from World War II "as a gigantic power that was in military possession of so much of Europe that the remainder lacked the space required for effective defense."[9]

During the 1960s, when Soviet and Warsaw Pact forces became, through modernization, armored forces configured for blitzkrieg, Western defense analysts began to worry that those forces might sweep defenders off the Continent—three days to the Rhine, and seven to the Channel. America's growing involvement in Vietnam from 1965 to 1973 heightened this fear.

NATO answered the middle 1960s threat with a huge deployment of American tactical nuclear weapons. In the late 1960s, some 7,000 of them were distributed in Europe—short-range missiles, bombs, intermediate-range missiles, nuclear artillery shells, atomic land mines, and more. NATO flexible response strategy emphasized "controlled and deliberate escalation," explicitly including first use of nuclear weapons. But this strategy, intended to intimidate the Russians, rested on faith in a clear American superiority, if not monopoly, in nuclear weapons, for only America's 1960s nuclear preponderance permitted NATO to develop "links" between strategic and tactical nuclear weapons. These were supposed to deter Soviet attack by the implied threat that if battle went against the West even with use of tactical nuclear devices, the United States would devastate the Soviet Union with its superior strategic nuclear forces.

Whether the Russians ever believed in this deterrent doctrine, no one can say. It is certain, however, that some of America's allies did not. Doubting American willingness to undergo even an inferior Soviet nuclear attack, the French under Charles de Gaulle withdrew from NATO's military arrangements in 1967. The French were the only nation actually to leave NATO's military structure because they doubted the American inclination to trade American cities for Russian cities for the sake of European cities. But other alliance members came to entertain a similar mistrust of American military commitments, a fact that has marked NATO policies and strategy since the middle 1960s.

In the 1970s, Soviet military gains once more forced strategic adjustments in NATO. On the Continent, Soviet land and air forces and tactical nuclear deployments compelled NATO to turn to North America for assurances of resupply and reinforcement from the earliest days of any potential war—a strategy of "rapid reinforcement." At last NATO's need to guarantee the sea lines of communication between Europe and North America acquired the same immediacy as its concerns for deterrence and continental position. By 1974, a Brookings Institution study put it with blunt accuracy: "The credibility of NATO strategy . . . rests, in large measure, on the certainty of timely U.S. reinforcements."[10]

Just as the Atlantic sea lanes became more important than ever before, however, NATO recognized that the West no longer possessed the undisputed naval mastery essential to reliable wartime communication between Europe and North America. To make matters worse, the high intensity of a modern war using smart weapons, with correspondingly high rates of material consumption, enlarged the potential reinforcement problem. It was entirely possible that war in Europe, if it should come, might be so short that seaborne supplies and reinforcements could not arrive in time to prevent defeat even if NATO could best the Soviet Navy. These concerns led quickly to NATO agreement on a strategy to parallel rapid reinforcement—the prepositioning of American military equipment in Europe (POMCUS). This would permit troops simply to be airlifted across the Atlantic in crisis or early in war.

By the late 1970s, as a result of evolving Soviet power—nuclear, conventional, naval—NATO's original strategic concept, in which alliance members shared naval tasks, the United States supplied strategic air power, and the nations of Europe provided men and aircraft, was thus completely overturned.

Political rhetoric of the 1970s notwithstanding, NATO strategy today remains largely a function of American strategy, and in particular of American capability vis-à-vis the Soviet Union. Over the past thirty years, NATO strategy has reflected American concepts of how to cope with Soviet military power, and now that NATO has come to rely explicitly on the United States, not only for air power and nuclear weapons but for men, machines, and munitions, NATO dependence on American strategy and forces can only intensify.

This places a special responsibility on the United States to shape its defense policy and its force planning with full realization of the implications for NATO. The Carter administration emphasis on NATO was, in this context, fully justified and if anything remained somewhat short of what may be necessary.

Because Europe's great states were relatively much weaker in the alliance's early years than they are now, this new distribution of responsibility seems unfair. New defense burdens have led, quite naturally, to a feeling in the United States that Europe's nations are looking for cost-free defense, courtesy of Uncle Sam.

But NATO's nations have no immediate alternatives to relying on the United States. The United States has the only world-class navy left in the West. None of the European states can take up a large share of Atlantic naval responsibilities before the end of the century. Germany has the technology, the seagoing tradition, and the economic strength to do more than at present. But Germany also has constitutional limitations against military deployments outside its immediate areas of vital interest. Moreover, Germany's navy has no ships larger than destroyers, of which it has only eleven.

Britain's days of world naval power are past, and its economy is too troubled to permit serious thought of naval rearmament. Its navy now boasts only seventy major surface warships, including three very small aircraft carriers suitable only for antisubmarine operations. Indeed, bowing to budgetary pressures in the 1970s, Britain gradually has reduced even its modest contribution of land forces on the Continent, the Army of the Rhine.

France has a first-class navy, but with fewer than fifty major surface combatants, it is not large enough to do more than meet commitments in the Mediterranean and the Indian Ocean. Further, French military and political independence pose a formidable barrier to reliable military cooperation in any case.

Thus naval operations in the North, Central, and South Atlantic remain the primary responsibility of the United States. There is simply no one else. And since NATO's military strategy indeed rests now as never before on the "certainty of timely U.S. reinforcement," that certainty in turn must depend on confidence in the ability freely to use the Atlantic seaways in crisis and in war. NATO's political and military health is directly related to the level of confidence Europe's leaders feel concerning those supposed certainties.

Alliances cannot always prevent wars, and they cannot always win them. But they are among the most important ways in which nations try to find a proper balance between land power and sea power, offsetting each other's deficiencies. Yet ironically, as the 1980s open, NATO countries—especially Germany—are judging America's reliability as a partner by its ability to handle crises in places such as Iran and Afghanistan. This is not completely logical, because what happens to NATO, and in NATO Europe, presumably touches on more traditional, more vital, more clear-cut interests of the United States, all of which would facilitate prompt and substantial response.

In the 1980s, military challenges growing out of unpredictable injuries to American interests around the globe may be the most important for informed public attention to military issues. Such challenges are far more likely to occur than either nuclear war or large conventional war in support of major allies; yet American forces do not now possess satisfactory capabilities to deal with the unpredictable, and the obstacles to obtaining such capabilities are very large. As indicated, America's responses to Iran and Afghanistan are being interpreted—by friends, onlookers, and enemies alike—as indicating trends in national will and strategic capability. *The political and strategic gravity, therefore, of small contingencies in the next few years will be out of all proportion to their immediate context.*

The conceptual difficulties of preparing against the unforeseeable are in some ways less abstract than considerations of nuclear strategy. But in their own way, these lesser conflicts present more difficulty. The defense planner is trapped by intellectual dilemmas that have practical consequences. Planners face the need to make choices about what capabilities to obtain—and what to forgo. Year by year, budgets force choices; it is simply impossible to buy or to do everything. Planners must choose the capabilities the forces will acquire, and in so doing they risk being wrong. It is always possible—and given the perversity of human affairs, likely—that unfolding events will give cause for regret about past military planning decisions.

Further, political-military contingencies rarely arise in the exact terms in which they are anticipated. It is relatively easy to think about situations that might call for military response from the United States. But it is much more difficult to anticipate the way in which the current political framework will present real and immediate choices.

After withdrawing from Vietnam, for instance, the American military spent most of the 1970s preparing for high-intensity war against well-armed opponents, probably in Europe. The eruption of troubles in Southwest Asia in 1979 and 1980 was an almost total surprise—a failure not only of military planning but of intelligence. Late in the fall of 1980, General Volney Warner, then commander of the Readiness Command, made a telling observation to *Newsweek*, doubtless intending to convey confidence and modest optimism: "If you look back a year and a half ago," he said, "we didn't even have map sheets for Southwest Asia. Now we have a better handle on the problems and by 1985 or 1986, we can probably get there and win."[11] With American hostages still in Iran, Soviet forces still in Afghanistan, Iran's great refineries reduced to burning rubble, and Iraq's important oil flow to the outside world also halted, there was little comfort in this well-meant assurance.

In March 1980, President Carter seemed to have found the answer to the problem of unpredictable but important hazards to American interests. He established a Rapid Deployment Force specifically to react quickly to overseas provocation. The RDF was particularly intended to give weight to the new Carter Doctrine—the President's declaration that the United States would use all means at its disposal to protect its vital interests in the Persian Gulf.

Within months of its creation, the RDF was well on the way to becoming a textbook example of what goes wrong when it is politically expedient to marry the unpredictable to the impracticable. For it quickly became apparent that the creation of an RDF neither solved the problem of predicting which future challenges were the likeliest to occur nor equipped the nation to deal militarily with situations such as those in Iran and Afghanistan.

The RDF started out with a clear focus on the Persian Gulf as its most likely area of operations. Within a few months, however, its charter widened. It was ordered to be the first-line American force for use on short notice anywhere in the world outside the NATO area. In accord with the magnitude of this new responsibility, the RDF's commander, Lieutenant General Paul X. Kelley, USMC, rose to the status of a "CinC," that is, a commander in chief of operational forces, with direct wartime access to the Joint Chiefs of Staff and the Secretary of Defense. The size of the RDF, originally set at 100,000 men, also grew, to somewhat more than 200,000 men, at least on paper. In reality, the RDF consists of 250 officers and senior noncommissioned officers at MacDill Air Force Base in Tampa, Florida. The soldiers, sailors, airmen, and marines assigned to the force come under its command only in emergency.

A number of practical and political problems immediately beset the RDF and its commander. Not long after accepting the command appointment, General Kelley dryly noted that the RDF's principal need was to become "more rapid." To help in this, the Army was ordered to supply the RDF with logistic support. This in turn caused the Chief of Staff of the Army, General Edward C. Meyer, to verge for a time on resigning in protest against the Army's support role. General Meyer would have preferred to take responsibility for the front-line fighting rather than for rear-echelon logistics. And, as the real problems confronting the RDF became clearer, Defense Department and press witticisms suggested that "Rapid Deployment Force" was a misnomer: the RDF seemed neither rapid, nor deployable, nor much of a force.

Creation of the RDF did not give rise to totally new additional forces. Rather, it called on each of the services to nominate forces to be made available to the RDF commander when he was ordered into action. The Army and the Air Force quickly complied. But the Navy and the Marines responded by noting that their major forces were fully committed. What the RDF's commander would get in an emergency would depend on where in the world he was going and what else the Navy and Marines were engaged in at the time. This meant that virtually from the outset, there was little possibility of conducting the kind of combined forces training essential to the RDF plan in the first place.

Of the Army forces assigned to the RDF's commander, to be used on his call, most were unready for combat. One nominally available armored division was in the process of acquiring a new tank. It had little of its equipment; it needed one to two more years to train its people in the use and care of new vehicles; still more time would pass before the supply problems for the new equipment were well in hand. Other units assigned to the RDF were rated as unready for combat because of severe shortages of noncommissioned officers.

Further, the Army and Air Force units assigned to the RDF were all also dedicated to support NATO in war. Thus any hope of using the RDF to deal with a small contingency outside the NATO area while prosecuting a larger war in Europe was completely illusory.

Deployability problems had another equally serious side: a

shortage of airlift. Major General Thomas H. Sadler, commander of the 21st Air Force at McGuire Air Force Base in New Jersey, said in September 1980 that America's airlift capacity was 25 percent to 30 percent short even for a limited war, and much less adequate for a larger war. The Air Force, according to General Sadler, had transports and cargo planes to move only one third of an army division at any one time—only 5,000 to 6,000 men. To move the 82nd Airborne Division to the Persian Gulf area, with a mere five days supply of ammunition and food, would take ten days of continuous air shuttling involving the entire available fleet of C-5A and C-141 aircraft. It would require 13 million gallons of aviation fuel per day for those ten days—about one third of the total daily fuel consumption in the United States. And to put a mechanized division into the Persian Gulf area—a division with more vehicles and heavier equipment than that of the airborne division—would take about twice as long, approximately three weeks.[12]

Amphibious forces, moved by sea, faced similar limitations on deployability. The amphibious shipping available on the East Coast of the United States at the end of 1980 was far short of what would be needed to move a Marine Amphibious Force (a Marine Amphibious Force consists of at least one Marine division). The United States owns amphibious shipping enough to move one and one third divisions, but the shipping is divided equally between the Atlantic and the Pacific oceans. To move a MAF, therefore, amphibious shipping would have to be transferred from one ocean to the other, which in itself would take a minimum of fifteen days.

There were other problems. Two Marines fresh from Washington staff jobs told me late in 1980 that planners for the RDF had not yet figured out how to transport fuel and supply water for the machines and troops of the RDF. Late in October, *Time* magazine reported that RDF troops sent to the hot Middle East would need twelve gallons of water per man per day, but that a means of providing it had yet to be devised.[13] Until that problem could be solved, any talk of deploying the RDF was only that—talk.

Because of these difficulties of availability, airlift, fuel, and water, at the end of 1980 the RDF functioned only on paper. The relatively small portion of it that might be deployable would be capable of landing only where unopposed. There could be no thought of airlifting elements of the force into hostile airspace or territory, no over-the-beach, World War II style of operation. Rather, the RDF would have to be received at substantial facilities in friendly hands. It would need time and safety to set up equipment, bring in additional forces over several days or weeks, and obtain the water, fuel, and other support necessary for beginning operations. Whether many situations calling for use of an RDF would have such favorable local conditions remained debatable but dubious. The Marines with whom I discussed this matter in the fall of 1980 were unanimous in doubting the usefulness of an RDF that could not deploy under fire or against opposition.

There was at least one attempt to explain how to use the RDF in spite of its limitations. In its issue of October 27, 1980, *Newsweek* published the views of unnamed experts who suggested wielding the RDF as a "blocking force." On detecting Soviet intentions to move military forces outside Soviet borders, the United States could try to put portions of the RDF in place first, to warn off the Soviets by threatening opposition and possible escalation. But the risks of such strategy remained uncalculated.

In the months following the RDF's creation, it was extremely difficult to think of places in the world, and situations, in which a force of such a size might seem usable, appropriate, apt. Congressional defense experts calculated in mid-1980 that the RDF would have a very difficult time even against, say, 10 divisions of Iraq's armed forces in any contretemps in the Persian Gulf. The possibility of war against a smaller Middle East power reinforced by Soviet military units was beyond realistic consideration. Serious estimates of how difficult, costly, and yet inconclusive a 100,000-man war, or even a 250,000-man war, could be were still to come.

The RDF's planners, despite their widening mandate, continued to focus on the Middle East and Persian Gulf regions through 1980. In August, Jack Anderson broke a story in which he insisted that the administration was preparing for a second military operation against Iran, one timed to boost the President to victory in the November election. Although the White House asserted that Anderson had merely learned something of the routine contingency planning and training involving the RDF, the story was not completely in error—at least, so I learned from a high military official. Third World nations also wondered about the intended uses of the new force. In the course of the Iran-Iraq war late in 1980, important Middle East nations—not only Iran and Iraq but Saudi Arabia, Kuwait, and Libya—expressed their view that American forces in the Indian Ocean suggested an American intention to take over the oil fields if the opportunity presented. Even America's military support for Saudi Arabia, defensive equipment sent at Saudi request, stirred ambivalence in the policies and outlooks of other Middle East nations.

At the end of 1980, the RDF remained more a staff than a force, useful for military planning rather than for military action. "I am getting down into the nitty-gritty of who goes on what airplanes and where he goes," General Kelley, the RDF's commander, told *Newsweek*. "This is very fine-tuned planning, which really has never been done in such detail."[14] The question was whether, in view of the real constraints on the force, anyone would be able to go anywhere. There was also the question of whether refinements of military planning were really the result aimed for in the creation of the RDF. It was little wonder that as 1980 drew to a close, military "detailers"—those officers responsible for assigning others to their next jobs—were discouraging promising officers from seeking duty with the RDF. "It's chaos down there at MacDill," one officer told me. "It would be a mistake for a competitive officer to hook up with such a shaky outfit."

One Navy commander told me of the growing tendency among his military colleagues to refer to the RDF as the new "Emergency Overreaction Force." Like the freezing of Iranian assets in the United States in the hostage crisis, it seemed to have the potential to backfire, causing unease in relations with lesser nations as well as overconfidence among national security managers. Whether its existence would, in time, predispose decision makers to its use remained an open but important question.

There was also the comment of one Marine colonel, who said, to me: "What is all this excitement about some kind of Rapid Deployment Force? We've had one for years, and a damned good one, too. We call it the Navy–Marine Corps team. The only rea-

son it wasn't given the job of getting back the hostages is that
interservice politics blocked the sensible response." This telling re-
mark had, for me, the ring of truth.

The difficulties of the RDF remain unresolved, and despite
the Reagan administration's investment of some $5.5 billion in
RDF-related programs in fiscal 1982, they are unlikely soon to
improve. For officials are spending money rather than confronting the matter's essentials. In February 1981, the Army, Navy,
and Air Force joined in recommending that the RDF be placed
under the command of the European Command and thereafter
operate from bases in NATO Europe. In this new scheme, the
RDF was to be a "flanking force" for NATO's extreme southern
areas—namely, the Persian Gulf and Southwest Asia. The meaning of this suggestion, however, was considerably different than its
plausible-sounding rationale. No one who remembered the way in
which NATO allies refused facilities to U.S. resupply efforts in the
1973 Arab-Israeli War could repose much confidence in an interventionary force having to operate from NATO bases. The plan to
place the RDF under NATO's umbrella was tantamount to admission that it could not be used to effect in most, if not all, of the
world, and it made the expensive RDF-related programs of the
budget seem questionable if not simply wrongheaded. As criticism
of this idea mounted, the administration once more narrowed the
RDF's focus to the Persian Gulf–Southwest Asia area. But it was
doubtful that even this would soon ease the political and practical
problems surrounding the RDF and its potential uses.

In the weeks before the presidential election of 1980, regular
revelations of RDF shortcomings perceptibly merged with larger
concerns about the readiness and adequacy of the entire American military. Military preparedness became a distinct issue—apart
from discussing the need for an RDF and from the debate over
what should have been done in Iran, or about Iran. Adam Clymer,
writing in *The New York Times* in August 1980, shrewdly observed, however, that the preparedness issue went well beyond
military matters in its political significance: "Not since the missile
gap of 1960 has defense policy been as much of a campaign issue
in a peacetime election as it is this year. And it's not just because
of what the Russians are doing and what the candidates think
about that. For both President Carter and his main challenger,

Ronald Reagan, arms policy in this campaign is a metaphor for leadership."[15]

Nonmetaphorically, the debate on preparedness gave focus to the nation's conventional military priorities in the 1980s. Critics of our military readiness pointed to shortcomings of manning, mobility, equipment. In spring 1980, the House Armed Services Committee flatly said that the United States "now fields a force with deficient military credibility." Former Secretary of Defense Melvin Laird, together with Lawrence J. Korb, charged in fall 1980 that the Army had only 78 percent of the necessary tanks; that it lacked 60,000 vehicles; and that the Air Force was nine wings short of having the aircraft it needed for "reasonable reassurance" of being able to carry out its assignments.[16]

Through the fall and the election season, public figures ventured their opinions. A confidential Army report on readiness was leaked to the press, indicating that of the ten divisions based in the United States, only one was ready for combat. Three others were "marginally ready," and six were simply unready, with deficiencies that would take considerable time and money to correct. Of the Navy's thirteen aircraft carriers, the great ships central to naval warfare, four were undergoing routine overhaul, a lengthy business taking as long as twenty-eight months per carrier. Of the nine remaining carriers, six were rated "marginally capable of combat," and three were rated "not ready."[17]

Confronting another aspect of the problem, General Robert M. Shoemaker, commander of the Army Force Command, expressed doubts about our ability to get reserves into action on time. Current plans, as we have seen, call for reserve units to be in action in Europe within thirty days from the outbreak of war. "That schedule," General Shoemaker said, "is faster by a factor of 10 than we've ever tried to do it before." The Los Angeles *Times* dryly reported that "Pentagon manpower officials concede they do not know whether the ambitious schedule could in fact be met." In view of the problems of sea and air lift previously discussed, I see little possibility that such optimistic assumptions and plans would prove out in practice. Similarly, as the ranking minority member of the House Armed Services Committee, Representative Jack Edwards, told *Aviation Week & Space Technology:* "If we went to all-out war, we've got enough spare parts to last us maybe 10 to

20 days. When you're flying those sorties like crazy, parts tend to wear out fast. We should have enough for 90 to 120 days, but we don't."[18]

Moreover, in September 1980, Admiral Harry Train, Commander in Chief, Atlantic Fleet, told the Los Angeles *Times* that the Navy had only half as many Phoenix missiles in stock as were needed to fight a war. More interestingly, he indicated that such figures were misleading, because "estimates of what the Soviets actually can use at any given time had been reduced to make U.S. missile procurement appear to be lacking less than it did."[19]

In other words, Admiral Train suggested that the standards used to measure the adequacy of war stocks and other indicators of readiness were subject to manipulation in order to make the actual condition of America's defense look better than it was. In a related observation, General Alexander Haig shortly after his resignation as commander of NATO forces in Europe pointed to what he considered foolishly low war stocks in the alliance. For many years, in the 1960s and early 1970s, the United States tried to get all its NATO allies to maintain ninety days' worth of selected war stocks—ammunition, fuel, spare parts, critical minerals, and the like. Because such things are expensive, this effort never came close to success. Eventually, to reduce the political embarrassment and tension surrounding the matter, NATO—and the United States—rather than meeting the requirement, reduced it from ninety days to between twenty-three and thirty days supply. "Now," General Haig noted in September 1980, "we're lucky if we have that." Thomas A. Callaghan, director of the Georgetown University Center for Strategic and International Studies, confirmed late in October 1980 that "In Europe, . . . supplies are so limited that the U.S. Army could not engage in a major tank war for more than eight weeks without either risking defeat or having to resort to tactical nuclear weapons. . . . That is too high a price to pay to retrieve a military disaster that might have been avoided by strong conventional forces."[20]

Furthermore, as *Time* magazine noted late in October 1980, American industry was in no position to respond quickly to orders for military supplies and equipment. Delays of fifteen to eighteen months were normal for ammunition, and more exotic items, such as landing gear for fighter aircraft, might take as long as three years to obtain. *Time* quoted an Air Force general: "There is some residual belief in the country that we could repeat what we did in World War II and turn out aircraft by the thousands almost overnight. It takes three years to build some airplanes now."[21]

The foregoing considerations of readiness, and of the ways in which it is assessed, came together just before the presidential election of 1980. In mid-October, the honesty—or lack of it—with which the government represents America's military condition finally became an issue in itself. On October 11, the Washington *Post* published news of a memorandum that Army Major General James H. Johnson had prepared for internal use in the organization of the Joint Chiefs of Staff. This memorandum said that Secretary of Defense Harold Brown was withholding from Congress a report showing broad failings in readiness while revising the readiness rating system in ways that would produce more favorable evaluations. "The secretary of defense has decided not to forward our readiness report synopsis to Congress. He has expressed concern that our current readiness reporting formula formats only emphasize the negative aspects of our military readiness. . . . The secretary has asked that we re-examine our readiness reporting system to develop a report format which places greater emphasis on the positive factors of our readiness."

This story brought an emphatic response from Secretary of Defense Brown and his spokesman in the Defense Department, Thomas Ross. Ross told reporters that the general's memorandum was a "complete garble and misinterpretation" of Secretary Brown's attitude. In a telephone interview that *The New York Times* published on October 12, Ross said: "The Secretary has given no order whatsoever for changes in the rating system, which he considers a very good and useful management tool." In a speech in El Paso, Texas, only two days before the controversial memorandum became public, Brown had argued that "readiness, understood as the capacity for rapid military response," was but one among other fundamental factors in defense. Size and composition of forces, modernity of equipment, and the ability to sustain forces in action were others, equally important in assessing the ability of the American military to fight and win.

Predictably, the matter of General Johnson's memorandum entered into presidential campaign politics. Governor Reagan's supporters held a news conference the day the story broke, in which they charged that the administration was attempting to cover its failings. Secretary Brown appeared on a Sunday national news interview program to affirm his conviction that the American military was "ready to go to war if necessary." But precisely because of the political context, it was difficult either to accept the assurances offered by the Secretary of Defense or to believe wholly in the conspiratorial manipulations suggested by the administration's political foes.

Carter and Reagan supporters agreed on one point in the readiness dispute—namely, that readiness reports were not a wholly satisfactory indication of the nation's military condition. As it happens, on this point both sides were right, though not to the extent, or for the reasons, they might have believed. The widening attention to military and defense matters in the nation's press and periodicals produced ample evidence in weeks before the election that present measures both underrated military readiness in some respects and overrated it in others.

In retrospect, the October 6, 1980, issue of *Aviation Week & Space Technology* cast a certain light on the clash between General Johnson and Secretary Brown. Buried in twenty pages or more of articles on reliability and readiness lay a summary of a new Department of Defense "mission-capable reporting system" for aircraft. "The new system," said *Aviation Week*, "computes the readiness rate for a particular aircraft by dividing the number of hours that an aircraft is ready to perform *in at least one of its missions* by the total number of hours the aircraft is possessed."° "This gives us the positive approach of visibility," said Joseph P. Cribbins of Army logistics. "On an attack helicopter, if the machine gun is down and the TOW missile is up, you can still go out and use the TOW. In the same situation under the old system, you'd call the aircraft operationally ready with reduced mission capability, but it would not show up positively that it was part mission capable." In sum, this is an elaborate variation on the old question of whether a partly filled glass of water is half full or half empty. Those who are attempting to defend their administrative record naturally insist that the defense glass is half full; those

---

°My italics.

attacking the record consider it half empty. When all is said and done, what the public needs to remember is that the glass really is only partly filled, whatever the perspective from which it is evaluated.

There were other indications that readiness reporting did not, and does not, adequately communicate present capabilities. Late in 1980, General Edward C. Meyer, the Army Chief of Staff, in commenting on the marginal readiness of so many Army divisions, asserted that "it is a waste of money to keep every division at full combat strength when the primary mission of most is to reinforce NATO units several weeks after any fighting starts." Yet General Meyer had made national news in earlier weeks by criticizing weaknesses in personnel, training, and equipment for producing what he called a "hollow army," a mere shell without the substance to do the job. On a more ambiguous point, Air Force officials noted that present mission-capable ratings, which show only about 50 percent of the Air Force's planes ready for combat, do not take into account the war reserve kits for each plane. Including these, 75 percent of the aircraft could be made "substantially" combat ready. But in my opinion, it is difficult to know whether a figure of 75 percent substantial combat readiness with use of war stocks is cause for satisfaction or for concern. We must also take into account an observation in *Newsweek*'s fall survey of the nation's defense. "Readiness ratings may miss the most dangerous deficiency of all—the thousands of military personnel who may be too ill-trained to be considered fully ready for combat. In . . . mobilization the shortage of seasoned personnel would magnify the problem a hundredfold: tens of thousands of draftees would have to be trained by an armed-forces infrastructure unequal to the task."[22]

The readiness debate in all its ambiguity brought a classic response from at least one senior officer. In a speech to the Association of the United States Army, in Washington, late in October, General Frederick J. Kroesen, commanding general of the United States Army, Europe, complained about the negative press the military was receiving. He feared, so he said, that critical assessments of the American military would encourage Soviet aggression while discouraging the morale of America's own men in uniform. "If you read something enough, you begin to believe it," the general said. And then he proposed his solution: Readiness should remain a classified subject.[23] It was exactly the wrong conclusion, for it could bring an end only to informed public discussion, not to military decay.

At the moment of the presidential election, the debate on readiness was unresolved, and perhaps unresolvable. Whether or not a military really is ready depends ultimately on what it must do. The inability to answer that question clearly and surely posed an insuperable obstacle to obtaining simple, satisfactory answers.

Yet the debate was important to the military's tasks in the coming decade. In bringing together conventional force concerns relating both to support of allies and to the unpredictable in America's environment, the debate illuminated possible missteps as well as desirable next steps. Apart from examining the problems of manpower and high-technology weapons, which permeate the readiness issue, it demonstrated, I believe, that America's needs in NATO and in the RDF are largely congruent.

This congruity, however, does not make those needs particularly easy to satisfy. In both NATO and RDF contexts, the United States needs considerably more naval power. Not only must NATO—and for now this means the United States in naval matters—have full use of the Atlantic sea lanes; there is also a great need for strategic mobility, both to serve European needs in war and to meet lesser contingencies. Air lift is not now, and will not be for many years to come, an adequate alternative to sea lift. It takes twenty-seven large ships to move one Army division. To move such large military units, airlift simply costs too much in time and fuel—that is, if airlift can do the job at all.

Although it cannot be the principal means of moving large military units in great numbers, increased airlift is nevertheless another extremely high priority. The Air Force has suggested three ways of improving its airlift capacity in the 1980s. One way, already in progress, is by strengthening structural members of the seventy-seven C-5A transports now in the fleet, both to increase load-carrying capacity and to extend service life from 7,100 hours to 31,000 hours. A second method, now well along and due to be completed in 1982, is the "stretching" of most of the 275 C-141 transport and cargo aircraft in the fleet. This involves adding two "plugs" totaling 23 feet 4 inches in length to the main fuselage section of the aircraft, thereby adding cargo space to the plane's original interior dimensions, which have caused it to "cube out"— that is, fill up with bulky objects—before its weight limits were reached. The added cargo space is roughly the equivalent of adding ninety new aircraft to the fleet, this without significantly increasing either operating costs or manning.

But in airlift, the third proposed program is the most important, and with this last there is political trouble. The Air Force, supported by the other services and by the Office of the Secretary of Defense, has been requesting funds with which to develop a new, large cargo plane capable of carrying the largest equipment now in the Army's inventory while using runways somewhat smaller than those required by the C-5A. According to present estimates, the military needs between 200 and 300 such aircraft in addition to the reworked C-5As and C-141s.

But there are signs of real congressional opposition to the CX—Cargo Experimental—program. For one thing, as now conceived, the CX, like the C-5A, will be able to carry only one of the new XM-1 tanks at a time. Yet, in another sense, some congressional opposition may be no more complicated than the memory of the last major cargo aircraft program, the super plane for super cargoes, the C-5A. This aircraft, built by Lockheed from the late 1960s through the middle 1970s, was one of the most scandal-ridden programs in defense history, with massive cost overruns and mismanagement. It has become a textbook case, literally used in defense management and business school curricula as an example of business/government collaboration at its worst.

Yet the simple truth remains that to deploy the forces and equipment that mean so much in modern combat terms, and to do so in any timely way, the United States must be able to move more than one third of a lightly armed division at a time. It is very difficult to think of situations in Southwest Asia or the Middle East, for instance, in which the quick insertion of 5,000 lightly armed troops with a couple of days' supplies could do more than get the United States in deeper. "With piecemeal efforts," one Army officer recently told *Time* magazine, "you run the risk of piecemeal defeats." Small wars, as I have suggested, are likely to be very hard for the United States to find. Furthermore, the abili-

ty to respond on short notice has never been the criterion for political importance or great power status. The reputation of a great
power reflects its ability to sustain its interests over time, not from
moment to moment.[24]

In addition to increases in naval forces and airlift, the United
States needs sharp increases in its war stocks. Here, too, there are
political as well as technical and fiscal dilemmas. In one problem,
routine items such as spare parts and war reserve stocks lack a
constituency in Congress. Therefore, they also lack reliable sponsorship in the military itself. Last year, the President's Office of
Management and the Budget reduced by $500 million the money
requested for operations and maintenance, the account out of
which such costs must be paid. Then the Congress cut the request
by another $1 billion. "There is nobody on the Hill watching op-
erations and maintenance," one Senate staff member remarked
last fall.[25] Such moneys are thus among the easiest targets in annual last-minute efforts to cut budgets. Representative Jack Edwards
told *Aviation Week* late in 1980: "I would hasten to say on any
given day in my committee, on a question of whether to buy 10
Grumman F-14 fighters or spare parts to keep what we've got
going, the 10 F-14s will win out any day." His remarks were
echoed by Senator John C. Culver: "Generally, there is greater
pressure to buy new aircraft than there is to make sure we have
the parts for those aircraft we already have."[26]
  The military also has a natural tendency to become enamored
of sophisticated new technology, even at the expense of present
maintenance and munitions needs. "We've been pumping too
much money into research and development, in wizard weapons
from Bill Perry's Toy Factory," one Air Force general told the
Los Angeles *Times.*° "We have not been buying enough replacement parts or air-to-ground munitions." In a parallel point, Walter Guzzardi, Jr., noted in *Fortune* that "Congress . . . encourages
our military's passion for new weapons because plants in the right
districts help the right constituents."[27]
  Further, increases in war stocks must be based on realistic cal-

---

°Dr. William J. Perry was then Under Secretary of Defense for Research and
Engineering.

culations of usage rates under conditions created by modern tactics and technology. Again, the politics of the issue can frustrate
prudent attempts to build up war reserves. In recent years, the
United States Department of Defense, reflecting the military's
and the Congress's disinclination to invest heavily in such stocks,
has created still another excuse for inadequate reserves. There is
no reason, so the current official rationale runs, for the United
States to maintain stocks sufficient for periods of war longer than
those provided for by the allies' own reserves, because the United
States cannot expect to fight successfully in Europe without allied
assistance. At first hearing, this argument has a sensible ring. But
NATO's defense depends much less on the stockpiles of Greece or
Belgium than on those of the United States, and for the United
States to say it will not provision its forces beyond the point for
which its allies supply theirs is *not* sensible. Surely American interests could not be well served by accepting the possible early
defeat of European allies because of their lack of military stocks.
By that logic, America's contribution to the world wars of this
century would have been much smaller, and the results much different. This is not defense logic: it is, rather, a political attempt to
reduce the unappealing necessity of buying such uninteresting
items as ammunition, canteens, bandages, fuel, trucks, and rations.

Further, along with naval forces, airlift, and war stocks, the
United States must invest in reducing the backlog of required
maintenance on major weapons. To the extent that such a thing
can truly be estimated, the American military at present is in ar-
rears about $40 billion worth of maintenance—including the cost
of spare parts. This means that a very substantial fraction of our
total weaponry now counts for little or nothing. Considering the
investment already made not only in purchasing the equipment
and weapons but in developing them, testing them, and training
people to use and maintain them, this backlog is hugely wasteful.
Reduction of the backlog would very likely pay dividends in usable forces far in excess of what could now be purchased for similar sums.

The need for more naval forces, additional airlift, enlarged
war reserve stocks, and reduced maintenance backlogs—and for
much more at every level of military organization and oper-

ation—leads to one large point: The impossibility of being prepared for every eventuality—whether in NATO Europe or outside it—puts a premium on the ability to improvise, to adapt. One classic definition of strategy placed this emphasis clearly and correctly. As General Helmuth von Moltke said in the days of Chancellor Bismarck and Imperial Germany: "Strategy is the practical adaptation of the means at hand to the ends in view." Other military theorists, notably Carl von Clausewitz, have stressed the high importance of having a military that is flexible and adaptable in action. And Philip A. Crowl, a leading historian of the United States Marines in World War II, has remarked a virtual law of military endeavor: The equipment bought in peacetime is certain to be used in war in unexpected ways for unforeseen purposes.

Together these observations suggest what I believe to be a truth: The only sure basis for response to unforeseeable eventualities is a high level of readiness, of preparedness. The military cannot improvise to meet the unexpected when its people and equipment are inadequate or inferior. Low levels of supply, training, and maintenance simply deprive the military of any capacity to respond quickly to the course of events. A high level of readiness—supply, equipment, manning, and training—is essential not only because great wars are possible but because lesser combats are certain.

It is impossible to design, or even to afford, a military that possesses every conceivable necessary capability. In a sense, the emphasis on the RDF has encouraged the American people in a comforting but misguided belief that it is possible to be prepared for everything. Also, in a generation of being the world's leaders, Americans have developed an expectation that their government should be able to deal with injury to American interests and citizens every time it occurs, and in every place. But for reasons already discussed, this expectation is completely inappropriate to present political and military realities.

Events in Iran and Afghanistan in 1979 and 1980 have taught us painful but necessary lessons about the limits of military power. In both instances, it has become clear that despite $2.6 trillion spent on American defense since World War II, the United States does not have global military reach. Further, and perhaps more important, the Iran rescue mission pointed up a fact often ignored not only by the public but by professionals in foreign-policy and military affairs. The point, simply, was this: Even in a very large military, critical capacities may be in very short supply. The Navy had only two operational squadrons of RH-53 helicopters, the type finally selected for use on the raid, squadrons with eight helicopters in each. (There were in addition a small number of RH-53s used for training.) The eight helicopters sent on the mission made up fully 50% of the operationally available RH-53 force, and the seven RH-53s that were lost correspondingly reduced the Navy's inventory of this important mine-sweeping helicopter by 44%. In the entire Air Force, there were only 114 qualified pilots for the 53 series helicopter, including flight examiners and instructors; of these, just 96 were current in long-range flight and air refueling techniques. Training for the mission began on November 12, 1979; an initial operational capability was not obtained until the eighth of February, 1980. Only at the end of March 1980 did the force reach a level of readiness and proficiency that would have permitted them to act within seven days of receiving the order to carry out a rescue attempt.[28]

So it was with the Airborne Warning And Command (AWACs) aircraft sent to defend Saudi Arabia in the Iraq-Iran war in October 1980. Eventually the United States will have thirty-four of these specialized and very expensive aircraft. But it had no more than twenty-four of them last September when the Saudi request for assistance came to Washington. The decision to send four AWACs to Saudi Arabia was the more important precisely because of the relative scarcity of this valuable asset.

In America's need for larger and readier conventional forces, there lies a serious danger, glimpsed at least in part by several of the commentators writing on defense late in 1980. As expressed by Walter Guzzardi, Jr., by Newsweek, and, a year earlier, by Jimmy Carter's former speech writer James Fallows, the danger was this: Large increases in moneys for defense might well result in a bigger military, but not a better one. Late in October 1980, even the Rand Corporation, long a defense think tank, warned that much defense spending seemed no more than an unthinking response to immediate irritations. Coherence, as well as money, was requisite to improved defense.

In approaching our conventional military needs, it is essential to take up problems in the right order. A simple example will illustrate how easy it would be to sacrifice military improvement to military expansion. The Navy needs, and in the 1980s will finally get, some fifty to sixty more ships. Indeed the Navy seems about to receive many more ships than that. To man merely another 50 ships, it must have approximately 10,000 more petty officers than it currently requires—and thousands more sailors as well. But the Navy, as set out earlier in this book, is now somewhere between 21,000 and 23,000 petty officers short. If the Navy gets more ships before it solves problems of retention, training, and leadership, it will very likely enlarge its troubles at least as much as its capabilities. And, similar situations can be found in all the services. It is essential to tackle—and to reduce—the problems of people and technology before undertaking significant force expansion.

In my view, therefore, and despite the lack of appeal these matters traditionally have held in America's military and political circles, maintenance and war stocks must be heavily weighted in the next three or four military budgets. Setting figures on matters such as this always invites argument. Also, it is important not to set figures on the basis of irrelevant standards of measurement, such as the gross national product. What the GNP has to do with necessary or adequate or even affordable levels of defense spending is something I have never been able to fathom. The great need, in setting figures on defense proposals, is to seek some basis of calculation that bears a rational relationship to the problem under consideration. I think that the maintenance backlog of some $40 billion, along with figures derived from estimates of war reserve requirements, make good starting points for realistic suggestions about new spending.

The American military stands in paradox: It is more capable of dealing with its less likely challenges—nuclear war and NATO war—than of dealing with its more likely, and more immediate, tests. Yet such a circumstance is completely compatible with the logic the professional military brings to its priorities. Military planning is an exercise in prudence. Military leaders and military planners believe that they must attend to the most damaging threats first, the more probable ones only as time and resources permit. Given the choice between spending a dollar to prevent future disaster or spending it to reduce lesser but more immediate risk, the military professional will unhesitatingly invest the dollar in insurance against future catastrophe.

If the American people want a military that is more responsive to immediate needs, one that can deal with lesser as well as greater security threats, they must take an interest, and a part, in 1980s military matters. Left to themselves, the military professionals, out of the best of motives, will continue to sacrifice the needs of the present to the fears of the future.

VII THE PRESCRIPTION: MEASURED MILITARY RENEWAL

Men secure peace by using their power justly and by making it clear that they will not allow others to wrong them.

THUCYDIDES

THE UNITED STATES is so clearly bent on improving its military in the early 1980s that it may seem unnecessary here to prescribe military renewal. Ronald Reagan campaigned on promises to seek "careful, measured renewal of our military strength" and to restore a "margin of safety" to America's security posture. His Secretary of State, Alexander Haig, solemnly declared in his confirmation hearings that "There are more important things than peace—there are things which we Americans must be willing to fight for." When President Reagan welcomed the former hostages home from Iran, he promised "every means of protection that America can offer" to its representatives in the future, and threatened "swift and effective retribution" for future affronts.

But there are risks in advocating military renewal—even "measured" military renewal—and these risks require both caution and clarity from advocates of military reinvigoration. There is a political as well as an intellectual danger in becoming preoccupied with military affairs—the hazard of habituation in seeking military answers to profound human, social, and political problems. In addition, as we have noted, there is the more mundane but practical risk that military renewal will result more in growth than in improvement for America's armed forces. Neither Reagan's election nor a national consensus on reviving national power constitutes solutions to America's defense dilemmas: manpower, weapons technology and modernization, nuclear concerns, and conventional readiness. How military renewal is pursued is no mere matter of procedure or process; instead, it is a vital determinant of substance, of results.

It is my conviction that the goal of military renewal in the 1980s must be to create a better military for America, not a bigger one. A better military would be one in which both officers and enlisted persons want to make a career; for all its glorification of the "citizen soldier," this nation needs the professional soldier more than ever. A better military would be one in which weapons worked. The way in which the military, industry, and the Congress now pursue weapons development and acquisition routinely dissipates the strengths of America's technology, industry, and management. A better military would be one in which America's forces could be promptly and properly deployed, employed, and sustained in combat; it is, as Larry Korb of AEI has noted, "immoral to put guys on the line" in Europe and elsewhere without adequate supply and support, and it is ineffectual as well.[1]

How, then, to pursue this ideal, an improved, renewed military?

True military renewal for the United States will be the product of sustained, careful attention to the intricacies of the manpower and modernization quandaries I have discussed throughout this book. It will not result from quick fixes—from hasty or optimistic infusions of money into defense. In the first days after the election of Ronald Reagan, John E. Cavanagh, senior vice-president and general counsel of Lockheed, asserted that "We need quick fixes." But he was wrong.[2]

In manpower, the quick fix takes two forms. One is the continuing call for reviving the draft; the other appears in proposals for large, across-the-board pay raises. But the draft at best would enhance the size of the military far more than its quality. In my view, this makes the draft fundamentally inappropriate even if it were politically feasible.

Pay raises are a vital component of any solution to present manpower ills in the American military, but only a component. It is certainly essential to get the military off welfare—and not simply by cutting back on welfare. Yet more money and benefits alone cannot solve the retention problems that constitute the most serious aspect of the military's personnel concerns. Manpower difficulties also reflect a pervasive problem of morale, leadership, and ethics within the military.

A Navy captain recently shared with me this telling anecdote. As maintenance officer of a Navy A-6 fighter squadron, this officer established the goal of making the combat systems of every plane in the squadron fully operational. With his commanding officer's approval, he adopted a policy of grounding any aircraft with a major system down. A-6 radars posed a particular problem; there soon came a moment when nine of the squadron's twelve planes were grounded because of malfunctioning radars; the squadron commanding officer ordered a change in maintenance philosophy and put the planes back into use. The maintenance officer had to explain to the chiefs—the mechanics—that the CO had changed policies, that the pilots would fly the aircraft as they were, and "lie a little about the condition of the 'birds,' so the squadron statistics wouldn't look so bad. The chiefs wouldn't look me in the eye," the captain told me. "I felt really small, and I know that some of those guys decided that day to get out of the military rather than be a part of that kind of an operation."

In the American military, leadership has come to revolve around the avoidance of racial incidents and the obtaining of respectable reenlistment quotients from subordinates. It will be the work of a generation to eradicate this legacy of laxity in morale and leadership.

Economics, demography, and internal morale together frame a cruel picture of the future problem in military manpower: costs will rise, available manpower will decline. These forces will accelerate the already strong tendency to offset manpower shortages through increased technological sophistication. But this in turn will make the American military more dependent on retaining skilled personnel. The retention problem thus remains the heart of manpower issues. No improvements in recruiting statistics, no amounts of pay raises, no package of benefits, can be allowed to distract from steady commitment to retaining the professional officers and enlisted personnel vital to a better military for America.

The quick fix in regard to weapons appears in both crude and subtle forms. In its cruder guise, it is the simple call for more—more numerous, more powerful, and, to be sure, more expensive weapons. Immediately after Reagan's election, the military services requested extra money—hundreds of billions of dollars—for missile submarines, aircraft carriers, the MX missile, a new bomber, strategic airlift, thousands of tanks, helicopters, air defense weapons, and more. But the subtle versions of quick-fix thinking in weapons matters were more interesting to survey. The National Contract Managers Association met in Washington, D.C., early in December 1980. The meeting reached a consensus, duly reported in defense industry periodicals, that "the Reagan administration should try to reverse, or at least soften, the adversary relationship that has spread as government and industry struggle to cut through the legal thicket on procurement."[3]

In another, more insidious form of the quick fix, some defense industrialists, especially in aviation, put forward versions of the old weapons acquisition shell game disguised in the latest management jargon. Hoping to capitalize on the new administration's sense of urgency about defense, aircraft manufacturers have advanced variations on the idea of buying inferior weapons now and improving them later. One version of this idea is called "P³," for *P*replanned *P*roduct Improvement; another bears the acronym "Plus," for *P*lanned *L*ifetime *U*pdating of *S*ystems.

The United States military needs sharp improvement in the reliability and maintainability of its weapons and technical systems. But the durable problems of weapons modernization and acquisition discussed earlier in these pages leave me profoundly skeptical about "buy now, fix later" methods. America's military, like any other military, must have upgrading and evolution of its equipment. But this is something quite apart from buying now what will not serve later, or even long.

America's military needs careful study of authentic operational requirements in order to avoid the old problem of demanding performance levels that exceed requirements and hence result in degrading reliability. Further, in my opinion, the government must substantially enlarge its direct investment in military research and development. This is essential if only to regain necessary momentum in basic scientific and engineering research, the momentum requisite for keeping whatever technological edge the

United States hopes to have. It has proven a thoroughgoing illusion to think that the government could transfer the costs of research and development to the private sector. One way or another, directly or indirectly, the government pays those costs, if not in dollars then in inefficiencies, lost industrial capacity, declining numbers of defense contractors, diminishing competition, and correspondingly diminished choices for defense officials.

In one sense, no major weapons program is a quick fix. It now takes twelve to fifteen years to carry a new weapon from concept to initial operational capability, and longer to complete a construction program on classes of ships, such as Trident missile submarines, large numbers of tanks such as the XM-1, or aircraft or missiles. But it is possible to spend a great deal of money on major weapons without solving, or even addressing, fundamental questions as to whether, or how, they will make America's military better. It is this blind faith that buying weapons will indeed improve America's military, and hence our national security, that makes major weapons part of the quick-fix approach to military adequacy. A prescription of military renewal must therefore assess major programs now under discussion.

M-1 TANK: Despite continuing engine problems, weight, and other development difficulties with the M-1 tank—until early 1981, the XM-1 tank—the Army wants to buy 7,058 of them in the early 1980s at a cost of approximately $2.7 million each. In general, there is a valid case for a new and better American tank: tanks now deployed in Europe are not a match for the best tanks deployed by the Soviet Union and its allies, and antitank weapons cannot truly replace tanks, as it is sometimes assumed. Effective defense of Europe will require the West to be able to take the tactical offensive, and this in turn requires tanks—lots of them.

It is possible, however, that the M-1, while a good tank as finally modified, might simply be the wrong tank for the American army. Its weight makes it impossible to transport by air at reasonable cost and in reasonable numbers. (To fly two M-1 tanks to the Persian Gulf from the United States would have cost $221,000 at the end of 1980.) It is clear that M-1 tanks, once deployed in Europe, will remain there. What is not clear is what tank the Army and Marines will use in contingency operations elsewhere in the world.

The Army would resolve the difficulty this way: buy the 7,058 M-1 tanks now, and if a lighter tank seems necessary in addition, the Army will be happy to develop and acquire that, too, in the middle or late 1980s. But as with most weapons programs, the need for urgency in M-1 acquisition is somewhat less than that portrayed by military leaders. The Army is in a hurry to get the M-1 in part because its development has extended over many years, in part because of the supposed imminence of threat posed by Soviet military buildups in Europe. But—and this is highly important—the usual summaries of the East-West military balance leave out of account some 4,000 tanks held in reserve by the West German government—reasonably modern, thoroughly usable tanks in good condition. The East-West military balance, while of concern, does not justify haste in completing the M-1 program.

Should America nonetheless spend upwards of $20 billion for a tank usable only in Europe? I think not. But I am certain that the Army and the Marines will need a more transportable tank for use in other areas at least as much, perhaps more, than they need the M-1 in Europe, and it may therefore be desirable to obtain far fewer M-1s than the 7,058 now called for.

B-1 BOMBER: Between President Carter's cancellation of the B-1 bomber program in 1977 and the 1980 election, the manned, penetrating bomber became a litmus test of commitment to improved defenses. Given the political character of the debate, the real questions in the Reagan administration from the first revolved not around whether to acquire a new bomber but around which aircraft it should be.

In my opinion, the cases for and against a new manned bomber are very nearly equally balanced. What seems clear is that the B-52s now in service have approached the end of their useful life. Further reworking of these ancient airframes will not produce an ideal weapon, and perhaps not even an adequate one. If there is to be a manned, penetrating bomber—and the American military's tradition of replacing central weapons systems type for type within the service structure virtually guarantees that there will be—then the nation's interest lies in obtaining an aircraft that can meet the admittedly demanding challenges of Soviet air defenses. Under the pressure of budget priorities, there will be a large temptation to acquire a cheapened version of the B-1—a plane whose capabilities would be reduced to save money on sophisticated electronics. Such a decision would be a serious error if it resulted in an aircraft that could not perform the tasks for which it was bought. And whatever aircraft is selected, it must also be equipped with a cruise missile carrier and launching system, to preserve the standoff option.

MX MISSILE: No decisions loom larger in the early 1980s either in fiscal significance or in strategic consequence than those associated with the proposed MX missile and basing system. Like many MX critics of the late 1970s, Reagan administration officials have indicated their interest in finding alternatives to the MX that would be quicker, cheaper, and less environmentally disruptive to deploy. In his first days in office, Secretary of Defense Weinberger reopened discussion of such ideas as installing ABMs to defend present Minuteman missile sites, or putting new missiles to sea on submarines somewhat smaller than the new Tridents or the old Poseidon boats.

Predictably, the Air Force opposes attempts to make the already deployed Minuteman force more survivable, either through ABM defense or through camouflage of some sort. It has also pointed out that MX missile boosters could be produced about as quickly as the production line for Minuteman missiles could be reopened (in both cases, about four years).

I believe the MX basing system so flawed in concept that it is unlikely to bring advantages in the 1990s that will have been worth the many costs of the 1980s. It is simply not clear yet what should be done instead. But until it is clearer, it would in my judgment be better to do nothing than to build the MX system as it is now conceived. If the United States errs in the early 1980s in matters of strategic missiles, chances are high that it will err by doing too much, too soon, rather than too little, too late.

Prospective decisions concerning the M-1 tank and the manned bomber have an important consideration in common, one that the MX missile may soon come to share. In the 1970s, both the M-1 and the B-1 soaked up huge amounts of development money. Before its cancellation in 1977, the B-1 had cost in excess of $6 billion to develop—this in dollars more valuable for having been spent before the sustained double-digit inflation of the latter 1970s. To this one must now add the $2.5 billion for bomber funding requested by the Reagan administration in fiscal 1982. The M-1 cost approximately $1 billion to develop and, as mentioned, it still faces problems that will be expensive to correct.

In theory, at least, development costs should not determine acquisition decisions. Like their civilian counterparts, military managers are taught that sunk costs cannot be recovered, and except for the convolutions that sunk costs occasionally entail for accountants, this is no more than folk wisdom: Don't throw good money after bad.

In practice, however, in the American military, development costs of several billion dollars make it almost impossible not to acquire at least some of whatever weapon is involved. The actual number of weapons purchased may be lower than originally planned or hoped, but an outright decision not to go through with purchase after highly expensive development is almost out of the question.

Congress has already made it clear that the manned penetrating bomber's development costs have reached the point of no return. The $2.5 billion in further development moneys included in the 1982 budget merely confirm this political truth. XM-1 development costs may also have risen to a point precluding a reduced buy. This consideration adds great importance to decisions on the amount of development money to appropriate for the MX missile system. President Carter, a proponent of the MX, included $2.4 billion for MX development in his proposed budget for fiscal 1982, an amount that in my opinion would have pushed the MX over the line between development and acquisition. The Reagan administration requested somewhat more than $2 billion for MX development in fiscal 1982, despite frequently voiced doubts about the wisdom and feasibility of the MPS basing plan. In all, this was a saddening demonstration of the momentum that weapons development programs can maintain in spite of their faults.

In the long run, I believe, the 1970s—the decade of the M-1, the B-1, and the MX—are not going to go down as great years for military research and development. If they had been better, America's military malaise might be both less advanced and more responsive to treatment.

TRIDENT SUBMARINE: The Trident submarine program poses questions somewhat different from those growing out of the M-1 tank, B-1 bomber, and MX missile programs. There will be a number of Trident submarines; of this there is no doubt. Eight boats are under contract, seven under construction, and a total of fourteen now planned. But the construction of the lead ship in this new class, the *Ohio*, is now some two years behind schedule, with a cost overrun of some $300 million. The possibilities of further delays, larger cost increases, and defective workmanship continue to present difficult questions: Should the government resume construction of nuclear submarines in Navy shipyards? What to do about retirement of Polaris-Poseidon missile submarines due to be replaced by new Tridents now certain to be years late in reaching service? Should Trident receive funding preference in relation to other strategic weapons, such as the manned bomber or the MX, if such choices become necessary?

Interestingly, there is at least a possibility that much of the controversy over delays in submarine construction revolves around a false—or at least unnecessary—issue. Years ago, when the first contracts for *Ohio*-class Trident submarines were being negotiated, Navy ship-building experts calculated that in all likelihood the lead ship could not be delivered before the end of 1981. But eager to close the deal, Electric Boat promised delivery several years earlier, and Navy officials accepted that overly optimistic projection. Whether the Tridents are really late, therefore, and how much, is a matter of perspective as much as of contract.

Despite the possible objection that government shipyards should not compete with private industry, I believe that the Navy should construct one or more nuclear submarines in Navy yards. There are several reasons why this seems to be a good idea. One is that private companies capable of building nuclear submarines are few, really only two—Newport News and Electric Boat. These companies have more contracts now than they can truly handle, which is one reason for the delays encountered in both the missile submarine program and the *Los Angeles*-class attack submarine program. Further, in its own construction program the Navy would gain up-to-date experience that would put it in a better position to evaluate the validity of its complaints about contractor performance on the submarines now under construction.

The question of retiring older missile submarines is closely connected to that of possible funding preference for Trident over MX or the manned bomber. Retirement of older missile boats before Tridents are available to replace them is the only way in which America's strategic forces are actually going to decline in the next few years—barring further catastrophes such as the explosion of the Titan II missile in Arkansas in 1980. Yet I do not believe that the retirement of older Polaris boats will alter strategic relationships to an extent that would invite Russian adventurism or miscalculation. But superpower strategic ratios have a political and psychological significance that transcends their operational characteristics. If the Trident program can really be speeded up by the earlier commitment of funds, then those funds should be made available even at the cost of deferring acquisition of a new bomber or the MX system.

ABM DEFENSES: If the MX is not built after all, it is virtually certain that a great deal of money will be spent to develop antiballistic missile defenses. The Reagan administration has indicated interest in such weapons and hinted that renewal of the ABM limitation treaty, due to expire in 1982, would not be automatic.

In the early 1970s, when the United States and the Soviet Union signed the ABM treaty as part of SALT I, the ABM systems of both sides were of questionable effectiveness. Neither the United States nor the Soviet Union much favored an expensive race to deploy weapons in which they had justifiably little confidence. In the decade since SALT I, there has been progress in ballistic defense technologies, but I remain skeptical about the adequacy of land-based systems. The real promise of the future seems now to lie in space-based systems using lasers or other devices to destroy weapons following a ballistic trajectory. These space-based weapons are still ten years or more in the future.

The ABM treaty is the one product of SALT negotiations in which a little restraint has brought great savings for both sides. It should not be discarded lightly. It seems to me, therefore, that the burden of proof lies on those who may wish to change the status quo by allowing the ABM treaty to lapse and then deploying ABM defenses in some form.

Unfortunately, the ABM, whether in land-based or space-based versions, is subject to the same political law I have discussed in relation to the XM-1 tank, the B-1 bomber, and the MX missile: If development costs rise high enough, they will in effect require acquisition and deployment. Hence it will be important to keep a wary eye on development funding for ABM defense throughout the 1980s.

FIFTH FLEET: Events in Iran and Afghanistan in the last two years have given substantial impetus to a long-held Navy desire to establish a permanent, large naval deployment in the Indian Ocean–Persian Gulf area. The Republican party platform in 1980 called for creation of such a fleet, which indicated considerable support for the idea even outside the Navy. In the first days of the Reagan administration, moreover, the Congressional Budget Office published a study that called, among other things, for the addition of three large aircraft carriers to the fleet. In budgetary implications, a decision to establish a Fifth Fleet and to build three or four new carriers to constitute it would be second only to a decision to build the full MX system. Four nuclear aircraft carriers with appropriate support ships could easily reach or exceed $50 billion in cost.

There are strong reasons for doubting the wisdom either of establishing a Fifth Fleet or of building three to four new aircraft carriers. *The aircraft carriers and other naval vessels deployed to the Indian Ocean and Persian Gulf throughout 1980 proved largely irrelevant to the working out of America's concerns ashore—in Afghanistan, in Iran, and in the war between Iran and Iraq.* These naval forces were not powerless; they could have inflicted great destruction on Iran, for instance, if that had been ordered by President Carter. But this was deemed inappropriate. And the question of how, in actual practice, large naval deployments in the Indian Ocean would advance America's interests in dealing with equivalent difficulties remains unanswered by those who favor creation of a Fifth Fleet.

Further, there is a sort of "chicken and egg" problem at the heart of the Fifth Fleet idea. Naval forces, like most major weapons, take a long time to build. Even if fully supported in the budget, American power in the Indian Ocean–Persian Gulf region would take many years to develop. In the meantime, for a decade or more, a Fifth Fleet would have to be composed out of forces drawn from the Pacific Fleet, the Mediterranean Fleet, or the Atlantic Fleet—all of which are fully committed in support of other vital interests and areas. Thus the dilemma: In the absence of new forces to make up a Fifth Fleet, its creation would prompt a view of America's interests that exceeds its resources and encourage the routine reduction of important naval deployments in other regions of the world. On the other hand, in the absence of the go-ahead for a Fifth Fleet, much of the rationale for these new forces would fall away.

It may be that the United States needs a large, permanent naval deployment in the Indian Ocean, larger than current forces can conveniently accommodate. But it needs first, and more, a clear idea of what purposes that deployment is to serve, and at what cost.[4]

Among the many risks of advocating military renewal, one towers above the rest: the risk of confusing the necessary improvement of America's military with pursuit of military superiority over the Soviet Union. There is much to worry about in this regard. The Republican party platform in 1980 called for commitment to such a goal. Reagan himself took refuge in a more ambiguous pledge to seek a "margin of safety." *Newsweek* contended that this phrase was campaign code for increasing arms spending until the United States enjoyed advantages in power equivalent to those it held in the 1950s. In contrast, Richard Allen, Reagan's National Security Adviser, insisted that the President recognized the "need to establish America's position in the world, not on the same basis as in the 1950s, the 1960s or even the 1970s, but on a new basis."

The goal of restoring American military superiority holds an attractive simplicity, best captured in a line Reagan uttered during his televised debate with Jimmy Carter on October 28, 1980. "A nation has never gotten into a war by being too strong," Reagan said. But this line, with its homely sensibility, represents an arguable reading of history and of politics. The history of great power relations in the modern world revolves around the successive efforts of Spain, France, and Germany to acquire hegemony in the West, and of Japan to do so in the East. Since World War

II, the United States and the Soviet Union have regarded each other with suspicion rooted in the political instincts fostered by centuries of resistance to hegemony, to nations that get too strong.

Beyond any doubt, an American drive for military superiority will spur ever greater Soviet efforts to avoid conceding the advantage. I do not believe that the United States can set a pace in defense that the Soviets will not match, whatever the cost.

Rather than military superiority, the United States must seek military competence, and the elements of such competence are only common sense. The American military must be able to put forces where they mean something in the context of the nation's interests. And it must be able to carry out the threats national leaders deem it proper to make. Military competence does not necessarily require worldwide, instant interventionary capability.

Regrettably, exaggerated expectations of an improved military are being nourished by the false promise of the Rapid Deployment Force idea. As we have seen, the RDF as now conceived is a substitute—and a poor one—for the thoroughgoing, force-wide conventional readiness the American military really needs.

In this regard, the recommendations of the military committee formed to evaluate the Iran hostage rescue attempt were both instructive and worrisome. The Special Operations Review Group, chaired by former Chief of Naval Operations James L. Holloway III, found much that could have been different or better. But to guide future efforts, the committee made only two general recommendations. In one they suggested that all future special operations be evaluated in advance by a board of people such as themselves—solid professionals having no direct responsibility for conducting proposed operations. This recommendation was scarcely surprising. Committees rarely find their functions unnecessary; everyone likes to be consulted.

In their other recommendation, the committee suggested that "A Counterterrorist Joint Task Force (CTJTF) be established as a field agency of the Joint Chiefs of Staff with permanently assigned staff personnel and certain assigned forces."[5]

In short, and according to the best judgment of top military professionals, the American military should not be asked to deal with the unexpected. This, plainly, is unsatisfactory.

Someone once wrote that "Most speeches on military subjects

are pretty much alike. There's usually something to arouse concern, something to point up the immediacy of the danger, and something to reassure that there is still time to solve the problem—but not much time." In concluding a book such as this, it would be easy to slip into that formula. But to do so would be contrary to the philosophy that has informed the work. As expressed throughout these pages, it is my belief that the real limits on choice, on change, and on solutions to defense difficulties are exceedingly narrow, and that to ignore these limits will lead not to fundamental change but to irrelevance. There is no possibility that the Department of Defense is going to adopt that quaint panacea of the Carter years, zero-base budgeting. Nor is the American military going to stop what it's doing and start over, or in some other way throw off the constraints on choice growing out of past decisions and present practices. The present style of military politics, and of budgetary politicking, virtually precludes basic change in the nation's military thinking and doing.

There are risks in military renewal, and limits on what is possible, but there are hopes as well. America can have a better military if it approaches the military's problems—manpower, high technology, modernization, nuclear dependence, and readiness—with patience, not haste, in the expectation of improvement, not perfection.

Almost everyone now realizes, however reluctantly, that better defense must be more expensive defense. Indeed, defense costs will rise significantly in the next several years apart from whatever is spent to increase forces and military activity. The cost of nuclear weapons manufacture has traditionally been charged to the Department of Energy and its predecessor, the Atomic Energy Commission. Such costs properly belong to defense, and will soon be transferred. Inflation continues; fuel costs alone for the Department of Defense increased some $3 billion between fiscal 1980 and fiscal 1981, almost solely through inflation's effects.

Moreover, increasing defense costs in the early 1980s may to a considerable extent reflect the cost of doing right what had been done wrong—or not done at all. General Frederick Kroesen, then commanding general of the United States Army in Europe, said in October 1980: "If we did everything that TRADOC [the Army's Training and Doctrine Command] established for us in their training literature—that which should be accomplished by a squad or platoon or company—by the time we get to the battalion level training we won't have any money."[6] It is simply not in the nation's interest to force the Army to choose between mastering small unit tactics or practicing large unit tactics, but such choices have become routine in America's military.

A number of other considerations discussed in earlier chapters also heighten the peacetime cost of military adequacy today: the need for quick response in some situations; the possibility of quick defeat in others, such as Europe; the vulnerability of the American industrial base in war against Russia. These mean that the United States must pay in advance, in peacetime, a growing proportion of the costs of future wars. This is a novelty for the American people. The early stages of past American wars were used to call up men and crank up industry. The nation's insulation from attack permitted it to raise, equip, and then reequip the fighting forces after the outbreak of war. Wartime costs were met by wartime financing.

In the 1930s, for instance, annual military expenditures before 1938 in the United States did not exceed $1 billion. Between 1941 and 1946, World War II cost the United States more than $260 billion. If distributed over the ten years before the outbreak of war in Europe, these costs would have raised 1930s military expenditures to some $26 billion per year, more than 26 times their actual level. Similarly, in the latter 1940s, American military costs were running about $12 billion per year; the war in Korea from 1950 to 1953 cost about $60 billion; meted out over the years between World War II and the outbreak of war in Korea, that amount would have more than doubled peacetime military expenditures.

The point simply is this: The necessity of paying larger portions of war costs in advance means that peacetime military expenditures must increase far more than peacetime expenditures or inflationary trends alone might suggest. To some people, this view may seem a depressing acceptance of war's inevitability. I can only say, without wishing to alarm, that I see no grounds for expecting a future free of war, or of the threat of war.

I have said that America needs a better military, not a bigger one. But the effort to improve the American military cannot be left either to the military itself or to the many experts eagerly advising those in office. For in the American military, reform or improvement invariably means expansion. Things that don't work, or don't work well, are rarely if ever eliminated; rather, they are expanded on the premise that they could work, and would, with more time, money, and manpower, even though it is clearly an error to expand weaknesses rather than strengths, whether in the military or in any other organization. This organizational instinct, finally, makes the military incapable of reforming itself from within.

I do not advocate permanent disavowal of any growth in the American military; circumstances may indeed warrant a larger military sometime in the future. But the retention of skilled professionals in the armed forces will not be easier in a larger military; it will be more difficult. Reliability and maintenance of high-technology weapons will not be simpler in a larger military; more weapons, new weapons, or more advanced weapons will demand greater, not lesser, excellence at every level.

These days it is difficult without a blush to quote Theodore Roosevelt, that feisty representative of a more confident age in America's past. But he understood this nation's military needs in a way peculiarly apt to the threshold of the 1980s. "Oh, if only our people would learn the need of preparedness," he wrote in 1904. "Mere bigness, if it is mere flabbiness, means nothing but disgrace."

The renewal of America's military in the 1980s will succeed only if the interested public ensures that improvement takes precedence over enlargement. There will be nothing quick or easy about this task. But only in this way, finally, can the nation's military meet the nation's needs.

NOTES

Figures on current Soviet and American forces have been drawn principally from three sources widely acknowledged to be reliable and authoritative: the annual reports of the Department of Defense; the annual survey of the military balance published by the International Institute for Strategic Studies in London; and the landmark net assessment by John M. Collins of the Congressional Research Service, which is entitled *U.S.-Soviet Military Balance: Concepts and Capabilities 1960–1980* (New York, 1980). To simplify footnoting, sources for figures in the text have been indicated only when the figures have been drawn or derived from sources other than these, or when there is significant disagreement among these principal references. In keeping with my view that most defense issues lie well within the grasp of the attentive public, I have cited easily available and popular sources wherever possible.

II: THE ENVIRONMENT

1. For a fuller elaboration of postwar American strategy, and the ways in which the Korean War altered it, see Thomas H. Etzold, "The Far East in American Strategy, 1948–1951," in *Aspects of Sino-American Relations Since 1784*, Etzold, ed., New York, 1978, pp. 102–126.

2. This widely quoted passage appears in *Nuclear Weapons and Foreign Policy*, New York, 1957, p. 7.

3. This observation, and the strategy to which it applies, are discussed in Thomas H. Etzold and Bruce W. Menning, "Force and Diplomacy in a Nuclear Age," *Army*, January 1974, pp. 10–15.

4. Dean Acheson, *Present at the Creation: My Years in the State Department*, New York, 1969, p. 374.

5. This figure is sometimes debated among experts. It is taken from Nikita Khrushchev's statement of January 14, 1960, to the Supreme Soviet, as published in *Pravda* the following day. See the discussion of this point in Adam B. Ulam, *Expansion and Coexistence: Soviet Foreign Policy 1917–1973*, 2nd ed., New York, 1974, p. 403.

6. Senator J. William Fulbright entitled his important critique of the Vietnam War *The Crippled Giant: American Foreign Policy and Its Domestic Consequences*, New York, 1972.

242 | NOTES TO PAGES 9-20

7. See the Department of Defense, *Annual Report, Fiscal Year 1981*, Harold Brown, Secretary of Defense, January 29, 1981, Washington, DC, p. 36.

8. Ibid., pp. 33-38.

9. The United Press International (UPI) story on this subject was carried in many of the nation's newspapers on February 15, 1980. General Richard Ellis, commander of the Strategic Air Command, had alluded to the study in testimony before the House Armed Services Committee on January 25, 1980. See also the *DOD Annual Report FY 1981*, pp. 73-91.

10. *DOD Annual Report FY 1981*, pp. 37, 97-110.

11. Ibid., pp. 37, 102, 103.

12. Paul H. Nitze, Leonard Sullivan, Jr., and the Atlantic Council Working Group on Securing the Seas, *Securing the Seas: The Soviet Naval Challenge and Western Alliance Options*, Boulder, Colorado, 1979, p. 3.

13. Figures on Soviet naval developments are derived from *DOD Annual Report FY 1981*, pp. 37, 103-108. Zumwalt's observation appeared in *On Watch: A Memoir*, New York, 1975, p. 466.

14. *DOD Annual Report FY 1981*, p. 75; John M. Collins and Anthony H. Cordesman, *Imbalance of Power: An Analysis of Shifting U.S.-Soviet Military Strengths*, San Rafael, California, 1978, chapter three, *passim;* and John M. Collins, *U.S.-Soviet Military Balance: Concepts and Capabilities 1960-1980*, New York, 1980, Part III, "Strategic Nuclear Trends," *passim.*

15. Although this Truman anecdote has never been newsworthy in the past, it has been known to Truman experts for many years. Some scholars doubt its accuracy. It nevertheless captures a widely shared perception of important shifts in Soviet-American power relations. Jackson's story appeared in *Time*'s issue of January 28, 1980, p. 13.

16. "Harry S. Truman and the Origins of Containment," in *Makers of American Diplomacy: From Theodore Roosevelt to Henry Kissinger*, Frank J. Merli and Theodore A. Wilson, eds., New York, 1974, p. 191.

17. Loss figures are taken from contemporary press reports. Figures on initial forces on both sides varied in press and periodical stories, but only slightly. The figures here are from the authoritative International Institute for Strategic Studies (London), *The Military Balance, 1980* (London, 1979).

18. *The New York Times*, October 9, 1980.

19. United States Arms Control and Disarmament Agency, *World Military Expenditures and Arms Transfers, 1968-1977*, Washington, DC, 1979. Findings are summarized in pp. 1-12, and an exhaustive presentation of data follows. Complementary information on this subject may be found in *World Military and Social Expenditures*, a biennial publication prepared by Ruth Leger Sivard under the sponsorship of the Arms Control Association, the Institute for World Order, and the Members of Congress for Peace Through Law Education Fund. The latest booklet in this series appeared in 1981. The Stockholm International Peace Research Institute also publishes important information on this topic. See *World Armaments and Disarmament: SIPRI Yearbook* (annual since 1969), published in the United States by MIT Press, Cambridge, Massachusetts.

20. *World Military Expenditures*, pp. 9, 10.

21. Ibid., pp. 2, 3.

22. Ibid., p. 159.

23. *Background Air Force Actions*, vol. 4, no. 3 (July 1980):1.

24. A hint of this problem, and the internal defense debate it has caused,

appeared in Richard Burt, " 'One-and-a-Half War' Strategy Now Means Just What It Says," *The New York Times*, February 3, 1980.

25. Land mines and lift capability both came in for comment in the report by Norman Kempster and Robert C. Toth to the Los Angeles *Times*, "Are U.S. forces prepared to fight?", which was picked up by other newspapers around the country and published September 14, 1980.

26. Princeton, New Jersey, 1966.

27. The most notable of these was *FM 100-5: Operations*, publication of which occasioned a large debate in professional periodicals concerned with Army doctrine.

28. New York, 1978, p. 326.

29. December 31, 1978.

30. *DOD Annual Report FY 1981*, p. 3.

31. *The New York Times*, July 2, 1980.

32. *DOD Annual Report FY 1981*, p. 14.

33. "Is International Coercion Waning or Rising?" *International Security*, Spring 1977, pp. 92–110; and "On the International Uses of Military Force in the Contemporary World," *Orbis*, Spring 1977, pp. 5–28.

34. CNO speech to the Society of Naval Engineers Luncheon, Washington, DC, May 1, 1980.

35. *Iran Rescue Mission Report*, Washington, DC, August 1980, pp. iv–vi and *passim*.

36. *The 1962 Lee Knowles Lectures*, given at Trinity College, Cambridge, London, 1962, p. 52.

III. THE PEOPLE

1. *A Report by Chief of Naval Operations Admiral Thomas B. Hayward, U.S. Navy, on the Fiscal Year 1981 Military Posture and Fiscal Year 1981 Budget of the United States Navy, 31 January 1980*, p. 7.

2. Washington *Post*, April 12, 1980. The Associated Press picked up George C. Wilson's by-lined story and brought it to nationwide attention.

3. *DOD Annual Report FY 1981*, pp. 268–270.

4. Speech to the Society of Naval Engineers Luncheon, Washington, DC, May 1, 1980.

5. Ibid.

6. "The Mental Gap in the Defense Debate," *Fortune*, September 8, 1980, p. 43.

7. See Melvin Laird, "People, Not Hardware: The Highest Defense Priority," Washington, DC, the American Enterprise Institute, 1980, p. 4. As Richard Nixon's Secretary of Defense, Laird presided over the transition to the all-volunteer force.

8. *DOD Annual Report FY 1980*, pp. 275–279; *DOD Annual Report FY 1981*, pp. 262–265.

9. These figures were released by President Carter's Secretary of Labor, Ray Marshall, in the fall of 1980, and cited, among other places, in *Air Force Policy Letter for Commanders*, Washington, DC, July 1, 1980, p. 3.

10. *DOD Annual Report FY 1981*, p. 266.

11. Ibid., pp. 266–268; *Time*, June 9, 1980, p. 24.

12. *DOD Annual Report FY 1980*, p. 281; *DOD Annual Report FY 1981*, p. 267.

13. Quoted in *Newsweek*, October 27, 1980, p. 52.

14. *Air Force Times*, November 3, 1980.

15. June 9, 1980, p. 25.

16. Juri Toomepuu, "Ready, Willing, Able to Fight," *Army*, January 1980, pp. 6, 7.

17. *DOD Annual Report FY 1981*, p. 267.

18. *CNO Report FY 1981*, pp. 27–30; *Newsweek*, October 27, 1980, pp. 52, 55; *Time*, June 9, 1980, pp. 24–36, *passim*; *Time*, October 27, 1980, pp. 29, 30; *Air Force Policy Letter for Commanders*, 1 July 1980, p. 4.

19. *Air Force Policy Letter for Commanders*, 1 July 1980, p. 1.

20. Quoted in *Navy Times*, May 12, 1980, p. 14.

21. Ibid.

22. *Background Air Force Actions*, vol. 4, no. 3 (July 1980): 16.

23. *Newport Daily News*, May 8, 1980.

24. Kenneth J. Coffey, *Strategic Implications of the All-Volunteer Force: The Conventional Defense of Central Europe*, Chapel Hill, North Carolina, 1979; DOD, *America's Volunteers: A Report on the All-Volunteer Armed Forces (AVF)*, Washington, DC, 1979. The higher figure of 370,000 appeared in *Time*, June 9, 1980, p. 29.

25. For important recent discussions of this problem, see Arthur Macy Cox, "Why the U.S., Since 1977, Has Been Misperceiving Soviet Military Strength," *The New York Times*, October 20, 1980; "How Much More Can Moscow Spend on Arms?" *The New York Times*, November 2, 1980; Drew Middleton, "C.I.A. Foresees Big Soviet Increase in Arms Outlay," *The New York Times*, August 3, 1980.

26. United Press International distributed the Boston *Globe* story on August 27, 1980. See *Time*, September 15, 1980; and *Air Force Times*, November 3, 1980, for additional stories and figures. On the disparity of Census Bureau and Selective Service figures, see Lawrence M. Baskir and William A. Strauss, *Chance and Circumstance: The Draft, the War, and the Vietnam Generation*, New York, 1978, p. 87.

27. *Strategic Implications of the All-Volunteer Force*, pp. 78–113, 150–166.

28. *The New York Times*, May 14, 1981. *Time* magazine had earlier endorsed a renewed draft, as had many other prominent persons throughout 1980 and 1981.

29. "The Reasons They Give . . . And the REAL Reason," United States Naval Institute *Proceedings*, June 1980, pp. 86, 87.

30. Laird, "People, Not Hardware," p. 13.

31. May 26, 1980, p. 20.

32. The following paragraphs draw on information and figures presented in Laird, "People, Not Hardware"; on *The Report of the Department of Defense Pay Adequacy Study*, Washington, DC, October 1979; and on *The Report of the President's Commission on an All-Volunteer Force*, Washington, DC, February 1980.

33. Quoted in *Time*, June 9, 1980.

34. *Newsweek*, October 27, 1980, p. 62.

35. *Time*, June 9, 1980, p. 26.

36. *Navy Times*, July 12, 1980, pp. 19, 20.

37. Commander F. J. Glaeser, USN, "Our One True Strength," USNI *Proceedings*, June 1980, p. 86.

38. Quoted in *Time,* June 9, 1980, p. 26.

39. Ibid., p. 31.

40. The survey was conducted by Hays Associates of Philadelphia, under contract with the Department of Defense. Data was gathered in 1979. The study is summarized in *Air Force Times,* July 21, 1980, pp. 1, 14.

41. *Navy Times,* March 24, 1980.

42. April 7, 1980, p. 19. The name of the author was withheld from publication by the paper's editors.

43. *Air Force Times* conducted a survey of 11,397 active duty and retired military people, which it said was the largest such survey ever conducted on this issue. Results were published in the March 31, 1980, issue.

44. Laird, "People, Not Hardware," pp. 10, 11.

45. Ibid., p. 11.

46. "The Reasons They Give . . . And the REAL Reason," pp. 86, 87.

47. These possibilities are discussed in very brief terms in *DOD Annual Report FY 1981,* pp. 276, 277.

48. "The Mental Gap in the Defense Debate," p. 43.

49. *Air Force Times,* July 21, 1980, p. 14.

50. Ibid., p. 30.

51. Letter of June 29, 1893, in *Letters and Papers of Alfred Thayer Mahan, Vol. II, 1890–1901,* Robert Seager II and Doris D. Maguire, eds., p. 114.

52. October 30, 1980.

53. *Air Force Policy Letter for Commanders,* July 15, 1980, p. 1.

IV: THE WEAPONS

1. Washington, DC, July 1976, pp. 1–1, 1–2.

2. October 27, 1980, p. 30.

3. Senator Robert Taft, Jr., *White Paper on Defense: A Modern Military Strategy for the United States* (prepared with the assistance of William S. Lind, staff aide to Senator Taft), Washington, DC, 1976, pp. H-1–H-8.

4. "The Price of Preparedness: The FY 1978–1982 Defense Program," *AEI Defense Review,* no. 3 (June 1977), p. 13.

5. *On Watch,* p. 145.

6. "The Muscle-bound Superpower," pp. 59–78.

7. "How Much Is Not Enough? The Non-nuclear Air Battle in NATO's Central Region," pp. 58–78. Quotation from p. 62.

8. "The Price of Preparedness," p. 13.

9. "The Muscle-bound Superpower," p. 64.

10. The text of the speech appears in a State Department public affairs publication series *Current Policy* (no. 220) under the title "Essentials of Security: Arms and More," September 18, 1980.

11. *The New York Times,* September 21, 1980.

12. Toomepuu, "Ready, Willing, Able to Fight," pp. 6, 7.

13. "Are U.S. Forces Prepared to Fight?" September 14, 1980.

14. Quoted in *The New York Times,* September 28, 1980.

15. Quotations from Lorenzini and Fox, "How Much Is Not Enough," pp. 61, 62, 67.

16. October 27, 1980, p. 67.

17. *The New York Times,* October 21, 1980.

18. The *Wall Street Journal,* February 28, 1980.

19. "How Much Is Not Enough," pp. 62, 63.

20. *Aviation Week & Space Technology,* October 6, 1980, p. 60.

21. Quoted by Lorenzini and Fox, "How Much Is Not Enough," p. 63.

22. October 6, 1980, p. 70.

23. Ibid., p. 75.

24. Ibid., p. 44.

25. *Arming America: How the U.S. Buys Weapons,* Cambridge, Massachusetts, 1974, p. 108.

26. "Ready for What?" June, 1980, p. 40.

27. Ibid., pp. 39, 40.

28. Quoted in Fox, *Arming America,* p. 108.

29. "The Muscle-bound Superpower," p. 64.

30. In its October 27, 1980, issue, *Newsweek* asserted that POMCUS was costing only $265 million per unit set. The figures here were furnished by the Department of the Army.

31. *Navy Policy Briefs,* February 1980, p. 2. The quotation was drawn from Secretary Hidalgo's speech to the House Armed Services Committee on January 31, 1980, in which he presented the Navy's fiscal 1981 budget and posture statement.

32. General Brown's comment appeared in *Time*'s story on the Navy's troubles, May 8, 1978.

33. *On Watch,* p. 314.

34. *The New York Times,* August 10, 1980.

35. October 6, 1980, p. 70.

36. *Arming America,* p. 302.

37. October 6, 1980, p. 70.

38. *Arming America,* pp. 74, 75.

39. Ibid., p. 160.

40. Ibid., p. 103.

41. Ibid., p. 296.

42. Ibid., pp. 98, 99.

43. Ibid., p. 99.

44. Ibid., p. 138.

45. Ibid., p. 87.

46. Ibid., pp. 128, 129. For the most up-to-date detailed treatment of the unhealthy interplay between defense and industry, see Jacques S. Gansler, *The Defense Industry,* Cambridge, Massachusetts, 1980.

47. "The Mental Gap in the Defense Debate," p. 44.

48. *Newsweek,* p. 55; "The Mental Gap in the Defense Debate," p. 44.

49. *Aviation Week & Space Technology,* October 6, 1980, p. 70.

50. Ibid., p. 54.

51. Ibid., p. 75.

52. See pp. 107 ff.

53. "International Control of Atomic Energy," January 20, 1950, in *Foreign Relations of the United States: 1950,* I, Washington, DC, 1977, p. 38. An excerpt of this important document also appears, with notes and commentary, in *Containment: Documents on American Policy and Strategy, 1945–1950,* Thomas H. Etzold and John L. Gaddis, New York, 1978, pp. 373–381.

54. Quoted in Gordon Thomas and Max Morgan Witts, *Enola Gay,* New York, 1977, p. 240.

55. Los Angeles *Times,* September 14, 1980.

56. October 27, 1980, p. 55.

57. *Aviation Week & Space Technology,* October 6, 1980, p. 56.
58. Ibid., p. 43.
59. Ibid., p. 75.

V: THE NUCLEAR ISSUES

1. June 5, 1977.
2. p. 8.
3. Princeton, New Jersey.
4. Figures from Korb, "The Price of Preparedness," p. 28.
5. *DOD Annual Report FY 1981,* pp. 77-79.
6. Collins and Cordesman, *Imbalance of Power,* pp. 50, 70.
7. "A Manual of Missile Capability," p. 38.
8. September 14, 1980.
9. *DOD Annual Report FY 1981,* p. 85.
10. September 21, 1980.
11. Matthew H. Aid, letter to the editor, *The New York Times,* September 28, 1980.
12. *DOD Annual Report FY 1981,* p. 67.
13. "A Manual of Missile Capability," p. 35.
14. Ibid.; and see Collins and Cordesman, *Imbalance of Power,* pp. 46, 50.
15. Collins and Cordesman, *Imbalance of Power,* p. 46.
16. This finding, mentioned earlier, was discussed in a UPI story of February 15, 1980, and was the subject of testimony before the House Armed Services Committee on January 25, 1980. See also the *DOD Annual Report FY 1981,* pp. 73-91.
17. *DOD Annual Report FY 1981,* p. 88.
18. "The MX Basing Mode Muddle: Issues and Alternatives," p. 20.
19. "The Mental Gap in the Defense Debate," p. 42.
20. "The Case for the MX," *Air University Review,* July–August 1980, p. 7.
21. Ibid., p. 6.
22. "M-X Information," a catechism published by the Office of Public Affairs, Secretary of the Air Force, July 1980, pp. 14, 15.
23. Ibid.
24. Korb, "The Case for the MX," p. 9.
25. "The MX Basing Mode Muddle," p. 21.
26. Quoted in *Air Force Policy Letter for Commanders,* Washington, DC, July 1, 1980, p. 1.
27. Ibid., p. 3.
28. *Air Force Policy Letter for Commanders,* Washington, DC, October 1, 1980, p. 1.
29. The quotation is from page 3 of the official DOD news release, No. 344-80.
30. *DOD Annual Report FY 1981,* p. 127.
31. "The MX Basing Mode Muddle," p. 25.
32. "Guidance for Discussions on the Military Aspects of Regulation of Armaments," JCS 1731/22, June 5, 1947. Published in *Foreign Relations of the United States: 1947,* I, pp. 485–486, the document's conclusions were republished with commentary in *Containment,* Etzold and Gaddis, eds., pp. 279–281.
33. Quoted in John Bartlow Martin, *Adlai Stevenson and the World: The Life of Adlai E. Stevenson,* Garden City, New York, 1977, p. 543.

34. "International Control of Atomic Energy," *Foreign Relations of the United States: 1950*, I, pp. 43, 44.

VI: THE CONVENTIONAL ISSUES

1. *The New York Times*, September 21, 1980. Secretary Brown's comments are from his speech in El Paso, Texas, on October 9, 1980, and were widely circulated by UPI in the following several days.
2. Raymond L. Garthoff, "On Estimating and Imputing Intentions," *International Security*, vol. 2, no. 3 (Winter 1978): 23.
3. *The Conduct of United States Foreign Policy in the Nation's Third Century*. Claremont, California, 1975, pp. 115, 116.
4. Philip Morrison and Paul F. Walker, "A New Strategy for Military Spending," *Scientific American*, vol. 239, no. 4 (October 1978): 60.
5. *The New York Times*, September 28, 1980.
6. *On Watch*, pp. 461, 462. Admiral Holloway was quoted in *Time*, May 8, 1978.
7. "The Military Role of NATO," Chapter 10 of *NATO After Thirty Years*, Lawrence S. Kaplan and Robert W. Clawson, eds., Wilmington, Delaware, 1981.
8. *The Military Balance, 1980–1981*, London, 1980, p. 115.
9. Kaplan, ed., *Isolation or Interdependence: Today's Choice for Tomorrow's World*, New York, 1975, p. 15.
10. Richard D. Lawrence and Jeffrey Record, *U.S. Force Structure in NATO: An Alternative*, Washington, DC, 1974, p. 65.
11. October 27, 1980.
12. Los Angeles *Times*, September 14, 1980; *Newsweek*, October 27, 1980.
13. October 27, 1980, pp. 29, 30.
14. October 27, 1980, p. 61.
15. August 24, 1980.
16. *Time*, June 9, 1980; *The New York Times*, September 21, 1980.
17. These items were reported among other places in *The New York Times*, September 21, 1980, and *Newsweek*, October 27, 1980.
18. September 14, 1980; *Aviation Week & Space Technology*, October 6, 1980, p. 70.
19. September 14, 1980.
20. Ibid. *Time*, October 27, 1980, p. 30.
21. *Time*, October 27, 1980, p. 30.
22. *Newsweek*, October 27, 1980, p. 61.
23. *Pentagram News*, October 23, 1980.
24. October 27, 1980, p. 30. "Happy Birthday, RDF—And No Happy Returns," Washington *Post*, February 25, 1981.
25. *Time*, October 27, 1980, p. 30.
26. October 6, 1980, p. 69.
27. Los Angeles *Times*, September 14, 1980. "The Mental Gap in the Defense Debate," p. 42.
28. *Iran Rescue Mission Report, passim*.

VII: THE PRESCRIPTION

1. Quoted in Holt, "What We Need for Defense," p. 62.
2. *Aviation Week & Space Technology*, December 8, 1980, p. 21.
3. Ibid.

4. I have discussed this subject at greater length in "From Far East to Middle East: Overextension in American Strategy Since World War II," *Naval Review*, May 1981, pp. 66–77.

5. *Iran Rescue Mission Report*, p. 3.

6. *Pentagram News*, October 23, 1980.

INDEX